THE CELL BUILDERS

THE CELL BUILDERS

H. Garrett DeYoung

DOUBLEDAY & COMPANY, INC.
GARDEN CITY, N.Y.
1986

Library of Congress Cataloging-in-Publication Data

DeYoung, H. Garrett.
The cell builders.

1. Antibodies, Monoclonal. 2. Hybridomas.
3. Immunology—Popular works. 4. Biotechnology—Popular works.
5. Oncology—Popular works. I. Title.
[DNLM: 1. Antibodies, Onoclonal—therapeutic use—popular works.
2. Neoplasms—therapy—popular works.
QZ 201 D529c]
QR186.85.D48   1986   615′.37   85-31096
ISBN 0-385-19657-1

To Carrie, with love

PREFACE

This is not a book about immunology, nor about cancer, nor even about the living cell. Rather, it is a personal drama that encompasses all three. It is the true story of how a few people met for a time on the fields of medical research to fight a battle—a single battle, not yet ended, in a war that will be waged for decades to come.

A note about the characters and events in this book: With one exception, everyone described is a real person. With their permission, I have used their real names and stories to recreate certain events as they were recalled to me. The single exception is the physician and cancer patient whom I've called Jack Christie. That is not in fact his name; at his request, I have embellished certain of the minor events, personal descriptions, secondary characters, and locales that together make up his story.

There were two reasons for his request: First, he and his family are very private people, and he agreed to share his story only under the condition of pseudonymity. Second, he knows very well that he dwells daily at the cutting edge of cancer research, an edge too often dulled by false promises and advertising hype. As a physician, he fears that even the use of his name could be taken as an endorsement of new (and still largely unproven) cancer therapies. But while a few details surrounding "Jack Christie's" story have been fictionalized, the descriptions of his disease and its treatment are real.

No book is written entirely single-handedly, of course. During

PREFACE

the past year and a half, dozens of people have provided me with their invaluable experience, judgment, and support. I owe a special debt of gratitude to my editor at Doubleday, the eagle-eyed Adrian Zackheim, for his nonstop encouragement and advice. My thanks also go to those who have volunteered so much of their time and energy to help me grasp the fundamentals of immunology and cancer research in the 1980s; here I gratefully acknowledge the kind assistance of Drs. Kenneth Foon, Robert Oldham, Richard Miller, and Paul Abrams—just four of the hundreds of researchers who have dedicated their lives to unraveling the cruel mysteries of cancer. At Damon Biotech, Marcia Amsterdam Kean was of invaluable help in arranging my interviews and personal visits. And without the patient thoughtfulness of Drs. David Kosowsky, Allan Jarvis, Nigel Webb, and the other men and women of Damon Biotech, this book would not have been possible.

If technical shortcomings or factual errors are to be found within these pages, it is not because they were ineffective teachers but because I was a careless student.

H. GARRETT DEYOUNG
Boston, Massachusetts
October 1985

A NOTE ON SCIENTIFIC MEASUREMENTS

Every scientist, regardless of specialty, speaks, writes, and even thinks in the metric system of measurement. Throughout this book, I have also used these terms rather than the more familiar American system of inches, feet, etc. In order to avoid frequent and awkward comparisons between the two methods, I offer the following "quick conversion" chart:

WEIGHT

The basic unit is the gram, approximately 454 of which make a sixteen-ounce pound. A kilogram is 1000 grams, or slightly more than two pounds.

LENGTH

A meter is about thirty-nine inches. It is divided into 100 centimeters and 1000 millimeters; a millimeter is in turn divided into 1000 microns.

VOLUME

Liquids are usually measured in terms of the liter, which is approximately one quart. A milliliter is one thousandth of a liter, or about one thirtieth of a fluid ounce, and a deciliter is a tenth of a liter (approximately three fluid ounces).

At last, at last—but that was long ago—Nature achieved it. After thousands of millions of years of selection, or thousands of billions, if that sounds better, she earned her Seventh Day. She built a spot of life, and it had a wall. There it is—under the microscope.

—Gustav Eckstein
The Body Has a Head

Nicodemus said to him, "How can a man be born when he is old? Can he enter a second time into his mother's womb and be born?"

—John 3:4

PROLOGUE

You, the edifice, were made from just two cells.

Father gave you one—a squiggly impatient thing so small that 400 of them lying end to end would barely reach across your thumbnail. Mother's was much larger. Only about 150 of them would cover a line that long. But you didn't need nearly that many. One was enough.

The cells came together in a silent kiss one day, sheltered inside of her. While she slept, perhaps, or combed her hair, or rushed off to work. The kiss was unheralded, unfelt (although Mother may insist that yes, she felt it, she knew). It made them one, to share their plasms and all the tiny organisms that lived and worked and throbbed within their fragile walls.

It was all very new for you, of course, but it had happened countless times before. The kiss was not unlike the first one, probably stolen hundreds of millions of years ago in some hot soupy stuff bubbling just beneath the surface of what would later be called Earth. Maybe it merely happened, like some say it did— by chance, by luck, by an eternal cycle of trial and error and starting over again. Or maybe it wasn't luck at all. No matter for now. The kiss cared nothing for science, naught even for the things of heaven. Only the new cell was important. The cell and the microspeck that decorates its center.

Coiled tightly within this speck, this nucleus, was the threadlike DNA—so thin that an incredible six feet of it was packed inside the new cell, and every one that was to follow. Mother lent some,

1

and with it perhaps her pale blue eyes or her quick laugh. From Father's share may have come the broad shoulders and the love of Vivaldi. Or perhaps an unkind defect of spirit or body; the speck comes to us with no warranties. Within a few hours, the two cells that had briefly been one became two again. The two became four. The four eight. And every time one cell became two, so did the speck and its cargo. Nine months after the kiss, there were billions of cells. Later, the billions would become a trillion.

At first, though, when there were just a few of them, no man could distinguish one cell from its neighbors. Each lived and divided only to make more of its kind. Each consisted of a rigid but flexible wall and a jellylike cytoplasm within the wall, made up of water, minerals, granules of protein and fat, and something called Life. Each cell knew from its birth what it needed to survive —water, of course, but also gases, electrically charged atoms and groups of atoms, enzymes, molecules called amino acids—and how to arrange for their delivery from elsewhere in the system. None had to be taught how to bring the bundles of atomic particles through its cell wall where they could be used and rebuilt into other bundles that were needed just as urgently elsewhere. No slackers here.

Then something happened. One cluster of cells—only a few hundred, perhaps—suddenly looked a bit different from the cluster next to it. A month or so after the kiss (you were about the size of a hefty housefly then), a few cells began to look like the beginnings of a brain, resting close to what just might later be an eye. Some other cells clumped together to suggest something like a heart. Elsewhere, yet other offspring of the kiss were preparing to form the red and white blood cells and platelets that would find their way to that heart, thence to carry life to the remotest outposts of your body.

Now the differences became more important than the similarities. In the pancreas, certain cells made the hormone called insulin; without it, your other cells would literally starve to death in a matter of days. Other cells set to work making chemicals for your brain—the neurotransmitters that would distribute information throughout the nervous system so that you might later know to stop the car at a red light, or pull your hand away from fire, or lovingly nurse your child, or recall a Whitman verse. Still other kinds of cells, each like the others guided by a portion of the DNA at its center, came together into the cartilage and skin and bone that holds the rest of you together.

And at some point in its cycle of division, each cell recognized where and when to stop. Where and when this muscle was fully formed, where and when those brain tissues were sufficient to their tasks. At that point, the cell knew that you, the edifice, were complete. What was needed now was maintenance—garbage to be eliminated, damaged structures to be dismantled and carted off and replaced, vandals and intruders to be foiled, heating and cooling and plumbing and electrical systems to be inspected and repaired. The constant growth once so essential to life would now threaten to destroy it.

The speck knows this. But we've said that the speck is sometimes imperfect, and so may order up the creation of an imperfect cell. An impatient bit of chemistry this, it divides long before its appointed time, creating two cells that look ever so slightly different from the ones surrounding it.

Most of the time the anarchy is detected and squelched by other cells. Now and again the rebels get away, each to divide into two of its kind. The two become four. The four become eight. . . .

CHAPTER ONE

Texas Medical Center
Houston
April 1981

In a cramped, semidarkened room on an upper floor, two men huddle over an instrument console that occupies the lower third of one entire wall. Near the center of the console is what appears to be a small black-and-white television screen. Prompted by a series of commands punched into a large keyboard at its base, the screen displays a succession of ghostly images. Each lasts several seconds, then disappears. Another slightly different one takes its place a minute or so later. For long periods of time, the silence of the room is broken only by the sharp plastic *clickety-click* of the keys and an occasional hushed comment about one of the images. A nurse wanders into the room from time to time to watch over the men's shoulders, then leaves to continue on her errand.

When they're not looking at the screen, the men glance into the adjoining room through a large window over the console. There a third man, wearing only a flimsy gray hospital gown, lies on his back on a narrow metal table. The head of the table leads into a massive upright steel-and-enamel structure with a large circular hole in its center. Bouquets of colored wires and clear plastic tubes blossom from the man's arms and chest, connecting him to a cluster of instruments along the wall. Directed every few minutes by the computer on the other side of the window, the table glides another inch or so into the hole, then halts; the man's

4

upper chest is now surrounded. A loudspeaker mounted over the door that connects the two rooms crackles to life.

"How you doing, Jack?"

The man on the table says nothing, but raises one hand slightly in reply. The loudspeaker cracks again.

"You're lookin' good, pal. Really first-rate. We got a nurse in here who's so excited about these pictures that we're gonna send 'em to that computer dating service up the street. Okay, gimme a big smile. Deep breath, hold it—here we go." The man at the CT scanner—medical shorthand for "computerized tomography"—console jabs another command into the keyboard.

At that instant, the first in a new series of energy pulses is released from the X-ray generator as it begins its race around the inside of the hole. By the time the rotating device has come full circle—a trip lasting barely a second—it will have released hundreds of individual pulses of gamma rays. Each burst travels painlessly through the man on the table and is received by the detector, a bit of crystal, mounted precisely across the hole from the generator, that moves at the same speed as the generator. Every pulse of energy carries a priceless bit of information about the mass of tissue it has just penetrated. The datum is absorbed by the detector and is instantly digested, analyzed, and sent to the computer in the next room. There, along with the data represented by the hundreds of other pulses that make up the scan, it is reconstructed into a new image.

"You can breathe now, Jack." The man on the table lets out his breath and shifts slightly in a futile effort to make himself more comfortable. As with most CT patients, the physical discomfort is nothing; it's the overwhelming claustrophobia, the sense of being swallowed up by the gleaming, silent enamel tunnel through which he's been gliding for the past half hour. He feels helpless, imprisoned, completely at the mercy of the invisible men in the adjacent room. For a moment, he's gripped by the urge to rip the tubes and needles from his body, wriggle his way out of the tunnel, leap from the table, and race to freedom.

In the next room, the new CT image unfolds on the screen. It begins at the top of the monitor and works its way down—a rough oval, densely packed with smaller black, white, and gray images. The clarity, the detail, is nothing less than startling. It looks as though someone had used a huge razor to slice through the upper body as cleanly as though it were a chunk of salami. The radiologists at the console, in fact, refer to each image as a "slice." There, slightly off to one side, you can make out the large chambers of the heart; the larger structures near the bottom of the oval, of course, are the lungs, forever frozen by the X-ray beam. At the bottom of the oval, the spine and its enclosed cord are clearly visible. If there are any doubts, the men can refer to the large charts mounted on the wall behind them, on which virtually every human structure is accurately drawn, in both color and black and white, and labeled.

The thin, bearded man at the console raps out a new set of commands on the keyboard. "Deep breath, Jack. We're almost there now . . ." The table slides another inch or two into the hole. Another burst of X-rays. Another slice. And another, and another. Barely an hour after the man in the hospital gown climbed onto the table, the two men next door have accumulated nearly fifty slices. Each is slightly different from the one before it, since it represents a slightly different cross section of the anatomy. Each is automatically transferred to videotape for close inspection later.

As a rule, a solitary slice will not provide the radiologists with much valuable information. When they are all viewed in a continuous sequence, however, they will etch an incredibly precise portrait of Jack Christie's interior: every bone, every organ (although the X-rays draw finer pictures of hard masses than of soft ones), and most of the large and small blood vessels. Not too long ago, only a surgeon working all day and much of the night could enjoy such a vista. But Christie had not been touched by a scalpel. Not a drop of his blood had been shed. He would feel no pain.

But there are many questions—literally life-and-death questions—that even the CT can't answer. What is the chemical condition of the millions of cells that made up each image? Is each of them working properly, churning out or taking up its allotted share of blood, minerals, proteins, gases, hormones, wastes? Are all the cells working together smoothly? Or is there a tiny, still unseen cluster of rogue cells that have set out on their own destructive course?

The men in the darkened room don't ask those questions just

yet; it's far too early for that, and they will review the pictures with several of their colleagues before arriving at their decision. Still, they can't help but wonder about the pale little masses—"like a bunch of marshmallows," someone remarks—that cluster about one of the large vessels in Jack Christie's upper abdomen. If the blurry spots are what the men think they are, there's only one sure way to find out. But unlike the CT scan, the biopsy scheduled for later in the week will be neither quick nor painless.

Jack Christie won't be escaping the knife after all.

Houston, Texas
April 1981

Fifteen miles west-southwest of the Medical Center, Jack Christie reached again for the coffeepot. Four cups already, he chided himself, and not even seven-thirty in the morning. As usual at this early hour, he was adorned in only two items of clothing—Jockey shorts and a sweat-stained Houston Astros baseball cap. He added a shot of skim milk to the coffee, then turned once more to the matter of his death. It was important to him that it be a tidy one.

There was the matter of the will, of course, although he had reviewed that document just a few months before—he doubted that there would be any changes. But he would also have to dig out his insurance policies, place a few discreet calls to his lawyers, and think about rearranging some of his investments so that they could be maintained by the rest of the family with a minimum amount of bother. He might occasionally be careless about his personal habits, but not about this. His financial affairs were always in top-drawer order.

And there was the family: How much should he tell them at this point? How much could they understand? His father would probably take the news with his characteristic aplomb, even make a few jokes about it. Then he'd take his grief and anger for a long private walk. But his mother mustn't know yet. And certainly not Mama Christino.

En route to the bathroom, he stopped at the bedroom door to study the sleeping woman. He still loved the way she slept, drawn up childlike in a tight little ball. Only the thick dark hair was visible, flowing across the pillow like a spilled bottle of ink; all else was hidden under the flowered sheets. She would have to know, of course. But not today. Probably not tomorrow. Maybe next week.

Even now, two weeks after the biopsy, he was a little surprised at how easy it had been to accept the news. It was as though the mechanic had popped into his room to tell him his car was ready. The oncologist had tried to take some of the sharp edges off the news by offering chatty gossip about some mutual friends and inquiring about Christie's family. Finally, it came out.

"Well, it's what you thought, Jack. Lymphoma, non-Hodgkin's. We're still not 100 percent sure of the exact cell type, though. Some of us think it's one thing, some of us think something else. We'll have some other guys take a look at it later this week, get a better idea of what we're working with here."

Standing now under the lukewarm shower, Christie gingerly ran his soapy fingertips across the pink incision that traveled from just under his breastbone to an inch above the navel. The thing was there, alright—a hard, lumpy bit of tissue at the lower edge of his rib cage, off to the left. Was it bigger than last week, or was it his imagination? As a physician himself, he'd known all along what it was: the tip of his enlarged spleen, pushing beyond its normal borders and pressing into his stomach. It partly explained why his usually ravenous appetite had fallen so dramatically over the past month or two. Along with the other symptoms —the feverish achiness, fatigue, periods of restlessness, the unusual lethargy—the picture had become so sharply etched ("classical," as his professors used to say) that any barely competent practitioner would have spotted it.

He studied himself carefully in the mirror as he prepared to shave. Not so bad for a man with only a couple of years to live, he thought, if you ignored the little potbelly and the "love handles" he'd sported ever since high school. The shoulder and chest muscles were still sharply defined, the jawline clean and smooth with just the slightest hint of softness. His coarse black hair was as thick as it had been as an undergrad, with only a few gray strands here and there to suggest that he'd just recently passed the thirty-year mark. And until a few weeks ago, he could still press 175 pounds, breeze through sixty sit-ups, then jog his six or eight miles, all before 6 A.M.

Still, he knew what the pathology report meant. He was now a cancer patient, just like one of those poor shits he'd seen in med school and in residency. For some irrational reason, he'd never liked them (though God knows he always did the best he could do for them, though sometimes it wasn't much). They lashed out at him and at the nurses, or they whined and cried. They complained bitterly—or even worse, turned mechanically to their long-abandoned prayers for comfort and reassurance. They asked the same unanswerable questions in the same raspy voices. And they all smelled, especially toward the end; you could smell their disease as soon as you walked into their rooms.

It wasn't that he didn't feel sorry for them. He did. Most of them, at least, though not so much for the ones he always thought had brought it on themselves, like the two-pack-a-day smokers. Most of them had done nothing to deserve their tumors. Biologically, they had simply happened to be in the wrong place at the wrong time, like the guy who walks out of the store just as a speeding car jumps the curb. Life was really just a goofy crapshoot anyway, and it seemed that a lot of the losers wound up in the cancer wards. Jack Christie liked to spend his time with winners, not losers.

Now he was one of them, or so they told him. Certain cells that made up his immune system's major line of defense—cells that had developed over hundreds of thousands of years to defend him against the countless would-be microscopic invaders he encountered every day of his life—had suddenly turned on him and were reproducing themselves long before the replacements were needed. Later he would learn that the runaway cells themselves were relatively normal in appearance and function; there were just too many of them, and they were crowding out and attacking their life-sustaining neighbors.

Having arrived at his own diagnosis during the previous few weeks, he had gone back to his textbooks to learn more about his cancer, this thing called lymphoma. The statistics weren't encouraging. Every year his particular form of lymphoma struck some twenty-five thousand new victims; every year it killed about ten thousand more. And while some of the patients were able to live more or less normally for six, eight, even ten years after diagnosis, they were the exceptions. The average life expectancy was only about three and a half years.

For now, he felt fine. Just the little aches he might otherwise attribute to normal wear and tear. Within a few months, the aches would become pain as the malignant cells pressed their invasion. The fatigue would grow into a bone-deep weariness. At some point in time, a simple cold might have him confined to bed for days. A flu virus could kill him. Depending on the chemical personality of his lymphoma, the cancer could spread to other parts of his body—his stomach, perhaps, or his bones. Or some of the cells would find their way to his lungs, where they would grow undetected and unreachable until the only treatment they could give him would be something to relieve his final torment.

Still, he regarded his cancer with a certain professional detachment. He was, after all, a scientist; his was simply another case to be treated and, if possible, solved. He buttered an English muffin while his mind reached back in time for names. Names of other men and women who had established themselves as experts in a field that boasted no experts at all just a few years before. Names of universities and medical centers. Names of drugs—new and perhaps dangerous drugs that nevertheless had seemed to rein in the growth of the faulty cells, even for a few months.

Eight weeks after the diagnosis, he was at last struck by the intimacy of his cancer. Pulling into his driveway late one hot and sticky June afternoon, the front seat of the MG stacked high with books and journals, he suddenly realized he wasn't the doctor in this case, but the patient. And he was probably going to die. Switching off the ignition, he stared at himself for a few minutes in the rearview mirror. He thought that perhaps he should cry. Or pray. Or be enraged at being struck down for no good reason.

Instead, he said simply, "Well, there goes the fucking ball game. . . ."

Boston, Massachusetts
April 1981

For all practical purposes, Boston's Route 128 begins about ten miles north of the city, in the town of Wakefield. From there it loops off to the west, then to the south and east. It ends in Braintree, some twelve miles south of the city, thus forming a giant half-circle around metropolitan Boston.

By the late 1970s, many of high technology's most powerful names—computer manufacturers, mostly, like Honeywell, Control Data, and Teradyne—had been drawn to property along the expressway, for several reasons. For one, they liked the region's pastoral setting that had somehow survived the rapid commercial buildup. And although your next-door neighbor was probably one of your hottest business competitors, 128 had an almost academic sense of community that you couldn't find in the city, nor in most of the suburbs. And there was the convenience. You could usually get to almost anywhere on 128 in less than an hour, whether you lived in fashionably rustic Duxbury on the South Shore or in snooty, old-money Gloucester to the north.

Inevitably, someone decided that the highway needed a new name. Something catchier than "Route 128," and more descriptive than the original "Yankee Division Highway," the title given in honor of the wartime Massachusetts National Guard unit. Something like the Silicon Valley south of San Francisco, the nation's other white-hot high-tech region. So a few blue and white road signs sprang up on Route 128 during the late 1970s, informing drivers that they were now racing along "America's Technology Highway." Apparently feeling that "Highway" was too limited, the word was changed to "Region" in 1984. Actually, neither title ever caught on; today, the road and most of the rocky terrain through which it cuts is simply "128."

Considering the neighborhood, word of a new high-tech company here attracts about as much attention as snow in February. One of the exceptions was when word leaked out that Damon Corporation was moving into the biotechnology business. To some of the money men along Boston's State Street, the decision had all the makings of an economic disaster. True, the company had once been the darling of the financial community. The outfit that couldn't seem to do anything wrong. The company that until recently had scored with not just one or two of its ventures, but with every one.

But this was 1981; Damon had started to run short of golden eggs in 1975. In those six years, it had become a sort of good-news, bad-news joke in some quarters: The good news was that Damon had made a lot of smart decisions. The bad news was that some of them had hit the market at the wrong time. The unofficial word along State Street was that the company that once couldn't do anything wrong now had trouble doing anything right.

If they had dug around a bit, the analysts might have uncovered more unsettling news. While the science-business called biotechnology was long on glamor and promise, it had so far proven to be painfully short on profits. Cetus and Genex, two of the major prophets of corporate biotechnology, not only had yet to earn their first nickel, but were frankly warning their investors and the media that it would probably be years before the red ink turned to black.

Even worse, Damon's greatest triumphs hadn't been in biotech, but in electronics, laboratory instruments, and instructional aids for high school science teachers. David Kosowsky, Damon's rapid-fire chairman, was an electrical engineer who had been blessed with either a good head for business or a heaping share of luck. But company insiders admitted that they had no blueprint for the new biotech business and almost none of the people needed to get it rolling. The whole life sciences staff, in fact, essentially consisted of just two people: a middle-aged coronary case and a young molecular biologist who'd been out of grad school barely long enough to know a stock option from a Form 10-K.

But there were other stories about Damon floating around Boston. For one, the company was assembling a powerful team of scientific advisers from MIT and Harvard to oversee the birthing of its new offspring. Elsewhere in Cambridge, moreover, there was talk about how Kosowsky had recently come to own an odd bit of technology developed by "some offbeat inventor" down in Virginia. Some of them were still discussing the paper the inventor had copublished the year before in the widely respected journal *Science*. In that paper, the two men had described how they had taken living, insulin-making cells from the pancreas of a normal rat, wrapped them in tiny starchy capsules, then injected them into diabetic rats. The capsules had seemingly served as a sort of biological Trojan horse, had apparently fooled the rats' immune systems into accepting them. And this acceptance lasted not for just a couple of days, but for three weeks—long enough for the insulin secreted by the transplanted cells to reverse many of the animals' diabetic symptoms.

To be sure, no one was talking about a "cure" for diabetes; it was much too early for that, and there were far too many unanswered questions. Even to the most cautious readers, though, the implications just couldn't be overlooked. Clearly, the *Science* authors seemed to be onto something, but no one—maybe not even the researchers themselves—quite knew what it was nor what to do with it. At Damon, Kosowsky was overheard to admit that when he'd first been told that the Virginia researcher was stuffing cells into capsules and keeping them alive, he'd stared over the tops of his glasses for a few moments, then asked, "So what?"

Still, Kosowsky sensed that there was something very unusual about the results, and he could never turn away from the unusual. And although he wasn't entirely at ease with the complex and confusing principles of biology, he'd had a lifelong fascination with medical technology. Even as the *Science* paper was being drafted, in fact, his curiosity had prompted him to visit some friends at Harvard and MIT, his own alma mater, for a crash course in cellular biology. And the more he learned, the more fascinated he became.

One thing he learned was that while other people had tried to encapsulate living cells for one reason or another, the things kept dying. The Virginia researcher had apparently found a way around that: Not only did the cells not die in his new process, but they seemed to thrive as though they were still in the body.

Kosowsky nodded.

If for some reason you want to grow a large number of living cells, he was told, you really have only two ways of doing it: First, you can put a few of the cells you want inside a living organism, hope that they "take root" and multiply, then retrieve them when you have enough. Or you can go to cell culture methods; basically, you put the things in glass dishes, give them lots of food, and keep them warm and clean. Hopefully, some of them will be happy enough to divide and make more cells, and some of those will divide and make even more cells, and so on and so on.

One problem with growing cells in organisms such as bacteria, the biologists explained, is that you need an awful lot of glassware to give you enough of whatever it is you're trying to grow. A bigger problem is that the cells will be contaminated with the other stuff made by the organisms' own cells, stuff the creature needs but you don't. You have to find ways of getting rid of that stuff, and it takes a lot of time and money to do that. Cell culture, meanwhile, is limited by the fact that living things don't like glass dishes. They much prefer their original environments, where they're closely surrounded by other living cells and bathed in oxygen-rich blood and minerals and organic chemicals like hormones that tell them what to do and when to do it. In fact, most of the cells in a glass dish will just up and die on you, no matter how hard you try to keep them happy, so you wind up with only a fraction of the number of cells you really want.

"Go on," said Kosowsky.

They told him that the Virginia inventor had apparently found an interesting alternative to animals and glass dishes, a new way of growing large numbers of cells and keeping them alive and functional for a long time. And since Kosowsky owned the technology, Damon could do the same thing.

Kosowsky asked the obvious question: "Why do I want to grow cells?"

"You probably don't," they replied. "You want the stuff the cells make, or can be coaxed to make—hormones, for example, or interferon. The more cells you grow, and the happier they are, the more interferon you can make. And there are a lot of people who will be happy to pay you tens of thousands of dollars for even a gram of the stuff, barely enough to coat the bottom of a shot glass."

Kosowsky knew a little about interferon, a protein made by certain cells in the immune system when they are invaded by viruses. Some people were calling it the new miracle drug to fight cancer, and Kosowsky's friends at MIT were right: Someone out there was going to learn how to make interferon—in water tumblers, not in shot glasses—and get very rich doing it. The problem is that everyone was now trying to make interferon. Even if Damon wanted to play that game, what could the company bring to a business that was already overcrowded with players?

"Well, but there's lots of other things no one's making," the biologists explained. "Monoclonal antibodies. Almost no one's growing monoclonals, and it's a lot like the interferon thing. There's a ton of money waiting for the guy who can figure out how to do it."

As a businessman, Kosowsky had for a while regarded monoclonal antibodies as even less promising than interferon. He knew that the tiny scraps of protein, first made by two researchers in England a few years before, were another important part of the human immune system. As such, they were being touted by some as the answer to a veritable shopping list of human ailments, and so stood to be every bit as profitable as interferon. As with interferon, however, the scientists were right again: No one knew how to make them in any quantity, or at least no one was talking about it if he did. The people who were making them at all were content to do so not in grams, but in millionths of a gram. Until someone figured out how to do much better than that, monoclonals were going absolutely nowhere.

Still, Kosowsky wanted to learn more about the odd little proteins that no one seemed able to make. The more he learned, the more intrigued he became. But what he didn't know—in fact, what only a handful of men and women knew at the time—was more intriguing yet. And if Kosowsky had been part of that small circle of researchers, he might have heard about two young doctors in California who were using the proteins to treat a form of cancer they'd been studying for several years.

Non-Hodgkin's lymphoma, it was called.

CHAPTER TWO

The 1970s had been the age of the computer. By the time that David Kosowsky had rolled Damon's dice onto the table of biotechnology, the 1980s had already been baptized as the age of the New Medicine.

To be sure, there were important differences between the two technologies. One was that the small personal computers conceived and born during the 1970s were being targeted to the individual consumer. Moreover, they were distinct products: You could go into a store, say "I want one of those," take it home, and plug it in. Biotechnology wasn't a product, but a process—a perplexing collection of processes, actually—for manipulating living cells, and was aimed at hospitals, medical centers, chemical companies, and biological researchers.

But there were also similarities between the two, especially their incredible rates of growth. New electronics companies had sprung up like mushrooms during the late 1970s, each of them geared to plug into its own derivative marketplace. A few years later it seemed that all it took to launch a new medical technology venture was two or three biochemists and a suitcase full of money. And there was a generous supply of both. As with electronics, most of these new companies struggled to stake out a unique piece of the health care landscape—new pharmaceuticals and diagnostic procedures, mostly, along with the unique chemical raw materials needed to make them.

By 1983, not even a decade after the first planned transfer of a gene from one type of bacteria to another, the roster of biotech companies in the United States alone had topped three hundred. And that didn't even include the nonbiotech startups—tiny new labs tucked into corners of new industrial parks, in which young men in Izods and Docksiders sketched new artificial organs and medical imagers for twelve and fifteen hours a day, six days a week.

Medicine was suddenly very big business.

And sitting at the very center of all the excitement was immunology. The Mother Lode. The Tree of Knowledge. The Source.

Few would ever have predicted even ten years earlier that such a dreary science could explode so brilliantly onto the medical stage. Even as researchers chalked up Nobel-caliber victories in other life sciences—molecular biology, genetics, brain chemistry, heart disease, cancer—immunology trudged along anonymously, without color and with few popular heroes. Certainly none to fire the public imagination, like a De Bakey or a Salk or a Barnard. In a world in which dramatic discoveries were being announced almost weekly, immunologists seemed content to measure their progress in decades. Immunology was the great black box—science jargon for anything that works but that no one understands. And, to be honest, it was a bore. Endless postulates and theories wrapped in the kind of obscure terminology guaranteed to turn off the uninitiated.

One East Coast biologist recalls that "even while I was in grad school in the mid-seventies, immunology just wasn't where it was at. It was too much of a mystery; there wasn't anything to get your hands on." And without something to grab on to, how could you know where you were heading, or realize when you got there? Just as important to the new breed of ambitious young Ph.D.s of the time, how could you expect to capture the attention of your colleagues and superiors—not to mention the megabucks in research grants routinely handed out by the major foundations and health institutes?

Yet it was immunology that held the answers to so many vital questions still confounding medical researchers. It had been known for centuries that every mammal has a natural defense system against bacteria, viruses, and other types of living and nonliving foreign matter—a kind of central processing network that diligently compares every incoming particle against its own cellular surroundings and promptly disposes of whatever doesn't jibe. If this system could be fully understood and controlled, the implications for other fields of medicine were enormous. Certain parts of the system could be switched off or otherwise regulated at will. Organ transplants might become as simple as setting a broken arm. Diseases such as rheumatoid arthritis and multiple sclerosis, in which the immune system apparently turns on its owner, could become as obsolete as smallpox. And if cancer was indeed "immunology gone wrong," as some researchers were saying, it might be possible to control the disease—perhaps even eradicate it—by setting the network right again.

But as the twentieth century moved into its final quarter, the system had given up only a few tantalizing clues about how it worked. Or why it sometimes didn't.

The lights, when they came on, only seemed that much brighter.

If immunology had long been lacking a unifying theory—a "handle"—neither had it comprised a blank page in medical history. Just an indecipherable one.

Observations had been recorded and questions posed by curious minds almost from the beginning of history. The ancient Greeks and Chinese, for instance, couldn't help but notice that once they recovered from certain diseases they never suffered from them again, even though they were in constant close contact with other victims. And legend has it that certain medieval Russians even developed a crude means of vaccinating their young women against the dreaded smallpox. (There was nothing especially chivalrous about this, by the way. It seems that the girls were the community's only exports. The economic value of a girl whose face bore the telltale scars of the disease would be seriously reduced.)

But knowing that something works isn't quite the same as knowing why it works. The first man to come close to explaining "why" was an eighteenth-century British physician, poet, and natural historian named Edward Jenner. If immunology can be said to have a father, it was indisputably Jenner.

The practice of smallpox vaccination had become so common

by the mid-1700s that almost anyone with a needle, a steady hand, and a friend with the disease could do it at his kitchen table. All that was required was to prick one of the actively growing pustules with the needle, then scratch a trace of the material under the skin of the person being vaccinated. Every so often the inoculation backfired, and the patient came down with a full-blown, sometimes fatal infection. Most of the time, he developed only a mild form of the disease within a couple of days. When he recovered, he could rest assured that he was protected against smallpox for the rest of his life.

It was a simple enough procedure, and we might still be scratching each other with infected needles if Jenner's curiosity hadn't been fired by another observation: There seemed to be large numbers of people who claimed to be unvaccinated, but who nevertheless did not contract smallpox during outbreaks of the disease. Either the rules of probability were being strained beyond reason, thought Jenner, or these fortunate souls were being protected by something else. And so they were; Jenner soon learned that virtually everyone who enjoyed an apparent natural immunity to smallpox had once been infected with cow-pox. True to its name, cowpox—the symptoms of which closely resemble those of smallpox—usually developed first in cattle, then spread to the humans who milked and fed them.

Intrigued with this mysterious relationship, Jenner conducted an experiment that today would almost certainly strip him of his medical license on grounds of simple ethics. He vaccinated an eight-year-old boy with matter from a milkmaid infected with cowpox; a few weeks later, he injected the youngster with a hefty dose of material infected with smallpox virus. Fortunately for both Jenner and the boy, the second injection had no effect. Whatever had been infecting the milkmaid was now protecting Jenner's young patient. That could mean only one thing: There were certain similarities between the two viruses (the term Jenner coined to describe the responsible organisms). Exposure to one of them somehow protected against the other.

Jenner was so delighted with his findings that he prepared large quantities of his cowpox vaccine and sent it to his friends and relatives along with instructions on how to use it. (One of the recipients was Thomas Jefferson, who reportedly called his family and Monticello neighbors together for a mass vaccination.) Jenner couldn't realize it at the time, but he had stumbled onto what are now called immunoglobulins, or antibodies—tiny bits of specialized protein that are called up by the body in response to invading particles and organisms.

Nearly two centuries and hundreds of researchers later, antibodies are more than ever at the heart of immunology. And while there is still much too much we don't know about these unusual fragments of nonliving matter, we are getting tantalizingly close; somewhere among us, in fact, there are probably a couple of youngsters—ten years old, maybe fifteen—who will one day neatly fit into place the final pieces of the puzzle. And when they do, they will almost certainly report that as with everything else in our bodies, the answer was there all along, in the genes.

Look at a cell for a few minutes under a simple microscope. It seems to be a rather uncomplicated thing. Its shape may be roundish or squared off, elongated or squat. Depending on the dye you use to accentuate its features, the landscape beneath the lens sometimes stretches out flat and uninspired; at other times, or with other types of cells, you find yourself hopelessly transfixed with the strange, almost surrealistic beauty. Plain or lovely, the most common impression as you stare down the tube is one of unearthly silence.

If you could burrow into the cell, however, you would find the environment anything but serene. Slogging through the semiliquid cytoplasm that gives the cell its shape, you would encounter hundreds of miniorganisms, all working independently yet in smooth concert with their neighbors: Structures and molecules with foreign-sounding names—endoplasmic reticulum, Golgi body, mitochondrion, ribosome, glycoprotein—whose combined function is to acquire, build, store, and release the energy and raw materials needed for the cell's survival.

Sitting in the midst of all this activity is the main object of our search: the roundish body called the nucleus, the cell's main "control panel" which houses the forty-six odd-looking chromosomes. Like the cell itself, these come in all different shapes and sizes—some long and slender, others short and stumpy. If you look closely, you will see that the chromosomes aren't really forty-six entirely separate bodies, but two sets of twenty-three each—a set from Mother, a set from Father. Consider them their very first gift to you.

Dig deeper now into the chromosomes. Each of them is made up of a length of a very large molecule called DNA—deoxyribonucleic acid—wound about itself so tightly that the DNA contained in all forty-six chromosomes of a single cell, laid end to end, would stretch an incredible six feet. An average-sized chromosome contains more than two thousand identifiable genes, each consisting of a discrete length of DNA (think of a mile-long length of string marked off in segments of two and a half feet each) and most of them responsible for the production of a single protein. Since we consist mostly of protein, it is easy to see why DNA is often called the "blueprint of life."

And how does a gene carry out such a heavy responsibility? A grossly oversimplified explanation (which is bound to induce exasperated shudders among biologists) is in the unusual chemical structure of DNA. If it is helpful to think of genes as marked-off pieces of string, it is even more so to visualize the DNA molecule as an infinitely long spiral staircase, the steps of which are made up of just four other types of molecules (abbreviated C, G, T, and A). Each step is a combination of two of these molecules, either C and G or T and A; all other combinations are ruled out. When it comes time for the gene—a portion of the "staircase"—to call for the production of a protein, other organisms within the cell decipher the order in which the steps follow each other. If "C-T-G" is read, a molecule of one of twenty different amino acids is produced elsewhere in the cell; if the order is "T-T-A," a different amino acid is produced; yet another will result from a "G-G-T" sequence, and so forth. As the amino acids are manufactured, still other cellular mechanisms string them together, rather like a pearl necklace, to form a protein. Small proteins may consist of only a couple of dozen amino acids, while very large proteins may contain thousands.

There are some other remarkable things about DNA. One is that it's chemically and functionally the same no matter where it's found, whether in a human cell, a bacterium, or a daisy. From the standpoint of a molecular biologist, in fact, the only difference between a petunia and an elephant is the amount of DNA in their respective cells, and thus how many different proteins can be supplied for their design and maintenance. That is, a single-cell bacterium might require only a thousand or so genes, located on a single chromosome, to carry out its simple life; we, on the other hand, require something in the neighborhood of one hundred thousand functioning genes in each of our cells. (Actually, there's enough DNA in each human cell to make more than a million genes, but so far researchers have been able to identify only a fraction of that number that are involved in protein production. The unused portions of DNA appear to be spacers or serve as control or regulatory sequences.)

Another of DNA's interesting features arises from the chemical nature of the "stairs." Since an A molecule joins only with a T molecule, and a C only with a G, one doesn't need the entire staircase to know the exact composition of a gene—just its right or left side. If one knows the sequence along one side of the staircase, the sequence along the other side is predetermined. Even more useful is the fact that if the structure of a protein is known—that is, its specific sequence of amino acids—a reasonably skilled biologist can actually manufacture the gene that produced it, simply by working backward.

The network of specialized cells which we call the immune system amounts to about a tenth of all the body's cells. Over millions of years of trial and error, they evolved to fill just two purposes: to distinguish between what belongs in their owner's body and what doesn't—between "self" and "nonself," in some of the science's lighter terminology—and then to destroy or repel whatever doesn't belong. The first task is carried out millions of times every day because every cell carries on its surface unique bits of molecular architecture, or markings, that are rather like fingerprints. Also like fingerprints, there's a vanishingly small likelihood that any two people will have identical cellular markings.

The second task is more complicated. According to the latest theories on this still baffling process, every human fetus contains a mass of bone cells (called stem cells) that develop, soon after birth, into specialized white blood cells called lymphocytes. The term arose from "cyte," or "cell," and the fact that these particular cells are manufactured mostly by the tissues of the lymph system, the labyrinth of vessels and nodes that collects and strains the body's various fluids, then returns them to the bloodstream.

One of the most unusual features of these cells—and the one that threw so many early researchers off the track—was their baffling diversity. Most other families of cells bear strong physical and functional resemblances to each other: One red blood cell or heart muscle cell looks and behaves pretty much like any other red blood or heart muscle cell. The closer one studied these lymphocytes, however, the more variety they assumed.

One type of lymphocyte, for example, took the name "T-lymphocyte" (or simply "T-cell," the T standing for the human thymus gland—the little organ located behind the breastbone that appears to give these cells their genetic instructions). Furthermore, there appeared to be many different types of T-cells. Some came to be called "helper cells" because they stepped up the activity of other parts of the system. Others are able to single-handedly destroy cellular invaders, and took the name "killer cells." Yet another class of T-cells was called "suppressor cells," since they had the power to switch the immune system off at appropriate times. If it weren't for these suppressor cells, in fact, our bodies would perceive as foreign and reject any particle that didn't bear the identical molecular markings borne by each and every one of our own cells—the food we eat, the dust we breathe, even the children we bear.

By the middle of the 1960s, it had become clear that in the cellular war between "self" and "nonself," the T-cells are the battlefield commanders. They issue the orders, maintain communications between the troops, coordinate offense and defense, even decide whether battle will be waged at all. But there's another major group of lymphocytes—the B-cells, manufactured by the bone marrow, the spleen, and other organs. (The B refers to the bursa gland in the chicken, in which the cells were first found.) While they bear some physical resemblance to the T-cells, they play much different roles in the body. If the T-cells are the generals, the B-cells are the foot soldiers, patrolling the tissues and fluids in search of foreign bacteria, viruses, and other living and nonliving invaders. Together, these outsiders are generally called antigens. (Strictly speaking, that term refers not only to the foreign organism, but also to any part of the organism that interacts with the immune system.)

No one knows for sure how many different B-cell "families" the human body can produce in its defense. A mouse can make about 10 million, so we're certainly able to design hundreds of millions. Probably more like a billion. Each cellular family bears some physical and chemical resemblance to other families; more interesting, and far more crucial from the standpoint of the immune system, are the differences between them. The most important of these differences is in the tiny strands of protein—the immunoglobulins, or antibodies—which are made by the corresponding B-cell, and that dot the cell's surface like individual bits of fuzz on a peach. Although all immunoglobulins belong to one of only five major groups, the antibody found on any member of a given B-cell family is unlike the antibody on a member of any other family. During the past few years, many of these antibodies have been analyzed and portrayed by computer. They assume a variety of physical configurations, but are usually represented in textbooks and scholarly journals as Y-shaped molecules.

Better yet, think of them as little lobsters, their tails stuck into the surface of the cell and their claws outstretched. At first, they all look alike. Looking closer, we see that the claws of each lobster are ever so slightly different from those of the lobster on the B-cell next to it. The claws are in reality receptors—unique bits of chemical architecture, each designed to fit comfortably with one and only one other molecule or small cluster of molecules.

The more we've learned about chemical receptors during the past several years, the harder it is to overstate their mind-boggling complexity or their importance to all living organisms. There is barely a single biochemical reaction—from digesting a sandwich to smelling a rose to the decision to turn off the radio— that does not employ a receptor mechanism at some stage.

Virtually every natural receptor is made up of several strands of protein that fold over and under and around each other to form a geometrically unique three-dimensional mass, not unlike a huge knot of tangled string. Each individual strand, moreover, consists of hundreds or thousands of molecules of amino acids; change just one amino acid and you change the geometry of its corresponding protein strand. You also wind up with a completely different receptor. So while a close-up photo of a given receptor would look like a hopeless jumble of chains and atoms, each one is painstakingly built and utterly consistent from one cell to the next. Significantly, it fits comfortably only with its structural mirror image, like a casting fits only with the mold from which it was made. Some receptors are so sensitive that they can detect a difference of a single atom in a protein chain consisting of thousands of different amino acids.

It is this incredible selectivity that enables an antibody to recognize and bind to its corresponding antigen. When and if the fit between them is made, a chemical signal goes out to other cells in the network. The result is almost certain destruction for whatever is trapped in the claw, and for every other molecule bearing the same bit of architecture.

To illustrate, assume that a foreign bacterium enters the system. We tend to think that one bacterium looks pretty much like any other. Not so: Like all living cells, each bacterial species is dotted with hundreds or thousands of its own marker molecules (that is, antigens) and other structures of varying shapes and sizes. Some of these play important roles in the organism's simple life—as a means of fastening itself to a cell so it can dig in and take up residence, for instance.

As the bacterium travels through its new surroundings, it is met by several defenders, any one of which might bring it to a speedy dispatch. It may run into a natural killer T-cell, which would usually mean instant destruction. Or it could be challenged by a macrophage—relatively large cells that serve as the immune system's "bouncers"—in which case it would be engulfed and digested on the spot.

If the bacterium eludes these guardians, however, its presence will eventually be detected by other types of T-cells. Basically, these decide whether or not the newcomer belongs in the environment. To do this, they introduce the organism, like a new guest at a cocktail party, to the system of B-cells. One by one, each of the millions of different B-cells tries to match its claw with one or more of the bacterium's marker molecules.

If none of the claws fit the markers, the invader is freed to carry on its business. More likely, several of the claws will make a fit—

one on one of the bacterium's markers, another on a different marker, and so on. When that happens, every B-cell that matched itself with one or more parts of the organism instantly leaps into action by signaling the mass production of another type of cell, called plasma cells. Aided by the helper T-cells, the plasma cells begin to crank out enormous quantities of every antibody that made the fit. The swarms of antibodies, all slightly different from each other since each corresponds to a different marker on the organism, launch a search for more bacteria. When they find them, they bind tightly to their respective markers until other chemicals in the body arrive on the scene to finish the job. Enzymes may be summoned to break down the organism; other cells attach to the invader and destroy it by literally punching holes in its membrane.

Once scientists had worked out the basics of this simple yet complex chain of events during the early part of the twentieth century, they were finally able to fully explain Jenner's two-hundred-year-old smallpox experiments: When a tiny bit of the virus is scratched under the surface of the skin of a healthy patient, it is followed within a few days by antibody formation (what is now called an immune response). Not only do the antibodies keep reproducing themselves for as long as the virus is present, but they can also recognize and bind to any other virus that fits its receptor—the cowpox virus, for example, which bears some geometric similarity to the smallpox virus. And although the number of antibodies in the blood serum gradually decreases after the immune response, the system never quite forgets the experience. It is always prepared to launch another response should the virus reappear, a convenient feat of biological memorization that is the basis of every vaccine.

As in every science, however, every new answer led to a dozen new questions. And one of the most baffling had to do not with immunology per se, but with genetics.

Scientists had known about genes, at least in a qualitative sort of way, since the late nineteenth century. They had also speculated that each gene somehow ordered and controlled the production of a single protein. One gene (or group of genes) controls the production of liver cells, another the color of the eyes, and so forth.

Once DNA's chemical structure was worked out in the 1950s, however, intuition could no longer suffice. Now geneticists could not only understand the exact series of chemical events by which each gene cranked out its protein, but they posed a new challenge to their colleagues: No human condition, they said, could be fully understood until it was explained in terms of genetics.

In many cases, the mechanics of the gene turned out to be relatively straightforward. But when researchers turned to antibody production, their explanations hit the biological equivalent of a brick wall: If there were literally millions of different sizes and shapes of antibodies (which would be needed if the immune system was to successfully defend against every possible antigen), that implied that millions of different genes would be needed, one or more for each antibody family. The problem is that the cell nucleus contains only enough DNA to make about a million genes; of that complement, only fifty thousand or so genes actually make all the proteins needed by the body, and only a few of those are antibodies.

So where were all these antibodies coming from?

Until the mid-1950s, the usual answer was that we are born with only a few "general purpose" antibodies, probably inherited from our mothers. Each time we encounter a new antigen, the body somehow creates an antibody to attack it—perhaps by one of the white blood cells pressing itself up against the antigen to get a molecular imprint which then serves as a model for the new immunoglobulin. Antibodies on demand, so to speak.

But while this series of events might smooth out some of the bumps in immunological theory, it didn't go nearly far enough. It certainly didn't explain the work of an Australian named Frank Burnet, who had found specific types of antibodies in laboratory animals that could never have been exposed to their corresponding antigens. If antibodies were made only to attack antigens that had already entered the body, asked Burnet, where on earth had these come from?

The answer came, in 1955, from Burnet himself and from a London-born Dane named Neils Jerne. And just as the geneticists had promised, the explanation was locked in the genes.

We have all the antibodies we'll ever need, supposed Jerne and Burnet, not because we are born with them—or even because we can whip them up when they're needed—but because we're born with all the genes we'll ever need to assemble them. The hook was the word "assemble." Since there are only five major immunoglobulin families, their staggering variety must lie only in the one or two areas of the molecule that actually did the work—the lobster's claws (now called the "hypervariable region" of the antibody).

Interesting idea. In 1955 a radical idea. But it has flourished with only a few modifications for more than thirty years because it explains with such wondrous elegance the genetics of antibody diversity. Within a given immunoglobulin family, the main part of the molecule—the body of the lobster, or the "constant region" —could be produced by a single gene. Maybe two or three. But there is room in the DNA reservoir for hundreds, perhaps thousands, of variable-region genes. When a particular configuration is needed to confront an antigen, these genes shuffle themselves about to create as many specific proteins as are needed to assemble the lobster's claws. In a way, it's like making keys: Starting with hundreds of identical blanks, you could create hundreds of different keys simply by changing the size and location of the notches.

This genetic explanation of the immune system also resolved another knotty problem: how the lymphocytes reproduce themselves. According to the old immune response theory, these cells were basically devoid of a genetic "personality." Confronted with an antigen, any one of them could blindly turn out whatever antibody was needed to dispose of it.

By the late 1950s, though, such a possibility had to be discarded. Cells just don't behave in such a random fashion—their physical and chemical natures must be ruled by the genes. If the laws of genetics didn't apply equally to all cells, then they weren't laws at all. A normal kidney cell, for example, could not divide itself into anything except new kidney cells. Nor could a healthy insulin-producing cell in the pancreas divide into a cell that made not insulin, but an enzyme. In the same way, it had to be impossible for one type of lymphocyte—that is, one that produced a specific type of antibody—to divide into one that produced another type.

Thus was born what has come to be called the "clonal" theory of the immune system. In the vocabulary of biology, a clone is a line of cells descended from a single cell, and genetically identical to that one cell. Extended into immunology, the clonal theory says that when a B-cell reproduces itself, every one of its offspring will be a genetic carbon copy, preprogrammed to make precisely the same immunoglobulin as its parent.

As antibodies became better understood, they also shed new light on the growing number of disorders, called autoimmune diseases, in which the immune system turns on its owner. For reasons which still aren't completely understood, a single lymphocyte, either T- or B-cell, may suffer a mutation during its normal process of reproduction; the mutation, of course, is passed along to every one of its descendants. As a result, these offspring fail to recognize the cellular markings of their owner. The pattern of self/nonself breaks down. While there is still no cure for these diseases, researchers now feel they have the next best thing—a growing understanding of how and why they happen.

Certain forms of anemia, for example, are known to be caused by the production of antibody (called autoantibody) that destroys red blood cells. Similarly, some types of juvenile diabetes apparently arise when autoantibodies attack the insulin-producing beta cells in the pancreas. More recently, the devastating disease called AIDS (acquired immune deficiency syndrome) now seems to be the result of a virus that either destroys or prevents the formation of T-4 cells, a kind of helper T-cell. Without these helpers, the usual B-cell response is permanently and fatally sabotaged. The system is easy prey to a form of cancer called Kaposi's sarcoma, and to whatever organism happens along— usually the hepatitis virus.

In early 1985, researchers at Brigham and Women's Hospital in Boston implicated a faulty immune system in another crippler, multiple sclerosis. Working with thirty-five patients, the investigators reported in the *New England Journal of Medicine* that certain T-cells in twenty of them were unusually active. While MS had long been suspected to be an autoimmune disease, the Boston findings seemed to clinch it once and for all: Rather than defending their owners against infection, the rebellious T-cells were apparently attacking the fatty material, called myelin, that insulates and protects nerve fibers. As the myelin is eaten away, individual nerves are exposed, just as an electrical wire is laid bare by a break in its plastic insulation. The resulting "short circuit" produces the disease's characteristic tingling and loss of sensation.

The ideas and theories came together like pieces in a gargantuan jigsaw puzzle. It is now generally believed that at least some types of cancer happen because of faulty suppressor T-cells that "switch off" the immune response when it needs to be switched on, thereby permitting the abnormal cancer cells to leisurely establish their foothold. That notion gained special credence in 1984. Researchers at Northwestern University and Harvard reported that they had slowed the growth rates of a type of skin cancer (caused by irradiation, which by the way also promotes the proliferation of suppressor T-cells) by chemically attacking the T-cells. A cure for this type of cancer? Not quite; for one thing, no one's yet figured out how to retard one part of the immune system while leaving the others intact. But it could be another piece in the puzzle.

And what of organ transplants? Might it one day be possible to readily implant a heart or a kidney from any person into any other person? The watchful T-cells now prohibit such procedures, at the cost of hundreds of thousands of lives a year. True, those cells can be weakened for a while with immunosuppressive drugs. But such drugs cripple the entire system, including the B-cells—the patient is a sitting duck for any of the thousands of organisms that find their way into the hospital room. One answer may be in the drug called cyclosporin A, discovered in 1972 by the Swiss pharmaceutical firm Sandoz. The drug appears to make such selective knockouts, although no one can explain exactly why. When we find out, it may become routine to design new drugs that act on just one kind of immune system cell, or one small group of cells, while leaving others untouched.

Of all the forays into immunology, though, few are as captivating as the ones that suggest connections between the immune system and the nervous system—especially the possible connections that could radically affect how our bodies react to emotional stress. In one sense, the idea is hardly a new one; most of us are aware of instances in which severe depression or bereavement is soon followed by a serious but seemingly unrelated physical disorder. It's also well known that many key organs of the immune system (the spleen and lymph nodes, for example) are richly supplied with nerve endings. And from a less academic point of view, it's hard to imagine that any system within the compact, highly organized human body would be completely isolated from any other system. The problem for immunologists and other researchers is that there still is no hard evidence that links emotional stimuli with immune responses. Nor is there yet a generally accepted explanation of how one system might react with the other.

But there are some fascinating recent experiments on the subject which seem to be building into a controversial new discipline, called psychoimmunology. And while many researchers still question (or flatly reject) many of its basic premises, others are convinced that the interplay is a vitally important one. According to a 1984 article in *Nature* magazine, in fact, "The more radical psychoimmunologists talk as if there is no state of mind which is not faithfully reflected by a state of the immune system."

But it is just that sort of universality that troubles so many researchers, most of whom insist not on strong hunches but on hard, reproducible experiments that prove beyond doubt a cause-and-effect relationship. It isn't enough to simply observe that emotionally distressed people also suffer immune deficiencies; among other things, you must also rule out the possibility that it may be the other way around, that it is an immune disorder that's causing the depression. To do that, it will be necessary to conduct a detailed, extensive study (probably several studies) that relate only the two sets of symptoms. At this writing, it seems that either such studies have not yet been conducted, or the results are still being examined.

Nevertheless, several of the tentative findings so far are hard to ignore:

In June 1985 a group of Boston researchers working with dental students observed that levels of a certain type of antibody dropped noticeably during final exams, but later returned to normal—that is, after the psychological stress had been removed.

Ohio State University scientists found a similar effect on medical students during their finals, including changes in the levels of helper T-cells and natural killer cells (which seem to act as natural agents against cancer).

Tumor cells transplanted into mice that have been subjected to repeated stress seem to grow faster and longer than tumor cells injected into nonstressed mice.

In 1984 New York researchers reported that lymphocyte activity was apparently much lower than normal in men who had recently lost their wives to breast cancer. The same phenomenon has been seen among patients hospitalized for severe depression.

There is also evidence—again, sketchy and inconclusive—that the communication network between the brain and the defense system operates in both directions. That is, physical changes originating in the immune system seem to produce effects in the brain, according to a group of Swiss researchers. They speculate that certain products released by activated lymphocytes may find their way to the brain, where they alter the rates at which chemical and electrical signals are passed from cell to cell.

Once armed with an account of how antibodies are made, how they sort through countless molecules until they find one and only one that fits, and how the cells that create them are themselves created, a few immunologists started to ask some intriguing questions.

Could we, for instance, get our immune systems to produce huge amounts of just one kind of antibody, then scoop out the antibody and use it to mount a massive attack on its corresponding antigen?

Maybe, they replied, but it would be tough. One reason is the varied molecular markings on most antigenic organisms—markings that set thousands of different B-cells into production, each of them a clone of a genetically different lymphocyte. In genetic terms, the body makes a polyclonal ("many clones") response. How do you sort through this jumble of proteins, find precisely the antibody you want, then isolate its factory—the parent B-cell —from millions of other factories?

And even if we could make lots of antibodies of just one kind, they asked each other, what could we do with them? Who would be interested in large quantities of proteins that recognize and bind to just one other type of molecule?

Every scientist knows that the hardest part of problem solving is asking the right questions. And once these last two were asked, the answers came quickly.

For example, you could generate antibodies in response to a single type of cancer cell—each of which displays its own unique chemical markings, just like other kinds of antigens—then inject them into a patient with that kind of cancer. It wasn't unreasonable to think that the antibodies would attack the malignancy in the body, just like they attacked a virus or a bacterium. And if you attached a potent cancer-killing drug to the antibody, it was just as reasonable to suppose that the drug would be released only to the cancer cells. The healthy tissues that surrounded the tumor—and that often suffered from the drug's crippling side effects—would thus be spared.

But while this and other possibilities were being explored during the late 1960s and early 1970s, there were two questions no one seemed able to answer.

First, how do you find the one B-cell you need to make all these identical antibodies?

Second, how do you get the B-cell to divide and grow outside the body so it produces all the antibodies you need? How, in other words, do you keep it happy?

CHAPTER THREE

Jack Christie's soft boyish face and large dark eyes make him look more like the lead guitarist in a college rock band than a physician. Only the occasional gray hair and the deep smile lines about the eyes and mouth suggest that he's well past thirty. He's not a tall man—five eight or so—and he makes few attempts to conceal the round belly that tugs at the buttons of his Western-style shirt. His wavy black hair is fashionably trimmed so that it hangs lightly on the ears and the back of his collar. Like many of his fellow urban cowboys, he is given to expensive high-heeled boots, designer jeans, and a blinding redundancy of gold neck chains.

Yet he was Boston-born, the first of four Christie children and the first of his family to arrive with the Anglicized version of Christino, the original family surname. His grandfather had streamlined the name upon arriving in America with his family in the late 1920s, convinced as he was that the final vowel would unfairly handicap his sons in the tight job market.

The young Jack was quickly caught up in the Italian tradition that says that the firstborn has a special obligation of excellence to the family. Accordingly, he announced at his ninth birthday party that he was going to become a doctor. His parents happily endorsed his decision, opened a special savings account for him at a bank off Central Square in Cambridge, and over the next ten years furnished him with a stream of chemistry sets, plastic anatomical models, and books with titles such as *So You Want to Be a Doctor.*

By his second year of undergraduate work at the University of Massachusetts in Amherst, it was obvious that the decision had been a good one. He was ambitious, bright, personable when the occasion required, and hard-working—qualities inherited from his father, Jack Sr., a phenomenally successful investment analyst in a Back Bay brokerage. His mother helped the boy develop other valuable features, including a spontaneous sense of wonderfully racy humor and an aggressive self-confidence that she managed to combine with a warm sentimentality.

Alas, that last quality was for many years foreign to the young Jack. While his intellectual skills were formidable, they were often overshadowed by what he still calls the "sharp corners" of his personality—the sudden emotional shifts, from icy insensitivity to gushy emotionalism and back again, that even today make him an unusually complex man. He admits that he has little patience with failure, his own or that of others. Yet he is still inclined to graciously overlook his shortcomings when the situation warrants—the time he blamed a poor test grade on a bad cold, for instance, even though he had done uncharacteristically mediocre work during much of that term. And while he is fundamentally aloof by nature (especially toward those he considers his intellectual and social inferiors), he may be unexpectedly moved by a passing circumstance. "You never quite know what to expect from Jack," one of his friends told me. "One day he's as warm and thoughtful as can be. We were in medical school, and I was so flat broke I was thinking about dropping out for a while. Jack learned about it and every week he slipped fifty dollars, seventy-five dollars into my mailbox, and I know that it was money out of his own pocket. Never mentioned it to me, never asked about being repaid.

"But a few months later he can act like he doesn't even know you, and couldn't care less if he did."

He was consumed early on by two passions: women and the need for material success (the latter of which earned him the nickname "Diamond Jack" during his last year of college). Many of his friends, in fact, had been chosen as much for their economic and professional standing as for their personal qualities; for his own part, he rarely felt the need for companionship. He preferred solitary pastimes like reading, bicycling, working out in the weight room at his father's club, and racing his twenty-one-foot *Victory* off Marblehead, reaching on the hot and heavy August winds that came to life off Bermuda and roared all the way to the Bay of Fundy.

And the women, bless them. They wandered into and through his life like the midwestern tourists at Old Ironsides, beginning when he was fourteen (and looking seventeen). By the time he finished high school, it was not unusual for him to be dating three or four girls at once, swearing eternal love and allegiance to each. For their parts, they were drawn to the soft boyish features, the trim physique still cushioned by just a trace of baby fat, the brazen self-confidence and unapologizing quest for riches. "Looking back, I don't know how I got through undergraduate school, let alone med school," he said once, shaking his head. "I mean, I just couldn't get enough of 'em, and finding 'em was never a problem for me."

He developed a direct, head-on approach to meeting girls in the Newbury Street singles bars, and it rarely failed him. Reasoning that most of the women he wanted to meet had already heard just about every opening line ever coined, good and bad, he would catch their attention another way:

"Hi, I don't get out much, but I'd like to meet a nice girl. You interested in meeting a nice guy?"

At this, the girl would hesitate a moment; she'd probably never heard it put quite that way before. Certainly not with such sincerity. Most of the men here came on as either insufferable bores ("I'm celebrating my raise—*finally* broke the sixty-K barrier") or pitiful wimps who had just ended a "really heavy relationship" and couldn't bear to stay in the apartment that night.

"Well, yeah, I guess I'd like to meet a nice guy. Are *you* a nice guy?"

"You won't find a nicer guy than me; no point in even looking even further. Fact, all my friends tell me I'm too nice, and that's why I wind up getting hurt so much. And that's why I'm looking for a really nice girl. Would you like a fresh drink or something . . . ?" By now the young woman had had time to notice the twinkling pale blue eyes, and especially the unusual mixture of cockiness and vulnerability—a curious amalgam which he knew most girls found appealing, because they had told him so.

Occasionally, the gambit backfired, of course. A few women found the approach rather tacky (but he noticed that they were usually the ones who left with Sixty-K). And there was the time when the attractive woman at the bar listened politely about his search for a nice girl, then said quietly, "To tell you the truth, I'm looking for a nice girl myself. . . ."

His father impressed the boy early with the importance of financial independence. To illustrate his point, he made Jack an offer: On each and every New Year's Eve until he was twenty-one, he would write a check to match whatever money Jack had saved during the year. "As long as you can pay your own way in life, no one's ever gonna push you around," he said. The youngster remembered. He cut lawns after his high school classes, baby-sat on weekends, worked evenings at the local Stop & Shop supermarket. Every dime he could spare went into his savings account.

He was a straight-B student at Tufts University School of Medicine in downtown Boston. As a self-recognized loner, however, he decided during his second year that he would probably never go into practice; research was more to his liking, or perhaps even teaching, if he could ever zero in on a specialty. Perched in one of Washington Street's topless bars a few months before graduation, he complained to another student: "Here I am, almost finished, and I still don't know where to go next. I like internal medicine, hematology, cardiology—I like almost everything, but you can't do everything. I gotta get off the pot and make up my mind." His friend nodded sympathetically—he had already decided on psychiatry—then took another tug at his beer and turned his attention again to the stage.

One specialty he ruled out right away—oncology, the study and treatment of cancer. Not that he wasn't fascinated by the wild and unruly process of cancer. He was often angered by the fact that no one seemed to understand why cells sometimes go crazy, continuing to divide long after the division process normally stops. Yet it was a wondrous process, in a way, like a tornado or a hurricane. Nature gone mad. He could stare at the cells through his microscope, even admire them for the way they clung to life while being assaulted by powerful drugs and radiation. The way they shed little bits of themselves, like sunburned skin, which then drifted through the bloodstream or lymphatic system until they found a suitable landing site at which to set up another tumor. And another.

Frankly, it was the patients he didn't like. They were—well, embarrassing to be around. Many of them were dying, and they looked and smelled like hell while they were doing it. He especially remembered a liver cancer case during his third year of medical school. The woman was about fifty-two, and had been pretty once. Now she spent most of her day weeping silently into her pillow, or just staring out the window. Her family made excuses why they couldn't visit today. Jack and the others knew why they didn't visit: They couldn't stand to watch her die a little more every day. When they did show up, they fairly gagged on the hospital small talk:

"How are you feeling today? You look great. . . ."

"I hear the food is pretty good here. . . ."

"When you get outta here, we're going to take you to the best restaurant on the North Shore. . . ."

But in their minds was: "Please die, Judith. Get it over with. We have parties to go to and children to raise and livings to make, and we can't really get on with it knowing about your pain." Jack often wondered what he would do if he was ever diagnosed with cancer. He would kill himself, that's all. Something from the pharmacy, probably, something fast and clean. No one would ever stand over *his* bed and search for those empty and harmless words.

The problem of a specialty was solved when he realized, during his fourth year, that there was one place he always enjoyed being —the emergency room. Most of his friends complained about the ER's furious pace, the need for hurried decisions, the endless stream of injuries and symptoms, the impersonality of it all. And there were too many Gomers in the business. "Gomers, that stands for 'Get Out of My Emergency Room.' Those were the doctors, older guys mostly, who were too lazy to read and keep up with things. So when you brought a patient with unusual symptoms into an ER, they would just do whatever was necessary to keep the guy from dying on the spot, then ship him somewhere else. That's a Gomer."

For all his disdain for the Gomers, though, he often worried that he might one day fall into the same trap. The thought of mediocrity, in fact, utterly terrified him. Could he ever become so lazy, so complacent? Wasn't it all too easy to get caught up in the glamorous mystique that surrounded his profession, to actually believe that you're every bit as brilliant as your patients think you are? "The Messiah Syndrome," some of the older physicians called it—a perilous mind-set that goes far beyond healthy self-confidence, even beyond irksome egotism. Again, it was usually the older ones who tried to guard against it; Jack especially liked the framed quotation, usually attributed to Benjamin Franklin, that one of his professors displayed next to the door in his office.

"God heals," it read. "The physician merely collects the fee."

"I keep it there so it's the last thing I see when I'm leaving to see a patient," the professor explained.

No, Christie decided, he must never become a Gomer. If he couldn't achieve excellence, if he couldn't be the very best, he would simply leave medicine.

He soon realized that he was being drawn irresistibly to emergency medicine, and for the very reasons that his friends disliked the field. To his mild surprise, he found that he could even learn from the dreaded Gomers, many of whom had managed to acquire special insights into certain medical conditions. And he loved the pace of the ER, the life-and-death challenges, the fact that almost no one was there for a trivial reason: A gunshot wound might be followed by a cerebral hemorrhage, a messy attempted suicide by a four-year-old whose leg had been shredded by the neighbor's dog.

And when the cases weren't horrifying, they could be downright hilarious (if not to the patient, then to the bizarre funny bones of the doctors and nurses). There was the woman who had become so enraged to find pornographic magazines in her eighty-six-year-old husband's dresser drawer that she tore off her wedding ring and hurled it at the poor man. The ring took a one-in-a-million bounce and ricocheted off the wall back into her open mouth and down her throat. The X-rays later showed that the ring had passed harmlessly into her stomach. Jack struggled to maintain a professional demeanor as he loaned the couple a bedpan and advised them to go home and "wait a day or two until nature takes care of the problem. . . ."

Jack's favorite was the middle-aged man who limped into the room one day with a glass thermometer inserted into his penis. "We couldn't get him to tell us how and why he'd put the thing up there, but I think he believed he had an infection or something. All he could say was, 'Please don't break it, *please* don't break it.' We got it out with a little mineral oil. God, we laughed about that for a month afterwards."

What he really loved about the ER, though, was the fact that he could see and practice just about every kind of medicine. "Sometimes they come in showing just the tip of the iceberg—very subtle symptoms, real puzzlers. The fun part for me was that you're usually the first one to see this guy, and a lot of what happens later will depend on what you decided in that first twenty or thirty minutes. It's a real rush." And there was another nice thing about the emergency room. You never had to get close to the patient.

Ever since he was a teenager, he'd been almost as fascinated by the world of business as by the world of medicine—a fascination no doubt inherited from his father and fueled by his own need for material success. His self-appointed required reading, even in medical school, thus included most of the business and investment periodicals; the little spare time he had was spent largely in economics conferences on the campus. In a way, business and finance was a lot like medicine, he told one of his girlfriends: "You have to keep up with it all the time, you have to learn to predict the kind of problems that might come up. Economics doesn't give you much room for error; it very quickly separates the sheep from the goats."

And so he was gratified to learn upon his graduation from medical school that he had become quite wealthy, thanks largely to his father's early custom of matching his savings account every year, then investing the sum in stocks and real estate. In mid-1978 Jack Sr. had heard that a new office park was being planned near Randolph, a growing community about an hour's drive south of Boston. A week later, Jack was told that as a participant in a new real estate investment trust, he now owned a piece of the development—a small part, yes, but within a year he could probably double his investment. As usual, his father was right. They agreed to sell the interest in the trust and invest the profits in new stocks issued by three young software companies along 128. "After that, it seemed like the money just kept piling up," said Jack.

He got an idea. Why not start a chain of off-the-street emergency clinics? Places staffed by smart young M.D.s (who would be required to buy into the clinic, of course, just like owners of gas stations or Burger King outlets), where patients could walk in with their twisted ankles, sore throats, and what have you. Life-threatening situations would be referred to nearby hospitals; conditions that weren't so serious would be treated and paid for on the spot. Not only could the patient avoid the overcrowded hospitals or doctors' offices, but the clinic wouldn't have to be as heavily equipped as those sites. That would mean lower costs, lower fees, and higher profits for the operators. Everyone would be happy. "It also would have been a nice balance of interests for me—a little medicine, a little business—and maybe make me some money at the same time." Following his graduation from Tufts in 1978, he immediately enrolled in a series of postgraduate courses at Harvard, with an emphasis on internal medicine.

It was one of the happiest periods of his life, he recalls, even with the heavy study load and the tiresome daily drive between classes and his apartment in the western suburb of Brookline. (He refused to ride the subway—the "T," as it's called in Boston —after the day that three teenagers tried to tear his watch from his wrist.) Compared to his grueling schedule in medical school, though, it was almost a vacation. He even found himself with extra time on his hands every week, time usually spent with his father, looking into stock market investments that might later help finance his chain of clinics. And for the first time in several years, he felt physically well. He'd lost weight during his last year at Tufts, and now turned to beefing up his 152-pound frame. To speed the process along, he took to stopping for lunch several times a week at a McDonald's on Huntington Avenue. He later claimed that "my usual lunch was three or four quarter pounders, a bag of fries, and a chocolate shake. I'd almost always have them gone before I got into the city. I didn't put on much weight, though—just a little potbelly after a couple of months."

He fell crazy in love the following year, at a beach party in Southern California.

It was customary for second-year graduate students to spend part of their training outside the network of Boston teaching hospitals. Most of Jack's friends chose to stay in the New England area, opting for New England Deaconess, Massachusetts General, or Children's Hospital (although several chose some of the prestigious New York institutions, such as Columbia-Presbyterian and Memorial Sloan-Kettering). Christie decided to combine a little pleasure with his work and signed up for two months with the University of California at San Diego. Another advantage of the UCSD tour was that he could now spend a little time with his twenty-two-year-old brother Paul. The younger man—"a real computer nut," as Jack described him—had just moved to San Francisco and was now a junior-level circuit designer with one of the semiconductor companies in Silicon Valley.

It was during his third week at UCSD that he was invited to join the Saturday night "Guzzle-and-Nuzzle"—the weekly beer party conducted on the Mission Bay beach, organized by a group of interns and nurses. He already knew most of the men and women there, but not the reserved young woman who spent the first hour hanging along the outer edge of the group. A tall, slender woman whose shining black hair mirrored the gold and crimson hues from the bonfire between them. The one who stole shy glances at him every few minutes as she laughed softly at the coarse hospital jokes.

She was without a doubt the most beautiful woman he had ever seen.

Eileen Pierce was the nineteen-year-old sister of Pam Pierce, the surgical nurse who had moved to La Mesa from Liverpool, England, two years earlier. Like Pam (and like thousands of other young Liverpudlians), Eileen had seized her first opportunity to leave the economically depressed city, and was now halfway through a planned four-month stay with her sister.

They strolled the beach together for four hours later that night, all the while keeping just the right distance between them: far enough apart to look "respectable," but close enough for their hands and arms to brush from time to time. They talked about Liverpool, about the hospital, about San Diego. He was fascinated by her throaty British accent as she described her hopes of moving to the States, perhaps going on to college for a business career. She was no less entranced with his Boston pronunciations, and allowed herself to cast her tastefully brief sideways glances at him as he spun his stories about New England and his family.

He didn't sleep at all that night. She later said that she'd never slept better in her life.

During the five weeks that remained of his UCSD study period, they spent almost every free hour together. He rented a car on weekends so they could tour Southern California, from Santa Barbara to Lake Arrowhead to Tijuana. It was on his last Sunday in San Diego, walking hand in hand through the city's touristy Old Town district, that he asked her to return with him to Boston.

"Is that a proposal?"

"Well, in a way, I guess," he stammered. "Look, I'm not sure I'm ready for marriage just now. I mean, I want to finish up the graduate work at Harvard, think a little about where to go next. I'm still a little unsettled, okay? But one thing I know is that I don't want three thousand miles between us just now."

They walked silently for a few more minutes.

"You want me to move in with you then? Live together?"

"Might be nice. Hey, you're going to be in the States for another two months anyway. You know what Southern California's like, why not spend the rest of your time in Boston? If it doesn't work out for you . . . if it doesn't work out for us, I mean, you can still fly home in time for Christmas."

He knew she would refuse, despite the flawless logic of his offer. It was too sudden for her. They'd known each other for barely a month. Pam would certainly discourage the idea, and what would her family in England think about such an arrangement? For all he knew, she didn't even care all that much about him. . . .

Eileen tossed her soft drink container into a nearby trash barrel, then removed her sunglasses as she turned to face him.

"I should probably start packing this afternoon, shouldn't I?"

They leased a two-bedroom apartment in the North Shore town of Swampscott, two blocks from the ocean, in January 1980.

There he soon learned that her country-girl sweetness had a hard edge of cool independence. She let it be known immediately that young and inexperienced though she was, she would not be dominated by him, nor would she in any way be dependent on him. She surely would not be like Katherine, her other sister, begging her husband for spare change or asking his permission to go out with friends for an evening at the cinema. By the time the plane had landed in Boston, in fact, she was planning a career in accounting. Like Jack, she respected money—not for its own sake, she said, but because "when you have money in the bank, it clears your mind to think of other things."

The decision to become an accountant was not an idle choice. Jack soon saw that there was a well-developed sense of order and precision about the young woman. She felt comfortable with numbers, liked the way they always added up and divided according to ancient unbreakable rules. The orderliness extended into her personal life as well. She became furious when she found her stationery on Jack's desk, or a pair of scissors left on the kitchen counter after he had clipped an item from one of his journals.

Indeed, most of their quarrels early in the relationship were about his personal carelessness—the dirty socks left under the sofa, the wet towels flung casually over the shower curtain rod in the morning, and that bloody awful Red Sox baseball cap he insisted on wearing around the apartment—or her fetish for neatness and precision. "I'm afraid to set my coffee cup down for a minute," he wailed. "As soon as I take my hand away, you've got it in the *dishwasher* for Chrissake!" Throwing down her towel, she retorted that "*someone* has to keep this place clean, so just help out a bit or keep your mouth closed!" He decided to keep his mouth closed.

But they agreed on many things—including a vigorous and joyous sex life (which at first surprised Jack, who had heard from his traveled friends of the Victorian sexual attitudes which are still so common even in many of Europe's major cities). Two weeks after they'd moved into the Swampscott apartment, they calculated that they had made love at least twice in every room of the apartment. And in the back seat of the car. In the garage. On the boat. Under a blanket on the beach. Once in the second-floor bathroom during a birthday party at a nurse's home in Revere.

One or two weekends a month they relaxed in the surrounding countryside—at his parents' vacation home in the Berkshire Hills close to the New York border, rock hunting in New Hampshire's White Mountains near Woodstock—or just attending warm-weather outdoor concerts on the Esplanade along the Charles River. And despite her homesickness, she laughed—great, throaty bursts of laughter that made him fall in love with her all over again every week. He didn't even mind when he found himself the butt of her laughter, like when he decided to grow his mustache.

"Why ever do you want a mustache?" she demanded.

"Well, I think I should look a little older, you know? Hell, I'm almost thirty. And a doctor. Don't you think doctors should look more—doctorly? Jeez, I look like I'm still in high school."

So he grew the mustache, a startlingly thin and grotesque bit of fuzz that even after two months could barely be seen from ten feet away. One night she found him grooming it in the bathroom mirror and couldn't restrain herself any longer. "You look like one of the boys at home that snuck a pint an' forgot to wipe his mouth," she giggled. He shaved the thing off the next day.

She took a secretarial job at a downtown brokerage firm while her immigration documents were completed—a perfect opportunity to begin learning about business and finance, she thought, and a chance to make a mark of her own in her new world. Jack returned to Harvard, dividing his time between class and working in the emergency room at Lynn Hospital, just a few miles from the apartment.

Roger Cook signaled the waitress for two more beers and grimaced at the falling snow that was now clogging the late afternoon traffic along Boylston Street.

"God, I don't know how I put up with this for thirty years," he said. "When I left Houston the other day, it was sixty degrees, not a cloud in the sky."

Jack Christie emptied his third glass in less than an hour and studied the man across the table. He hadn't seen Cook since they'd graduated from Tufts, and had been surprised to receive his phone call the day before. Texas seemed to agree with him, that was certain; he sported a handsome tan that immediately set him apart from Boston's pale white and gray February faces.

"I guess it sounds corny, but I think I'd miss the seasons here," Jack shrugged, nodding toward the window. "Even this. How long you in town, Rog?"

"Just 'til tomorrow afternoon, after the seminar. I always thought I'd miss the seasons too, but I don't. Not when I see on TV that Boston's getting another foot of snow and ten degrees. And I'll tell you something else about Houston, pal—they're crying for experienced doctors and nurses, I mean crying for 'em. And they've got the money to recruit them. The town's growing so fast the hospitals and medical schools can't keep up. Some of the hospitals are even offering to pay relocation costs and the first few months' rent for the right people."

Jack found it easy to ignore Cook's sales pitch at first. While Boston itself had few claims on him, he had never thought seriously of leaving New England. True, the weather was notoriously disagreeable for five or six months a year, especially during the cold, damp winter and spring seasons. But he liked the variety of the region—the mountains to the north and west, the sea to the east, New York City just a four-hour drive to the southwest. And he liked New Englanders. Good, plain people whose roots and traditions went back hundreds of years. Solid people.

Still, he had more than once overheard others talking about the growing surplus of physicians and other health care personnel in Boston—a surplus that might soon erupt into increased competition for patients and prestigious teaching posts, and perhaps even lower incomes. And although he had never aspired to become wealthy in medicine (his investments were already taking care of that), neither did he think it right that physicians should have to claw at each other like used-car salesmen for what amounted to loose change.

Nor was Roger Cook the first to sing the Sunbelt's praises. A few months before, another friend had urged Jack to consider Texas or Arizona as the setting for launching his chain of franchised emergency rooms. There was no shortage of venture capital, the friend had promised, and the region's upscale lifestyle and rapid population growth promised as much business as he could handle. "Texas drivers are even crazier than in Boston," the friend confided. "You could probably do a hundred thousand a year just on auto accidents."

Somewhat to Jack's surprise, the adventurous Eileen agreed that it might be worth a try—for a year, anyway. They could always come back. In June 1980 they took a two-bedroom apartment in an elegantly landscaped complex off Westheimer, a mile from Houston's chic Galleria shopping plaza.

It was in early December 1980 that he first suspected that something was going wrong. He and Eileen had flown from Houston to San Francisco for the long Thanksgiving weekend, staying with his brother Paul and his new wife in their apartment near Ghirardelli Square. The two couples spent Friday afternoon shopping in Chinatown, then much of the night at Pier 23—the two-by-two tavern on the Embarcadero that had, according to Paul, the "most uncomfortable seats and the best live jazz in the city." The next morning, Jack set out for the Embarcadero on his usual morning jog. This time, he was exhausted by the time he had passed Fisherman's Wharf, barely a half mile from Paul's apartment.

He wanted to blame the beer and the late hours of the night before. But he had been unusually tired for the past month. He often dozed off in front of the television before 9 P.M., and he found it difficult to stay awake through a two-hour movie. Considering his long hours and hectic schedule at the Houston hospital, however, he reminded himself that there was nothing so unusual about being tired at the end of the day. Hell, Eileen was tired most of the time too, what with her business classes two nights a week and her job at a downtown bank—and she was eight years younger. He would take some early vacation time after New Year's, he promised her, maybe spend a week or two with Pam in California.

But the other symptoms were harder to shake off. The occasional mild fever. The painless, slightly swollen lymph nodes. The achy listlessness. The waning of his usually robust appetite. The nights when he woke up at 3 A.M. to find his sheet and pillowcase soaked in sweat. The pound or so he was losing every week, so that his once snug-fitting cords were now slipping off his hips. Looking at himself in the full-length mirror, he saw that he was involuntarily getting thinner. He decided that he had fallen victim to some kind of infection; that would explain many of the symptoms, especially the nodes. He would have it checked.

It got worse later. They spent the 1980 Christmas holidays with Eileen's parents in Liverpool, after a three-day layover with his parents in Boston; on the way back to the states, they stopped in London for a few days to visit one of his former professors from Tufts who was then working at the National Heart Hospital. On their second night in the city, they decided to try one of the small theaters in Mayfair, near Berkeley Square. He fell noisily asleep during the second act. Not once, but three times. They had dinner at a tiny, smoke-filled pub just off Picadilly Circus later in the evening. He had been ravenously hungry earlier. Three bites into his sole almondine, however, he suddenly felt bloated. Most of his plate—about fourteen dollars' worth, he calculated—was taken away untouched.

On the afternoon of February 18, 1981, he stopped for his usual quarter pounders and fries at a McDonald's on Westheimer and carefully set them up on the MG's passenger seat. Creeping through the heavy I-610 traffic toward the hospital, he got only partway through the third burger. The food just wasn't going down as easily as usual. He was feeling uncomfortably full, just as he had in London. For some reason, he slipped his fingers inside his shirt and felt around his stomach. There it was, just under the rib on the left side. The merest protuberance of tissue, trying to balloon past its normal boundaries. He knew instinctively it was the tip of his spleen. That was hardly an alarming discovery, however, especially if he was right about harboring some kind of infection.

About the size and shape of a small porterhouse steak, the organ is one of the body's most versatile and hardest-working organs. It is also one of the least understood. The spleen not only appears to produce red blood cells in some cases, but it also destroys them when they've become worn-out. In so doing, it converts the cells' oxygen-carrying hemoglobin into the yellowish bilirubin, which is then sent to the liver and incorporated into bile needed to break down fats in the diet. The spleen is also a key manufacturing site for lymphocytes and antibodies, and is thus a vital part of the body's defense system. The enlargement, Jack surmised, could be due to any number of conditions—infection, of course (which was the most likely), or an acute inflammation. In the latter case, the swelling would be due to the extra supplies of healing blood that are rushed to the tissues after an injury or some other kind of damage.

As he swung the MG into the hospital parking lot, the possibility of a tumor crossed his mind briefly. His first impulse was to rule out that diagnosis; the spleen is actually a rather uncommon primary site for such disorders. Solid tumors that begin elsewhere in the body, however, may shed some of their cells into the bloodstream, thus spreading to eventually include the spleen and other organs.

But there were other cancers besides the solid tumors. There were the various forms of leukemia, in which certain white blood cells grow at phenomenal rates, replacing the body's blood-forming tissues, crowding out normal cells, and eventually spreading to to other organs. There was the group of malignancies called lymphomas, so named because they came to life in the tissues of the lymph system—probably from a single mutated cell. The cancerous cells often spread quickly throughout the lymph tissues and soon packed their way into the widely distributed nodes, the pea-sized sacs of tissue that cleansed and filtered the lymph fluid as it coursed its way back to the bloodstream. The malignancy typically moved on later to the spleen, the liver, the bone marrow, and elsewhere. He thought too of the lymphoma called Hodgkin's disease, a type of cancer marked by giant tumor cells and a gradual erosion of the immune system.

As usual, he felt better after this speedy though superficial review of his symptoms. He now had something he could analyze and test, something to put into a test tube or culture dish, or look up in his textbooks, or perhaps attack with an antibiotic. He would do nothing for now, he decided—just keep an eye on things for a week or two, hoping they would improve.

They didn't. The night sweats continued, the general weakness worsened. He lost two more pounds in less than a week. His sex drive waned noticeably, so even Eileen knew something was terribly wrong. He waved off her worries: "Just working too hard, I guess."

Ever since childhood, though he never knew why, he'd harbored an almost psychotic terror of hypodermic needles. At one time he'd convinced himself that the fear would subside during medical school; it got worse. Now, clamping his eyes shut against the gleaming glass and steel, he had another doctor at the hospital withdraw ten cubic centimeters of blood for a full analysis. Normal red cell count. Normal blood chemistry and protein. No infection. The series of lymphangiograms—X-rays of the lymphatic system—were similarly inconclusive. He went back to his texts and reference books; involuntarily, he kept coming back to the sections on lymphoma.

"A group of malignant tumors characterized by neoplastic proliferations of the various cell types endogenous to lymphoid tissue," one of them read. "Hodgkin's disease is considered to be a type of lymphoma. Lymphomas are classified on a morphological basis according to the cell of origin of the neoplasm, the degree of differentiation of the tumor cells, and the overall architecture of the involved lymphoid tissue. The etiology of lymphomas remains unknown." And a little further down the page, he read: "Most commonly, the liver, spleen and other lymph nodes become diseased as evidenced by their increase in size."

Another book described some of the common symptoms, including the night sweats—probably caused by the body trying to rid itself of the microscopic by-products being discarded by the cancerous cells—the weight loss, the fatigue. Yet another talked about incidence, cure rates, and survival time. The various lymphomas accounted for only about 5 percent of all cancer cases, but some forms ranked among the most aggressive forms of the disease: Of the tens of thousands of new lymphoma cases a year, less than half will survive five years after their diagnosis. In fact, the mean survival time for one form of the malignancy, called non-Hodgkin's lymphoma, was just under four years.

The literature review brought him to the point at which most physicians turn elsewhere for help. "The more I read about it, the more positive I was that I was dealing with some kind of lymphoma. But you can't remain objective anymore when it gets that close. You have to start questioning your own judgment." In late March, he called one of his former professors at Tufts, a middle-aged hematologist for whom Jack had developed a special affection and admiration during medical school. More to the point, the man had written more than a dozen technical papers on lymphomas and was considered one of the nation's top authorities on the subject.

The professor listened as Jack described the primary symptoms, then fired a series of questions into the phone.

"How are the nodes?"

"Slight swelling, sort of comes and goes. Nothing certain on the lymphangiogram either."

"You've run through all the blood tests, of course?"

"Nothing unusual—everything normal."

"And no recent infections?"

"Nothing I'm aware of, nothing that's shown up so far."

"What about a nodal biopsy?"

Jack had thought about that and had shrunk from it. He wasn't about to have someone piercing one of his lymph nodes with that damn needle, anesthetic or no, unless it was absolutely unavoidable. "Uh, no, not yet. I wanted to check out everything else first."

Silence on the other end of the line.

"Well, you should have it looked at, Jack. You've got lots of good men down there, you know; if it was me, I'd probably want to see the biopsy and maybe a scan."

The hematologist gave Jack the names of three physicians associated with the Texas Medical Center.

The CT was ordered for the following week. Jack told Eileen that he would be attending a two-day emergency medicine seminar at Baylor University. And while he was there, he added, he might as well stop in at the Medical Center for a quick checkup. "Gotta be some kind o' virus," he shrugged.

Technically, the operation is called a laparotomy. Some doctors still refer to it as "a blind date with the abdomen," because you're never quite sure what you're going to find inside. A week after Jack Christie's CT scan, the surgeons at Houston's Rice University Medical Center prepared to find out more about those queer-looking marshmallows.

The surgeon, a Pakistani whom Jack had never seen before and would never see again, started by drawing the scalpel through the top skin layers, from a point just below the breastbone to an inch or so above the navel. Picking up another knife, he then repeated the incision through the fascia, the fibrous layer just below the skin. The muscle came next; the Pakistani chose not to cut it, though—too bloody. Instead, he pushed it aside like so much spaghetti, and cut carefully through the final layer of tissue, the peritoneum, to avoid nicking the bacteria-ridden intestine just beyond.

From time to time, a nurse reached into the wound with an electric cauterizer to stop the bleeding. The instrument gave off a sharp *bzz* whenever she touched the tip to one of the severed vessels.

The organs were now exposed. The surgeon studied them carefully, looking for obvious signs of disease before going any further, then slid his hand into the opening to gently examine each of the residents. The stomach. The gallbladder. The intestine. Satisfied that all was in order, he snipped off a tiny piece of the large, firm reddish brown liver, and placed it carefully into a nearby tray. A piece of the purplish spleen came next, a more difficult cut because of the organ's spongy texture. Into the tray.

Someone from pathology would be up shortly to retrieve the bits of organ. They would be frozen, then sliced into pieces so thin as to be transparent. The papery tissue would then be stained with a drop or two of dye and placed under a microscope.

The surgeon closed the wound carefully. The peritoneum first, then the fascia. Since the fascia was under considerable tension, he used individual pieces of thread from start to finish; if one stitch gave way, the others would keep the closure intact. For the final sutures, he selected a very fine silk thread and took what seemed to be an especially long time completing his embroidery. "He's a nice-looking boy," the Pakistani explained. "We should give him a nice-looking scar, yes?"

Jack was right, the pathologist told him the next day. The sections of liver and spleen had confirmed it. Non-Hodgkin's lymphoma—specifically, a form of B-cell lymphoma. It explained the "marshmallows" he had seen on the CT scan; they were really enlarged cancerous lymph nodes lying at waist level, close to the spine.

"But there are lymphomas and there are lymphomas," the man

continued. "Based on the type of cell we found, I don't think it would hurt to be fairly optimistic about the outcome."

Jack's studies of a few weeks earlier had refreshed his memory on the subject of B-cell lymphomas. The pathologist was right; a little optimism wasn't at all out of order. Although half to two thirds of lymphoma victims will eventually die of the disease, cures were being reported. Even those patients who weren't cured were having years added to their lives with new treatment methods. The therapies often amounted to little more than holding actions, but they gave researchers precious time to find still more treatments.

Two days after the laparotomy, he wheeled himself to the hospital library and found the *Index Medicus,* the two-inch-thick volume that compiles the titles of thousands of reports from hundreds of medical journals every month. He found the major heading "Lymphoma," and began the long process of note taking. By late afternoon, he recorded the titles of thirty-two reports describing the treatment and outlook for his malignancy. It took the better part of the next morning to find the bound back volumes that carried the actual reports (except the four that were missing) and photocopy the articles.

"The diagnosis really hadn't hit me yet," he said later. "It was as though I were tracking down some information about someone else's disease, like it was just another patient. Except for the incision from the laparotomy, I sure wasn't feeling sick. Matter of fact, I felt pretty good, and just wanted to get out of there and go back to work."

Back home, he spread out his books and photocopied articles and set out to learn more about his disease. He found out that non-Hodgkin's lymphoma is characterized by different cell types. Some involved large cells, some small. The cells might be spread throughout the system ("diffuse"), or they could be localized in the lymph nodes. Seen up close, the malignant cells might assume a typical cellular appearance (that is, "well differentiated") or they might be odd-looking things that don't really look like any other kind of cell. They could be cleaved—the cell nucleus sort of split down the middle, suggesting a B-cell origin—or noncleaved. And some forms of the disease involved only B-cells, some only T-cells, some a mixture of both. Each form of the cancer had a preferred treatment program and its own prognosis. The pathology report described his own cells as a sort of mixed bag of cell types, but predominantly "small cleaved, diffuse, well differentiated"—basically normal, in other words, but far too numerous, reproducing themselves too quickly.

And what of treatment? Here again, there was no clear answer. The cancer was not especially fast-growing; it was an "indolent" type, they told him. Some researchers had made a good case for simply doing nothing in such cases. The disease seemed to move along at its own rate no matter what you did, they said, and a patient like Jack could be assured of at least three years, maybe much longer. Others took the opposing viewpoint: New drugs and combinations of drugs had achieved remarkable results in the previous few years. Many patients were actually being cured. Jack was young, and reasonably healthy in spite of his diagnosis. To do nothing was foolish, if not criminal; he had very little to lose with treatment, and everything to gain.

It took two months for the whole crummy thing to catch up with him, for him to realize that at the age of twenty-nine he suddenly seemed to be much closer to the end than to the beginning. He finally allowed himself a bit of self-pity.

"It was all over, and I didn't know why. I'm not sure I ever went through the denial stage—I'd seen the reports, I knew what they meant—though I think there was some of that for a while. But there was plenty of anger, the sense that it was all so damned unfair. I had everything going for me. I was young, had a nice career underway, a beautiful girlfriend, financial security. I'd always been a good guy, I think, never hurt anybody, then *blam!* you get shot in the ass with something like this. With all those Gomers running around, why me?"

For some reason, he thought of Ken Foon. The men had met at a seminar in San Diego two years earlier, during Jack's stay in California. Foon was on a fellowship at the time, studying oncology and hematology at UCLA and on his way to becoming an assistant professor of medicine. Four or five years older than Jack, Ken was one of those guys who seemed to get on well with everyone—easygoing, enthusiastic, personable, and brighter than most.

If Jack remembered correctly, Foon had recently left California for the National Cancer Institute and was now somewhere in the Washington area. A few phone calls narrowed it down further, to the town of Frederick, Maryland.

"Hello, Ken? This is Jack Christie. We met in San Diego a couple of years ago, remember? Well, I think I've got a little problem. . . ."

CHAPTER FOUR

Middle age arrives early on 128—usually around a company's tenth birthday. When it happens, the company has pretty much the same options as an individual: It can ignore the event and maintain a steady-as-she-goes attitude. It can veer off into an entirely new lifestyle to prove that it still has the old pizzazz. Or it might use the occasion to take careful stock of its past—both successes and failures—in order to better shape its future. It was in 1976 that Damon Corporation of Needham Heights, Massachusetts—at the tender age of fifteen one of 128's senior citizens —opted for the third choice.

In fact, Damon was down with a mild case of the jitters— something new for a company that had become accustomed to having almost everything go its own way. It wasn't so much that things weren't going right. It was more that the things that had gone wrong had gone very wrong. Crucial developments hadn't materialized; predictions about the fickle marketplace had fallen far off the mark; critical social and economic trends hadn't developed according to the corporate schedule.

Almost from the very beginning, Damon had managed to stay close to the top of 128's roster of star residents. It had started out in 1961 as Damon Engineering, a small electronics company spawned by David I. Kosowsky, then six years out of MIT with a doctorate in electrical engineering, nine years after leaving the City College of New York, summa cum laude. Kosowsky still considers himself privileged to have had Jerome Wiesner as his doctoral thesis advisor—*the* Wiesner, later to become White House science advisor to John Kennedy and president of MIT. Following his graduation, the young Kosowsky signed on with a small electronics company. By the mid-sixties, Damon had branched into several profitable technology-related fields, including electronic instruments, high school science educational aids and scientific hobby kits, and joint publishing ventures.

There was nothing significant about the name Damon, by the way. Kosowsky explained that "The company I'd worked for was called Hermes Electronics, and I wanted a name that carried on the idea of mythology. So when I was getting ready to start the new company, several of us sat around one night going through mythology books, came up with Damon from the story of Damon and Pythias. It sounded good, and was easy to pronounce."

No one argues the point that as Damon's chairman, Kosowsky gets most of the credit for its success during the 1960s and well into the 1970s. A native of New York, "Dr. K" seems to have fit quickly and comfortably into the affluent Newton-Wellesley-128 environment. He has by all accounts been twice-blessed. First with the quick and analytical mind of the engineer—something he says he probably inherited from his father, one of those rare talents who could instantly multiply and divide large numbers in his head—then with the crackling managerial style of the archetypal CEO. Even more remarkably in these parts, he appears to enjoy the wholehearted respect—in some cases, even affection—of most of his employees, both past and present. "David's like most engineers in that he's a 'concept person' rather than a 'people person,'" recalled one former employee. "I never thought he was entirely comfortable in one-on-one situations." Another middle executive at Damon explains that "he can be a tough guy to work for, but he's always fair. Just don't ever try to lie to him—he'll never forgive you for that."

Physically, Kosowsky is one of those men who fuel the common belief that males are luckier than females because they get better-looking with time. Now in his middle fifties, he is built hard and sparingly. His thinning gray hair, rather than detracting from his looks, is a patrician complement to his sharp features. Even in the relaxed surroundings of his tasteful second-floor office, he is an animated conversationalist. He shifts his position frequently and gestures vigorously to accent his points. When his listener fails to grasp a subtle scientific point, he quickly snatches up a pencil and paper to translate the concept into a crude but enlightening diagram. He can be a charmer when the occasion demands it. He also admits to being impatient—sometimes to the point of rudeness—with men and women he perceives as functioning below their capabilities.

For all the company's early successes, Kosowsky says that Damon had been sailing awfully close to the wind during the mid-1970s, partly because of his own uncharacteristic misreading of medical care in the United States. Although primarily an electronics company, Damon was never far removed from the fortunes of the national health care system. After all, most of the company's key instrumentation customers were hospitals, clinics, and medical researchers. Another reason was that Kosowsky had always nurtured a personal fascination with medicine and biology, and sat on the boards of directors at three major Boston hospitals. And as something of an expert in medical sociology and economics (if not technology), he couldn't shake his gambler's hunch that that industry was overdue for some big changes.

The entire network of products and services that was loosely called health care delivery, in fact, was nearing the end of a giddy fifteen-year ride. It had been an incredible era, one probably never to be seen again. An era during which no price was too large for medical progress, no mission too daunting. Americans had walked on the moon; after that, what could be so difficult about eliminating heart disease, curing cancer, wiping out birth defects? Richard Nixon had even declared all-out war on cancer; who would have thought that like the war in Southeast Asia, it would take much more than bold men and barrels of money to win it? The government sent one blank check after another for educating new doctors, creating new research laboratories and home medical care programs, raising gleaming new hospitals that would never be more than half full. It was the Great Society all over again. "Looking back, some of the goals we set for ourselves seem rather spectacular," a grinning Kosowsky said later. "But hey, those were the days when you could do spectacular things."

Also like the Great Society, it couldn't last. One wonders now why more of the experts didn't see it coming, especially when it came to hospital care. Sliding down into his high-backed leather chair, Kosowsky planted his feet on top of his desk and shook his head as he recalled it. "You've got all this money floating around, okay? So for years and years, hospitals could spend almost anything they wanted to run their business.

"What fascinated us most was the fact that the cost of, say, a blood sugar test in a typical hospital was many times more than if that test was run in an independent lab. The hospitals knew that they'd be reimbursed by the government or collect it from the patients; where was the incentive to cut costs? We thought that was insane. It *couldn't* go on." At some point, he thought, hospitals would be forced to account for their costs; if they didn't assume the cost-control responsibility themselves, the government would take care of it for them. And when that happened, hospitals and clinics would suddenly have to find new, less expensive products and services.

And so only eight years after its birth, Damon launched the largest of its businesses—clinical diagnostics, the general term for a variety of products and services aimed at helping physicians, hospitals, and clinics perform standard diagnostic tests more quickly and efficiently than they could do themselves, and at a much lower cost.

Like most good ideas, Kosowsky's was a simple one: Damon would buy up dozens of small and medium-size medical laboratories and equip them with the company's own instruments and personnel. For an industry anxious to cut costs, there would be at least two advantages. The first was that like any company—and unlike hospital lab personnel, who by and large felt little responsibility to reduce costs—Damon would be strongly motivated to find less expensive laboratory methods; the hospital, of course, would share in the savings. The second advantage was that of efficiency: A company that maintained forty or fifty labs couldn't help but uncover faster, simpler, or more dependable procedures which would be shared by all the labs in the network.

Convinced that he was on the right track, Kosowsky set out on a buying spree that netted the company more than a hundred privately owned clinical laboratories, most of them based in small hospitals. "When these cost-control measures became law— 1974, 1975, we figured—we'd be all set. By doing things faster and more efficiently, we'd *make* a little money, the hospitals and insurance companies would *save* a little money, and everyone would be happy. Wonderful idea, right?"

Except for one detail. Kosowsky's predictions about cost-containment materialized not in the mid-1970s, but the early 1980s. The new rules took form as what are now called DRGs, or "diagnosis related groups." Under the DRG policies set by the federal Department of Health and Human Services, Medicare would no longer reimburse hospitals according to their stated costs. Rather, reimbursement would be according to a fixed schedule of fees. And the fees would be set before the procedures, not after. If the government decided that twenty dollars was a reasonable fee for a particular blood test, for example, then it was up to the hospital to provide that test for twenty dollars, or less. If the hospital could run the test for fifteen dollars, it stood to make five dollars on each test; if the cost went to twenty-five or thirty dollars—well, too bad.

It was almost precisely the belt-tightening system that Kosowsky had foreseen nearly fifteen years before. Unfortunately, Wall Street has no prizes for the company that nearly make the grade. Damon's stock plummeted from $70 in 1972 to a paltry $3.62 in 1980. "But the '70s was a bad time for most companies," Kosowsky said. "No one's stock was doing all that well. Still, when your stock drops that far, people figure you can't be doing anything right."

Kosowsky's first order of business, then, was to sell off some of the hospital labs he'd accumulated during his ambitious buying spree and reorganize the others into a leaner and more manageable network. But another answer (one that actually wouldn't present itself until later) might be in diversification—a dramatic move into a new business to shore itself up among its stockholders and the Boston and New York financial communities, and at the same time set the company off on a new growth path. Given his interest in medicine (and given the fact that medical technology was already promising to eclipse computers as the growth industry of the 1980s), it was inevitable that Kosowsky would ultimately be drawn to what was already being called "the new biotechnology."

And just what was this new biotechnology? Basically, it rested on the fact that every plant and animal cell not only absorbs nutrients from its surroundings, but also creates something in the self-maintenance process. Depending on the cell's genetic instructions, the product may be an enzyme needed to break down its food, or defend itself; a cell may manufacture and secrete hormones—insulin, for example—that are sent to other cells within the network; or it may be the simplest kind of wastes, which are then picked up and carried away for disposal. Simply stated, the new biotechnology was the science of persuading these cells to create products they don't ordinarily make, or to make them in much larger amounts than usual.

Until the mid-1970s, it was necessary to find a particular organism (or group of organisms, usually bacteria) that secreted a particular protein that could be used to bring about a desired result. The yeast that goes into a loaf of bread, for example, actually consists of certain organisms that secrete certain enzymes. These proteins break down the starchy molecules in the dough, meanwhile giving off carbon dioxide that makes the bread rise.

With the New Biotechnology, it was no longer necessary to restrict oneself to a predetermined range of organisms. Two scientists, Stanley Cohen and Herbert Boyer, had proved that for the first time in 1973 by chemically moving a gene from one type of bacterium into another type; more importantly, the transplanted gene continued to make its product in all the subsequent bacterial generations. That meant that if for some reason you want large quantities of the bread-making enzyme, all that is necessary—in theory at least—is to isolate the appropriate gene from the DNA in a yeast cell that produces the enzyme, then move the gene into an organism that grows much larger, or much faster, than the original yeast cell. The faster the new "host" cell grows, the more enzyme it produces. The same principle applies to any other protein you want to make. Do you want large quantities of human insulin? Simply find out which one of the 100,000 or so functional genes in the human cell makes (or "codes for") insulin—once an exhausting chore, but now a surprisingly straightforward and largely automated assignment—transfer it from its original segment of DNA into a strain of sturdy fast-growing bacteria, then stand back.

To make such a transfer, of course, the molecular biologist needs the appropriate gene—that is, an assembly of molecules linked together in a specific sequence. If the biologist already knows the sequence (which is increasingly the case, thanks to new analytical techniques), he may choose to make the gene himself in one of the new "gene machines"—automated electronic devices that can be programmed to chemically assemble the appropriate molecules in any order.

If the genetic sequence is unknown, however (or if the laboratory isn't equipped with one of the costly machines), the biologist needs only a supply of DNA containing the gene. And since DNA from one source is identical to DNA from any other, almost any source will do (as long as insulin was included in the donor's repertoire of proteins)—a tiny bit of human tissue, for example, the cells of which have been slowly reproducing in a warm nutrient solution in a small cone-shaped flask. To get at the DNA, the biologist first transfers a few milliliters of the murky "soup" to a test tube, then places the tube in a centrifuge and switches it on. After a few seconds, the centrifuge rotor reaches a speed of tens of thousands of revolutions per minute, hurling the cells to the outstretched bottom of the tube with a force approaching 40,000 g. The cells are soon packed into a small, hard pellet at the rounded bottom of the tube.

Now the biologist pours off the clear liquid over the pellet, adds a few drops of another liquid, and redisperses the cells. Into the tube goes a small amount of a chemical abbreviated as EDTA, which weakens the walls of the packed cells; next he adds a little detergent (not all that different from the one under your kitchen sink) that dissolves the fatty portions of the cell walls. Thus disrupted, the cells release their contents, including the DNA, into the tube.

The mixture now contains not only the separated DNA, but every other molecule (proteins, mostly) once contained within the cell. The biologist rids himself of these interesting but unwanted contaminants by adding another chemical to the tube, which causes the proteins to knot together into a tangled, viscous mass. Another ride in the centrifuge separates the contents into several distinct layers, the top one of which contains the sticky, viscous DNA. Once this layer is removed and purified, the researcher (if he's a thoughtful soul) may stop for a moment to reflect on the wondrous nature of the gummy gray wad of stuff he holds in his hand. For within that wad is every bit of information he would ever need to construct, protein by protein, a new living replica of the man or woman from whence it came.

The biologist wants to produce only a single protein, however. To do that, he dips into a class of chemicals called restriction enzymes. Dozens of these enzymes are now available from commercial suppliers of biologicals, and there's nothing especially exotic or mysterious about them. Like all enzymes, these molecules "recognize" and bind to just one cluster of atoms (in much the same way that antibodies bind to their corresponding antigens), then split them apart at a very specific intersection of atoms. If you know the chemical structure of the insulin gene—that is, its precise sequence of amino acids, from one end of the gene to the other—you can purchase restriction enzymes that when mixed with the DNA will chemically "snip" both ends of the gene from the DNA molecule. It's rather like going along a picket fence until you find the picket that's a bit shorter, or taller, or fatter, or thinner than the others. Run through a sequence of chemical separations and *Voilà!*, you have a mixture containing only insulin genes. Another series of reactions introduces these DNA fragments into the cell wall of a bacterium (perhaps by hooking the gene to a virus which invades the organism), and in the process splices the new gene into the bacterial DNA. Once inside, the new gene will be reproduced in every succeeding generation of the bacterium, there to order up the production of its unique protein.

Without fully realizing it, perhaps, Damon had already positioned itself in biotechnology. Since 1973 the company had maintained a research agreement with Dr. Franklin Lim, a researcher at the Medical College of Virginia in Richmond. A small, intense Taiwanese in his late forties, Lim has been described as almost a caricature of the mad scientist—a brilliant theoretician wrapped in wrinkled gabardine whose laboratory methods sometimes bordered on the bizarre, but who nevertheless had an uncanny way of coming up with fascinating results.

Under the agreement, Damon had first commercial rights to whatever Lim developed. And Lim's work had been an interesting bit of business indeed: He had learned how to take various nonliving materials, such as chemicals and enzymes, and fully enclose them in microscopic hollow balls fashioned of different types of polymers. The resulting microcapsules could be so small —perhaps only a few millionths of a millimeter in diameter—that hundreds of thousands of them would fit comfortably inside a thimble.

Lim wasn't the only researcher working in microencapsulation. In many ways, in fact, the process was old stuff. Some forms of carbon paper were nothing more than ink-containing capsules that burst open to release the ink when struck by a typewriter key. And Lim himself had used the principles to invent what later came to be called the LiquiSol—"liquid-solid"—line of Damon's diagnostic kits. Basically, the kits consisted of chemical reagents enclosed in hollow, porous microspheres; when the spheres were mixed with a sample of fluid from a patient, other chemicals in the fluid flowed into the pores and reacted with the enclosed molecules. Since all chemical reactions are accompanied by some measurable phenomenon—a color change, perhaps, or an electric current—an automated instrument could be used to quickly calculate how much of a reaction had occurred, and therefore how much of the corresponding chemical had been in the patient fluid sample.

In 1978, Lim was reporting back to Damon that he'd designed an interesting variation of his encapsulation method, one that could be used to safely encapsulate not just chemical reagents, but perhaps also living cells. To his knowledge, no one had ever developed such a process (although it had already been proposed by other researchers). His LiquiSol technology certainly couldn't do it; the cells would be destroyed instantly by the heat needed to evaporate the liquids in which the polymer was formed, or by the toxic organic chemicals he used to form the polymer coating. If he was to enclose living cells, he needed an unusual type of polymer, one based entirely on water.

The answer, when it came to him, literally called him out of a sound sleep one night. "It was too simple," he said. "I couldn't wait to get back into the lab to try it."

When he did try it, he chose enzymes as the encapsulated material. Like all proteins, enzymes consist of chains of amino acids—hundreds or thousands of them arranged in a precise sequence. To chemists and biologists, the most critical result of this arrangement is that the chains fold up and over and around one another—in much the same fashion that cell receptors are created—to give the enzyme molecule a distinctive geometric shape. It is this shape that enables an enzyme molecule to "mate" and react with just one other chemical structure (called the substrate).

But enzymes are notoriously sensitive to outside influences. Mix them with the wrong chemical, or expose them to excessive heat, and the amino acid chains will first disassociate from one another then refold into a completely different shape. As a result, the new molecule is useless as an enzyme.

To test his encapsulation process, Lim mixed a solution of enzymes with a purified version of a common chemical extracted from seaweed, called sodium alginate. As they mixed, the alginate surrounded and clung to the molecules, rather like chocolate syrup surrounds and clings to a scoop of ice cream. When he dribbled the coated enzymes into another water-soluble chemical, calcium chloride, the alginate was converted into a gummy, Jell-O-like substance.

The final step was the critical one: building the spherical capsule around the gummy droplets. To do that, Lim mixed the coated cells with a third chemical, called poly-L-lysine, or PLL—basically a water-soluble conglomeration of molecules of the amino acid called lysine. Lim knew that the alginate that enclosed the cells contained a large number of negatively charged chemical groups called anions; the surface layer of the PLL, however, was loaded with positively charged groups, called cations. Mixing the two should bring the positive and negative groups together into a tight network—"like pulling up a zipper," he said later.

But there was no point in completely enclosing the enzymes. For the capsules to be useful as an analytical tool (that is, measuring how much of a corresponding substrate is in a sample), Lim had to allow these other chemicals to get inside and react with the entrapped molecules, and a way for the new reaction products to get back outside to be measured. He speculated that he could fill both requirements by designing pores into the membrane, pores large enough to allow the necessary molecules to flow in and out, but small enough to keep the enzyme inside. The pores, moreover, could be formed in the polymer simply by altering the conditions of the reaction; larger pores could be obtained by stopping the reaction before the "zipper" was pulled all the way up, or by choosing another polyamino acid, one that reacted only partially with the alginate. In the final step, he washed the mixture in yet another chemical that dissolved the unreacted alginate inside the capsules and let it flow out through the pores.

Under a microscope, the hard little capsules that were left resembled plastic Whiffle balls, with the enzymes trapped inside. And by controlling certain parts and ingredients of the process, Lim found he could vary not only the enzyme concentration within each capsule—from just a few to hundreds of thousands of molecules—but also the size of the pores in the capsules.

And the enzymes remained completely undamaged. If such dainty things could survive the process, asked Lim, *why not living cells?*

If you're not in the business of raising cells, it may be difficult to grasp the significance of such a notion. Even Kosowsky—a bright engineer but something of a neophyte in the nuts and bolts of biotechnology—didn't quite know what to make of the news. "When they told me that Frank was thinking about encapsulating living cells, my first reaction was, 'Gee, I didn't know they *couldn't* do that.' My second reaction was, 'Why do you want to do it anyway?' "

Perhaps Kosowsky didn't fully understand that the commercial success of the new biotechnology hung on a very few, very fragile threads. One of those threads was the maddening tendency of all living cells to die when they are placed in a new environment. Even in the cleanest and most carefully controlled laboratory, the glass dishes and flasks that are used to grow, or "culture," cells are about as hostile an environment to living tissue as the back side of the moon is for us. Cells that thrive and multiply happily in the body go into a sort of shock when they touch glass. They were meant to be in a living, breathing body. There they flourish on the blood and minerals and proteins in which they are bathed and fed; there they also communicate with each other through a complex and still not understood system of electrical and chemical signals.

Even today, the phenomenon of the cell has never quite been duplicated in the laboratory. Perhaps it never will be. One reason is that no scientist has ever been able to achieve the kind of cell densities—the number of cells that can be packed into a given volume—that occur in nature. Human body cells typically grow to a density of about a billion per cubic centimeter (roughly the size of your fingertip); the best laboratory cell culture method can produce only a few million. On the tiny scale at which cells live, that's the difference between a Manhattan subway car at 5 P.M. and an isolated cabin in the north woods of Maine. Unlike subway commuters, however, cells like being packed closely together. Only under those conditions can oxygen and nutrients and enzymes flow unhindered from one to another; only in such congestion can waste products be carried away to other parts of the body for elimination or recycling. For living cells, separation is certain death.

There are other ways of growing cells or cellular products. Bacteria such as the common intestinal bug called *Escherichia coli* are often very adept at housing transplanted genes and serving as miniature factories for producing the protein; in fact, that's how most of the recent crop of genetically engineered drugs and chemicals have been manufactured. But "bacteria can't make any protein for which we happen to have a gene," one biochemist explained. "They're very simple organisms, you know; they just don't have all the necessary 'construction equipment' for building any and all proteins. It would be like trying to manufacture a new Cadillac using only a hammer and a screwdriver."

Another problem comes when you want to remove the product. How do you retrieve it from all the other normal products and debris that the organism has invariably produced along with it? It can be done, of course, but only through lengthy and expensive purification procedures that drive up the cost of the product.

And if your product is one day to be injected into a human—insulin or interferon, for instance—there's an even bigger problem: The immune system of the recipient might not see your hard-won wonder drug as "self." It will bear the unmistakable cellular markings of another species. The recipient's system of

T-cells and B-cells could turn on the newcomer and try to destroy it, perhaps wreaking havoc on the patient in the process.

Lim's encapsulation technique was burdened by none of these problems. As a cell culture method, it promised to be simple, clean, and cheap. Damon owned it. But what to do with it? "We had what we considered to be a very important answer," Kosowsky explained. "But at that time no one was quite sure what the question was."

There were plenty of questions all right, and it was Paul J. Vasington's job to ask them. As an experienced cell-culture scientist and vice president of Damon's diagnostics division, Vasington was also fascinated by the new encapsulation technique. He knew firsthand the problems of growing cells in such hostile environments as glass dishes; if the cells could somehow be grown in friendlier surroundings, it might mean an entirely new means of producing interferon or other valuable cell products in bacteria. It could even be a revolutionary new cell-culture technique for cancer researchers and other medical explorers, many of whom were frustrated by the maddening tendency of cells to die at just the wrong time.

The new science called drug delivery offered another opportunity for Lim's process. Vasington knew that every drug, no matter how effective in treating disease, was in a sense limited by its own efficiency. The drug called vincristine, for instance, is a powerful anticancer drug that works by destroying rapidly dividing tumor cells. But an injection of vincristine doesn't seek out only tumor cells; it attacks *all* rapidly dividing cells in the body, such as those that line the gastrointestinal tract and those that produce hair follicles. That's why chemotherapy patients often suffer such violent digestive problems during treatment, and why they lose much of their hair. These side effects could be eliminated, thought Vasington, by placing a few molecules of a drug inside Lim's capsules, then imbedding them close to a tumor. As the drug oozed out of the pores, nearly all of it would be limited to the immediate area.

During the summer of 1978, Vasington and his boss, vice president Edward B. Lurier, flew to San Francisco to attend a conference of the American Association of Clinical Chemists. Wandering through the exhibit areas, they happened onto Frank Lim.

The three men agreed to meet for dinner later that evening at Ernie's on Montgomery Street. They talked for more than two hours that night about Lim's work, Vasington at first pushing the researcher toward the idea of creating new diagnostic and analytical devices based on encapsulated enzymes.

Lim nodded slowly at the suggestion. In fact, he'd been thinking the same thing, and had successfully put several types of enzymes inside his little Whiffle balls; the new process would be a logical addition to Damon's business, a profitable adjunct to the LiquiSol products.

But the wiry researcher had other ideas too—especially the one about encapsulating and growing live cells. What he *really* wanted to put inside his capsules, he told Lurier and Vasington, were human liver and kidney cells. If they continued to function, and if he could get them to grow to the kinds of densities that were typical of living tissue, he would possibly have found the key to an important new cell culture method. One that sidestepped all the existing problems of culturing cells in glass dishes and eliminated the costly drawbacks of growing them in animals. The new biotechnology would have a priceless new tool for advancing itself.

Lim had another reason for wanting to grow liver cells—the intriguing idea of an artificial liver. Other researchers were already closing in on an artificial heart; a doctor in Philadelphia had reported several successful cases of artificial tendons; Lim was sure that the bulky dialysis machines that served as artificial kidneys would one day shrink in size and cost, or be obsoleted by portable, inexpensive units for millions of kidney-damaged patients.

Why not an artificial liver? A conglomerate of living cells that could take over for the thousands of organs lost every year to cancer, alcoholism, hepatitis? To be sure, it would be a massive undertaking that would probably take years of experimentation, then several more years of trials in animals and in humans. But the logistics were of almost secondary importance; he first had to get healthy liver cells to grow to large densities, then "package" them. Perhaps inject them into damaged livers, where the capsules would allow them to grow into masses large enough to take over some of the lost function. When he had described the idea to one of the directors of his lab in Virginia, the man could barely control himself: "You do that, Frank, and I'll see you in Stockholm in five years!" It's doubtful that the director was wholly serious (Nobel prizes are rarely accorded so quickly), but neither was he entirely joking.

For the forty-seven-year-old Lurier, Lim's work had a very special meaning, one that went far beyond the mundane world of business: His popular and vivacious wife Beth, just forty-four, had died of heart disease the year before as a complication of her lifelong diabetes. Making matters worse was the fact that Lurier's twenty-year-old son Eliot was a victim of the same disease. Having watched his mother suffer through the many trials of her diabetes, the young man was possessed with a growing awareness of his own fate. He knew that diabetes was much more than two shots of insulin every day. It could mean devastating damage to the nervous system. Impotence, perhaps. Circulatory system abnormalities that in some victims leads to heart disease, blindness, even gangrene. Worse yet, he knew that there was still little or nothing that could be done for him. He had become depressed, angry, fatalistic.

When Lim turned to the idea of encapsulating liver cells, then, a light had gone on somewhere in the back of Lurier's mind. Not liver cells, not kidney cells, but *pancreas* cells. Specifically, the ones called beta cells whose job it is to produce insulin in the healthy body.

Lurier was a businessman, not a scientist; he didn't even have a college degree. But he had learned, through research triggered by painful personal experience, a great deal about diabetes— especially the severe form known as "juvenile-onset" diabetes that accounts for about a tenth of all known cases of the disease. He knew that insulin is normally secreted by the beta cells— located in the pancreatic tissues called the islets of Langerhans— in reply to rising levels of blood sugar, such as after a meal. In the nondiabetic, the insulin breaks the sugars down into new molecules that can be converted to fuel by the body's cells. If the pancreas produces a defective kind of insulin (as in adult-onset diabetes), or fails to produce it at all, as in the juvenile-onset form, the sugars accumulate in the blood while the cells that need it for fuel go hungry—a condition some have called "starving in the midst of plenty."

Lurier also knew that simply injecting oneself with insulin was a dismal substitute for a properly functioning pancreas. One important reason is that the twice-daily injections cause sudden rises in insulin levels, then a steady decline as it is consumed by the body. Blood sugar rises and falls several times during the day, however, in a roller coaster pattern that is easily handled by the normal pancreas. So no matter how faithfully the diabetic administers the insulin, no matter how carefully he guards his diet, the blood will usually contain either too much sugar or too little. And even though no one knows for sure how the body is damaged as a consequence, there are several theories. The sugar may react indirectly with proteins in the body, for example, forming products called glycosylated proteins that interfere with normal proteins, lay down residues in the blood vessels, and lead to abnormal types of tissue.

And what are the long-term results of these varied assaults on the body? Lurier knew the statistics all too well: Diabetics are seventeen times more likely than nondiabetics to suffer kidney disease. Eight out of ten of them will lose some or all of their vision, the possible result of the excess blood sugar being sucked up by blood vessel membranes in the eye; the sugar's devastating effects on other blood vessels make diabetics especially susceptible to gangrene, and they run at least twice the average risk of heart disease and stroke. For the diabetic, said the first-century Greek physician Aretaeus, "life is disgusting and painful, a melting down of the flesh and limbs. . . ."

Even today, Ed Lurier admits to an obsession with the disease. Talk with him about almost any other subject and he's simply a balding middle-aged businessman, his roundish face rather impassive, sometimes remote. Turn the conversation to diabetes and it's as though someone plugged his finger into a wall socket. He leans forward across the desk, his hands flitting back and forth like slender little birds. You leave with the feeling that diabetes, the "melting down of flesh," is Lurier's personal dragon, and he lives for the day when he can slay it single-handedly.

It was Lurier's feverish sense of mission that Frank Lim remembers about that night at Ernie's. And by the time the coffee cups had been refilled for the third time, Lurier's moving enthusiasm had won over both men. "He wasn't interested in liver cells, or kidney cells," said Lim. "He jumped on the idea of pancreatic cells, perhaps as the basis of a cure for diabetes. My God, he had tears in his eyes. I felt I didn't have any choice but to go ahead with it."

But Lim's commitment was less than wholehearted, he said later. He was sure that he was hot on the trail of an artificial liver. What a coup that would be, not only for his own career but also for the medical world. It might go into the books alongside the artificial heart, and if there was a Nobel in it, so much the better. But whether it was he or someone else who finally invented it, Lim was convinced that the artificial pancreas (which is precisely what it was, regardless of the final form it might take) that Lurier was envisioning that night at Ernie's was much further downstream. To delay work on the liver cells and turn instead to pancreatic beta cells might pay off in the long run, or it might not. But it would definitely put his other research program on hold, perhaps for a year or more.

As the men parted on the sidewalk outside the posh restaurant, Lim promised Lurier and Vasington that he would try to have some preliminary results within six months. Returning to his Virginia laboratory, he immediately set to work on new variations on his process. And as the living encapsulated material, he chose red blood cells, largely because those cells are so easily damaged. The least bit of trauma can "lyse" the fragile membrane—rupture it so that its precious cargo of oxygen-carrying hemoglobin spills out into the surrounding fluid. If the red cells stood up to encapsulation, Lim reasoned, it was likely that any cell could survive.

In order to extend his work into pancreatic cells, though, he would need a steady supply of healthy islets. He would also need money—and substantially more than he was receiving from the Damon grant—for equipment, chemicals, and laboratory animals. Lurier assured Lim that he, Lurier, would find the money. He knew several academic and commercial researchers right in Boston who would be happy to join forces with Lim, he said.

It was one of those promises that was much easier to make than to keep. As Lurier made the rounds of diabetes researchers in Boston and in other cities, he crashed into one wall after another. Frank Lim was hardly a "name" in diabetes research, Lurier was told. Where had he worked? Where had he been published? What made him an authority on the disease? Moreover, a lot of diabetes researchers were heavily invested in their own projects; everyone, in fact, seemed to have a personal favorite in some stage of completion. Especially disappointing to the academically naive Lurier was the growing competitiveness of diabetes research—the unspoken but palpable warning that said, "If it isn't invented here, we're not interested."

That wasn't all. While Lim was unquestionably an original and innovative thinker, his methods sometimes seemed fearfully unscientific. He appeared to have forgotten (or perhaps couldn't be bothered with) one of the first principles of scientific research. One of Lim's colleagues described it this way: "When you run any kind of experiment, you have dozens of things called variables—conditions that can be altered pretty much at will. You can change the temperature, you can change the pressure, you can change the concentration of a solution, and so on.

"But if you really want to know what's going on in this experiment, you can change only one of these things at a time; everything else stays the same. If you keep everything else constant and raise the temperature, and something happens that didn't happen before, then you know that what happened came from the temperature rise. If you change the temperature and the pressure and you make something happen, how do you know why it happened?"

In Lim's impatience to put his theories into action, though, such simple precepts were often brushed aside. "Sometimes he'd have all these experiments running at the same time, variables all over the place," the coworker went on. "He got some interesting results, but it was hard to know how they'd come about. Even he couldn't always duplicate them." Another colleague was more blunt: "His data were lousy. Just lousy. He should've gone back to double-check some of his results, but rarely did."

Little wonder, then, that Lurier met so much resistance from so many prospective patrons. Everywhere he went—in Boston, New York, California, even a giant pharmaceutical company in Denmark that was regarded as a world pioneer in diabetes research—the story was the same. "I never realized how much effort is going into what amounts to basic research," Lurier complained. "It seems that no one's doing applied research—no one's trying to put what they've learned to work on diabetics." At first frustrated, he became angry, then furious at what he considered a blind resistance to the new, the unusual, the unproven. "I know I made a lot of enemies during that period. I was the maniac, the nut trying to sell this wacky idea." To make matters worse, Kosowsky himself confessed to serious doubts about the project, wondering how it could ever be made to work. And even if it could, how would Damon possibly benefit from it? It was only after several visits with diabetologists at Children's Hospital in Boston that he became convinced of the technical feasibility of the experiments.

As for the commercial payoff, said one colleague, "There are about ten million diabetics just in the United States—four or five times that many worldwide. If you can offer even 2 or 3 percent of these people an alternative to insulin injections, something that controls or eliminates these horrible complications, the humanitarian implications alone are just overwhelming. And it doesn't take a genius to grasp the potential dollar value of such a therapy."

A year after his meeting with Vasington and Lim in San Francisco, Lurier's "wacky idea" hit a receptive audience at Connaught Laboratories in Ontario, Canada—the company that had first manufactured insulin in 1921, and that had since become considered among the top two or three corporate leaders in diabetes research. They were interested enough in the concept to at least run their own series of experiments with Lim. At their end, the tests would be managed by a reserved, soft-spoken Connaught researcher named Anthony Sun.

From a purely technical standpoint, the matchup turned out to be a stroke of genius: Sun was already the author of several papers on diabetes treatment and was regarded as one of North America's leading authorities on the elusive artificial pancreas. He was also many of the things that Lim was not—well-organized, methodical, self-effacing, a stickler for accuracy and experimental reproducibility. Most important from Lurier's perspective, he had credence.

There is even today some confusion about whose experiment it was. What is remembered is that Sun, working in his Ontario laboratory, would surgically remove pancreatic islets from several adult rats, then freeze the cells and send them to Lim in Virginia for encapsulation. Lim would then return the capsules to Sun, who would implant them in diabetic rats.

Sparks began to fly between the two men almost immediately. Part of the antagonism was due to the personal and cultural differences that still separate the Taiwanese from the mainland Chinese—differences that are not unlike those that divide the northern United States from the South. But the hostility between Lim and Sun, said Vasington, seemed several orders of magnitude greater than could be explained by their respective heritages: "Sometimes I could hardly bear to be in the same room with them."

The professional differences were, if possible, even deeper. Lim claimed that the islets he received from Sun were either dead or close to it. Sun shot back that the islets he had sent Lim were perfectly healthy, but had come back to Toronto dead.

Sun settled the dispute by flying to Virginia to observe first-hand Lim's encapsulation procedure; he would make the encapsulation himself, using Lim's principles. A few weeks later, Sun reported that he had encapsulated insulin-producing islet cells; now the experiment could get under way.

Sun placed some of the cells—the "controls"—off to one side to grow in culture; the rest he encapsulated with the same process Lim had used for his red blood cells. The coated cells were washed to dissolve the gel remaining inside the capsule, then allowed to multiply.

A few days later, Sun examined the cells. Both batches were secreting insulin at about the same rate. The encapsulation process apparently hadn't harmed the islets; those cells, in fact, would keep producing insulin for fifteen weeks.

Sun's final step was to inject both types of cells into another genetic strain of rats that had been made diabetic with the chemical streptozotocin. As he had hoped, diabetic symptoms—high blood glucose, excessive water consumption, high urine output—were alleviated in all the rats after implantation. After five days, however, the symptoms returned in the animals that had received the unencapsulated islets; the cells were being rejected and destroyed by the rats' immune systems. The other rats were still almost symptom-free nearly three weeks later. For some reason, the capsules had not only allowed the islets to grow before implantation, but they were also protecting the cells from the immune system long enough to allow them to "take root" in the animals.

By all measures, the experiment was a success. The encapsulated islets indeed "cured" diabetes, if only for a few weeks. Much more work was required, of course; a cure lasting three weeks is no cure at all—only the faintest promise of one. The personal relations between the two men, however, never recovered; each remains convinced that the other had almost scuttled the whole program.

In a sense, the capsules represented another "black box"—it worked, but no one was entirely sure why. Lim offers his version of what happened: "When the encapsulated islets enter the body, the cells of the immune system see the capsule, okay? First thing. Why don't they attack it? I think it's because the capsule is made up of groups of amino acids, things that are already in the body and therefore 'accepted.'

"After a few weeks, the capsule breaks down. The islets are released. But by now, the immune response has subsided. The T-cells and B-cells have dropped their guard, so to speak, so the new cells go unchallenged."

Translation, according to one of Lim's colleagues: "Who really knows why it works? By all rights, it shouldn't."

The islet experiment was published as a two-and-a-half page article in the November 21, 1980, issue of *Science* magazine. While Lim and Sun acknowledged that a great deal more work remained to be done—the best method of inserting the encapsulated islets, for one—they closed on an optimistic note: "Further studies should provide significant information in all of these areas and may lead to the use of islet transplantation in the treatment of human diabetes."

There was a story going around for awhile that certain Connaught people wanted Vasington to appear as one of the paper's authors because of the support he'd given the project. (If true, it was an odd gesture; by tradition, only researchers who perform the actual work are so cited in technical journals.) At any rate, recalled a Damon observer, "Frank Lim flatly refused. I think his ego wouldn't permit it." Vasington settled for a brief note of thanks tucked at the end of the article.

The results were enough to convince Kosowsky that he was onto something. The exact nature of this "something," though, was still anyone's guess. Most important, could it ever be developed into something more than a laboratory curiosity? And for God's sake, could it make money?

One of the men who was hired to help answer those questions was a tall young molecular biologist named Dr. Allan P. Jarvis, Jr.

If you meet Jarvis today, you suspect that he might have once been one of those gangly kids who spent his teen years catching his feet in throw rugs or bumping into doorjambs. Not that he's an awkward man; in fact, his movements and gestures tend to be gracefully deliberate, almost like those of a dancer. There's just something about his lean angularity that suggests an early clumsiness. He speaks with the same kind of deliberation—so softly that you sometimes have to strain to hear him. Although a native of the Boston area, there's only a trace of an accent (most often the insertion of an *r* between two vowels, such as "We sawr an opportunity . . .").

Jarvis had heard through the scientific grapevine about the experiments under way by Sun and Lim. He was fascinated. Unlike Lurier, however, Jarvis had no special interest in pancreatic cells, nor in diabetes in general. What captured his imagination was the unusual package that the two men had used to enclose the cells and apparently keep them alive and healthy for so long.

When Jarvis first contacted Damon in early 1980, it was a result of a nagging curiosity on his part about how basic research is conducted within a business setting. With a solid background in both human interferon and the new techniques of genetic engineering, he wondered how companies would develop and eventually commercialize such potentially beneficial drugs. Yet with all of these questions, he was still dedicated to basic research in the field of molecular biology, was quite happy where he was, and didn't fancy himself a businessman.

After his initial interview with Vasington, Jarvis thought that he could see a way to use the capsules to produce valuable proteins like interferon using procedures similar to those worked out by

Lim for the production of insulin. Closer to home scientifically, he inquired of Vasington about the possibility of borrowing the technology to further his own research at the Worcester Foundation, out toward the center of the state.

As a researcher at the Worcester Foundation for Experimental Biology, the thirty-one-year-old Jarvis was looking for new challenges. Since leaving the University of California at Davis in 1974, he had spent most of his time studying gene expression—how genes behave and manifest themselves at various times during the development of an organism. There are several ways of studying such puzzling events; Jarvis chose to do it by working with the little animals called sea urchins. The beauty of sea urchins, he explained, is that "it's easy to see the various stages of development. Therefore, you may be able to alter the cells' development at some point in time—by changing their nutrient supply, for instance—then determine what effect that alteration has on the subsequent development of the organism."

And how could he change the nutrient supply while holding everything else constant? One way was to encapsulate sea urchin cells in Lim's microspheres. If he could put cells into, say, ten batches of spheres, all with different pore sizes, he could create a tenfold variation in nutrient flow; in effect, he would have the results from ten different experiments, but have to run only one.

Interesting idea, said Vasington. But why didn't Jarvis come to work for Damon, and bring his library of cells with him? That way he could carry on his gene expression research right in Needham Heights, and maybe at the same time figure out what to do with these capsules. And while he was at it, maybe he could look into the feasibility of producing interferon for the company.

Jarvis was hooked by Vasington's proposal. Early in his research career, he had worked extensively with interferon—one of the chemicals produced by many types of human and animal cells in response to infection by a virus. There was even some talk about interferon as a "wonder drug" for cancer, since it seemed to slow the growth of some types of tumors. But by the late seventies, said Jarvis, "everyone was working with interferon, trying to purify it, trying to clone it into bacteria, and trying to get enough of it to run clinical trials on cancer patients. The field was getting too crowded, so I switched over to studying gene expression through developmental biology." With that caveat, Jarvis joined the company in March 1980 with the title of molecular biologist.

In a way, it was a homecoming for Jarvis. He had left Boston for California almost ten years earlier, lured away by the academic quality of the genetics department at Davis. He was also convinced that he'd had enough of Massachusetts. Especially the area around Newbury, tucked away up in the northeast corner of the state, where he'd been born and raised. For all its popularity with midwestern tourists in search of "Old New England," the region is a portrait of small-town America. By and large, the older ones like it that way; it is intolerable for many of its teenagers, especially the wheelless ones who can't negotiate the thirty-five miles or so into Boston on a Friday or Saturday night.

So Jarvis had grabbed his chance for the University of California and the opportunity to study the genetic control of the increasingly popular interferon. He then moved on to do research at Memorial Sloan-Kettering Cancer Center in New York and the Worcester Foundation in east-central Massachusetts. Perhaps predictably for a man nearing middle age, coming home wasn't nearly as bad as he thought it would be. "I feel comfortable here now," he said. "Maybe I'm mellowing."

"He wasn't the only candidate for the spot, but he was the first to be formally interviewed," said personnel director Kathy Fay. "I also thought he was the brightest. He asked some very interesting questions about the company, things we hadn't thought about. Even if we hadn't hired him, we would've wanted to stay in touch with him."

Jarvis learned early on that he had no laboratory space dedicated to encapsulation; he would have to share the second-floor laboratories with other researchers in the diagnostics division. The good news (and the dream of every researcher) was that he was given the money he needed to create one. Buy the equipment, hire the assistants, plan and execute the experiments, beginning with the encapsulation of his own collection of cells.

One of the first of his hirees was twenty-five-year-old Terri Grdina, a native of Cincinnati who had come to Boston with her husband, a postdoctoral fellow at Harvard. Anyone wanting to grow cells could hardly have picked a better research assistant,

Jarvis recalled. She is still remembered as "the person with two green thumbs in cell culture"—the person who seemed to have a sixth sense about what cells needed to thrive and grow. "You can read all the lab manuals you want on this topic," said Jarvis, "but cell culture can be taught only up to a point."

Grdina seemed to know it all instinctively. She knew that before the cells could be enclosed in the capsules, they had to be grown to a certain density on glass plates. Some types of cells, however, couldn't be permitted to grow too long or they would start to die off; it was largely up to her to know (or learn) when that point was reached.

She also knew that young cells are relatively undifferentiated—that is, there is little in their physical appearance to distinguish them from their neighbors. At some point in their development, they begin to divide at a slower rate. It is at that point that they step up the production of whatever it is they are being grown to make. The problem is that increased production requires extra energy; eventually, the production will slow down. The true cell culture aficionado, therefore, is able to distinguish—often by just looking at the glass plates on which the cells are growing—when they are ready to be encapsulated. Grdina knew: "I guess it sounds a little nutty, but you start thinking of these cells almost like they were your kids. Every one's a little bit different from the others; you get to know what they need, when they need it. Most important, you have to like this kind of work." She loved it.

They spent the first nine months repeating and verifying Lim's original experiments, using red blood cells and certain types of rat and mouse cells. Then they turned to the several cell lines he had carried with him from Worcester, modifying the process where necessary to accommodate the special needs of particular cells: erythroleukemic cells (transformed blood cells that produce the oxygen-carrying molecule hemoglobin), the cells called human diploid fibroblasts that manufactured the chemical called beta-interferon, human lymphoblastoid cells (immature cells that later develop into lymphocytes) that produced another type of interferon, called alpha-interferon.

Somewhat surprisingly at first, Lim's encapsulation process worked on every cell, or could be slightly modified to make it work. In packaging the fibroblasts, for example (which make up the body's connective tissues, such as skin and cartilage), Jarvis knew that such cells needed to grow under special circumstances; the cells needed a firm surface on which to spread out and anchor themselves. His solution was to encapsulate these cells along with small amounts of a connective tissue component called collagen. Inside the capsules, the additive formed a sturdy fibrous matrix that provided the cells with a sort of molecular platform on which to attach and grow.

And the work was fun, said Grdina. "We knew that no one had ever tried a lot of this work before. It made me feel like we were really pioneering something." At first, she didn't even mind the twelve-hour days and six-day weeks—time required to watch over her "children," making sure they were getting the right nutrients and growing properly in the dishes. She could usually tell how well they were doing just by looking at them. "Cells that were growing well in the capsules had a sort of opaque appearance," she said. "If they weren't doing well, the capsules were transparent, and you could see these little specks of cellular garbage piling up in their interior."

If there was ever any question about their goals, Kosowsky kept them well informed. He wanted a commercial product, he said, not just academically interesting observations. Sitting in his second-floor office of the red brick building in Needham Heights, he found himself staring out the window at the Charles River flowing through the wooded area across the road, asking himself over and over: "Do we want to grow cells? Or do we want the products the cells make?" The answer seemed obvious.

He was in the lab almost every night around 5 P.M., pulling up a stool and questioning Jarvis about the day's results. As an engineer, Kosowsky was accustomed to getting answers in a short period of time; he seemed to resent the fact that when cells move at all, they do so at their own pace; they utterly refuse to be rushed and often answer your urgings by just dying on you. Sometimes he wasn't even sure what questions to ask, so he asked questions that led to more questions. He knew little about the biological principles at first; he learned, from Jarvis and Grdina and Vasington, from friends at MIT and Harvard. And on Friday afternoons, he seemed to become depressed, Grdina recalled, because he knew that the work would slow down over the weekend.

Jarvis and Grdina made up the entire encapsulation program for most of the first year. They worked together seventy and eighty hours a week, and she developed an enormous admiration for Jarvis—his intellectual skills, the soft-spoken New England reserve that didn't quite mask the underlying ambition, the streak of quiet competitiveness with which he approached his work. "I always had the feeling that this was a personal challenge to him," she recalled. "It's true that we had a lot of fun—it's always like that when a new project is underway—but I also think Allan would've been devastated if we'd come across some cells we couldn't get to grow with this process."

Fortunately for both of them, they got along personally as well as they did professionally. She teased him about his squeaky-clean preppy image and the fastidious, almost squeamish way in which he approached the cells. He poked gentlemanly fun at her long, curly blond hair—"Anyone ever tell you you look like Rod Stewart?" he asked—and the too lean physique that for a while had driven her to sign up for a Nautilus program in nearby Newton.

But fun or no fun, she was getting tired after only nine months. Little by little her spirits were drained by the long days and nights of baby-sitting cells, repeating experiments then repeating them again, translating Jarvis' ideas into yet another series of tests with a new polymer or a different nutrient or a longer or shorter reaction time. During the Friday night happy hours, she plopped down in a booth with the other Damon technicians and biologists at a bar and grill in Newton, complaining that her personal life was drying up: "Allan just keeps giving you more and more work until you finally want to scream, 'Arghhh, I can't do anymore!'" No sooner were the words off her tongue than she was seized by a brief pang of guilt—while she was relaxing with friends over a glass of beer, Jarvis was still in the laboratory.

But at work, she had kept her growing anger and frustration to herself. He was thus taken completely by surprise when she turned in her notice—all the more so when she revealed that she had accepted a lower-paying job, with fewer hours, at another biotechnology company.

She may have suspected all along that he wouldn't have much trouble talking her into staying. And if she left, who would take care of her cells?

By the end of 1981, Jarvis confidently assured Kosowsky that in his opinion, the company indeed seemed to have a commercializable process (or at least a reproducible one). To Jarvis' knowledge, there was not a single type of cell that couldn't be manipulated inside Frank Lim's little capsules, then grown to densities at least ten times greater—in some cases a hundred times greater—than in any other cell culture method.

Neither Jarvis nor Grdina knew it at the time, but much of their work had been a mere warmup for what was to come. The real payoff for the odd little capsules was based not so much on the cells that had flowed through the laboratory during the previous year, but on an unusual series of events that had transpired six years before, in a windowless basement laboratory in Cambridge, England.

CHAPTER FIVE

On the morning of November 14, 1984, in a second-floor meeting room of Manhattan's plush St. Regis Hotel, two men were being pummeled, prodded, and pushed by a mob of reporters and photographers.

One of the men—a slender, bearded six-footer whose thinning white hair belied his thirty-eight years—seemed to find the event wholly distasteful. Shifting his weight back and forth several times as though to ease his aching feet and legs, he'd never realized how hard it was to smile for hours on end. Just as his eyes recovered from one battery of flashbulbs, another crew rammed its way to the front of the room. Handed him things to hold. Told him where to direct his gaze. Smile. Don't smile, look serious. Stand back a bit. Come forward just a step.

Most press conferences were harmless bores. This one was turning into a bloody carnival.

Nevertheless, the white-haired man knew as he took his seat in the front of the room that he was an important guest here. His hosts had gone to great expense to bring him five thousand miles to New York and put him up for almost a week. He could endure the rudeness and silly questions for another hour or two.

His name was being called.

"Dr. Köhler," a reporter asked, almost begging for a snappy quote for the afternoon edition, "how does it feel to win the Lasker Award only a month after sharing in the Nobel Prize?"

The crowd fell for a few seconds into an embarrassed silence.

Near the back of the room, another reporter shook his head. "Oh God, it feels just awful," he whispered to the woman next to him. "All that fame, all that filthy money. Yech! Poo!"

Georges Köhler glanced at the small bird-faced man seated next to him, and they exchanged self-conscious grins. Köhler stood and answered the reporter in a heavy German accent.

"It's a very great honor, of course. I could hardly believe it. . . ." For a few seconds, he struggled vainly for more words. Words he hadn't already uttered dozens of times, at dozens of other press conferences.

Too late. The reporter had his quote and was heading for the rear door with a package of press handouts under his arm. Köhler returned to his folding chair as another man in the audience jumped to his feet.

"I have a question for Dr. Milstein. Sir, could you explain briefly the significance of your invention? What exactly are monoclonal antibodies, and why are they so significant to the medical profession?"

Squinting through his massive horn-rimmed glasses into the spotlight at the rear of the room, the small man stood and tried to pick his questioner out of the crowd. Compared to Köhler, Cesar Milstein seemed positively miniscule. Five five, perhaps, and no more than 130 pounds.

"Monoclonal antibodies are proteins made by an artificially produced cell, called a hybridoma," he began. His voice had an odd, almost soporific cadence—his native Argentina tinted with more than two decades among the British.

Twenty years Köhler's senior and the star of hundreds of press conferences, Milstein had already been a minor celebrity when Köhler was still an undergrad. As the recipient of dozens of awards—including today's $15,000 Lasker Award and last month's $193,000 Nobel, both shared with his young colleague— he exhibited none of the painful self-consciousness that fairly oozed from Köhler's pores.

"We made the hybridoma by combining a white blood cell—a lymphocyte—with a type of cancer cell called a myeloma," Milstein continued. "So all of the antibodies made by this hybridoma are identical, since they all come from the one lymphocyte. And they are made for very long periods of time, you see, because of the immortality of the cancer-cell parent."

Some of the reporters were getting restless. Even though Milstein had furnished them with black-and-white diagrams to help them get through his little lecture, the whole thing was getting too technical, with too many strange words. Antibodies. Lymphocytes. Myelomas.

"Why do we think these antibodies are so important?" Milstein went on. "The reason is that when the body is invaded by an antigen . . ."

Antigen. More Greek.

". . . it produces thousands of different antibodies to defend itself against the antigen. That's called a *polyclonal response,* and the antibodies are polyclonal antibodies since they are made by clones—exact genetic copies—of many, many different kinds of cells. But there are times when we'd like to have large numbers of just one kind of antibody, all made by clones of the same cell, that attacks just one antigen. Since all these antibodies are made by genetically identical cells, they are called monoclonal antibodies. The hybridoma allows us to make these proteins, and in very large quantities."

There followed a dozen or so more questions, some of which were directed at the three other guests of honor at the front of the room. And like all well-done press conferences, the question-and-answer session was followed by a fairly acceptable lunch.

Most of the reporters were reasonably satisfied with Milstein's explanation. As they filed out onto East Fifty-fifth Street, however, a few veterans suspected that they'd heard only a very small part of the hybridoma story. They knew what most scientists had known for centuries—that discoveries of this magnitude usually come through either old-fashioned hard work and sweat, a sudden flash of genius, or through a lucky accident. Usually, there's a bit of all three. The mysterious hybridoma was one of those cases.

The reporters couldn't help but realize that even in the medical research circles of the dizzying mid-1980s, the hybridoma was clearly something out of the ordinary. For one thing, the Nobel Committee had singled it out for its prize in medicine and physiology only nine years after its discovery, barely half the usual length of time required for official recognition in Stockholm.

86

Early in that time span, moreover, Milstein and Köhler's hybridoma was being heralded as nothing less than revolutionary—"one of the most important methodological achievements in biomedicine of the 1970s," according to the Nobel Committee. It promised to finally let some daylight into the mysterious black box called immunology, and in the process give birth to dozens of new techniques for finding disease months or years earlier than ever before. In some cases, perhaps, even cure those diseases. By the time of its fifth birthday, the hybridoma had launched an entirely new industry, the value of which was said to be heading for half a billion dollars a year by 1987. Two or three times that number by the turn of the decade.

All thanks to two men who had wanted not to spawn an industry, but only to find out a little more about these chunks of protein called antibodies.

Few of the reporters at the St. Regis that day took note of the gaunt-looking man with mousy brown hair and cavernous eyes who had shared the stage with Köhler and Milstein. He fielded only one or two questions, directed largely in deference to his position and to the fact that he too was in New York to receive a $15,000 Lasker Award. So only a few of the reporters that day ever realized that except for Dr. Michael Potter, there might never have been a Köhler or Milstein.

In which case the newsmen would today be buying their own lunches, and sure as hell not at the St. Regis.

Basically, there are two kinds of researchers: The one who hopes to make some money from his labors—preferably lots of it —and the one whose greatest reward is simply to move his science ahead, even by just an inch or so. By all accounts, Georges Jean Franz Köhler was and remains of the second breed.

He first arrived at Milstein's laboratory (officially the Laboratory of Molecular Biology, part of the British Government's Medical Research Council) in 1974. Then twenty-eight and the new recipient of a Ph.D. diploma from West Germany's University of Freiburg, he was a confirmed academic, completely disinterested in the world of business. (Years later, when he learned that he had been named to share in the 1984 Nobel Prize, he attended a reception in his honor wearing jeans and sweatshirt, his usual working uniform.) He wanted only to continue his postgraduate studies in the genetics of the immune system; after two years, he planned to move on to the Institute of Immunology in Basel, Switzerland. While in England, however, he wanted to do his work under the leadership of Cesar Milstein (a decision inspired by a Milstein lecture in Basel the year before).

His choices couldn't have been more inspired. The complex of aging buildings on Cambridge's Hills Road has long been considered an academic Eden—a congested cluster of tiny, seemingly disordered offices and laboratories within which some of Great Britain's greatest scientific minds labor side by side with the empire's most mediocre new graduates. At the time, the complex was presided over by the great Frederick Sanger, the first person ever to receive two Nobel Prizes for chemistry.

Unlike most other research sites around the world, Cambridge prides itself on the fact that it has always remained unsullied with commercial interests (a mentality that still grates on many British businessmen who claim to see England slipping disastrously behind its high-technology competitors in Japan and the United States). For the disinterested academic, however, the place was pure heaven. Never mind commercial interests, they were told; never mind if there's a market for what you learn, there are others who will chase down markets. Never mind the Japanese, the Americans, the West Germans. Describing the place ten years later, Milstein himself happily recalled the atmosphere as one in which he could "do good experiments, and not worry about the rest."

That didn't mean that Milstein cared nothing for the real world. In fact, he had argued for years against the barriers that had been set up between basic research (learning how and why something happens) and applied research (how that learning can be put to work in the real world). He had spent all his career at Cambridge, except for two years at the National Institute for Microbiology in Buenos Aires during the early 1960s; he had returned to Cambridge when four of his staff were fired for joining a trade union. Since then, he had established himself as a brilliant researcher and one of immunology's new dons. A few years before Köhler's arrival, for example, he'd published a pivotal study on immunoglobulin structure, showing that an antibody's combining sites—the "lobster's claws"—were immutable, and that this immutability was somehow dictated by the genes. To prove it, he'd combined a mouse B-cell with a rat B-cell. The new hybrid B-cell still produced antibody, but only rat or mouse antibody—no combinations. In his mind, that proved that the genes regulating antibody production seemed to stay together, even when the cells that carried them were combined with cells from another species.

For the first few months of Köhler's tenure in Cambridge, Milstein had him perform a series of routine antigen-antibody experiments. Laboring in the windowless basement laboratory, working with cell cultures that Milstein and others had grown in glass dishes over the years, Köhler dutifully carried out the suggestions of his superior.

But he was growing frustrated. At night he complained to his wife Claudia that he didn't seem to be doing the kind of work he'd hoped to do. In order to learn about how the genes control immunity, he said, he needed huge supplies of cells that produced lots of a single kind of antibody—the defender proteins—which were in turn developed against a single known invading antigen.

But there was no such cell. It was true that every B-cell turned out antibodies of a single design, but Köhler knew that those cells don't survive very well outside the body. They usually live only a few days in culture, dividing six or seven times, then die. Another drawback was that while any given line of B-cells produced identical antibodies, no one could precisely identify the corresponding antigen; there could be hundreds of thousands of possibilities. Maybe millions. Tracking down the responsible antigen would probably take years of tedious testing. Köhler didn't want to invest that kind of time.

Milstein had other cells, however. Like most biologists, his collection consisted not only of cells he himself had cultivated, but also cells received from other researchers all over the world. Frozen cell cultures, in fact, go from laboratory to laboratory like so many baseball cards in a schoolyard. And among Milstein's culture collection were a couple of cell lines developed by Michael Potter, an American researcher with the National Cancer Institute in Bethesda, Maryland.

Potter had been pursuing his own work in the immune system since the early 1950s, first with the University of Virginia Medical School and then with NCI. As a research tool he had selected mouse plasmacytomas, malignant cells that began in the mouse's antibody-producing plasma cells, turned out large amounts of antibody, and were long-lived. The problem was that such tumors were very rare—much too rare to serve as a reliable source of antibody for researchers; it was, someone said later, like trying to keep the nation supplied with oil from one 100-barrel-a-day well in Oklahoma.

But by the late 1950s, Potter had found a way to generate such tumors at will, and thus a constant source of antibody. Another cancer researcher, Dr. Thelma Dunn, had found that plasmacytomas could be created simply by placing a small plastic disc under the skin of a mouse. Since the disc could not be absorbed and broken down by the mouse's cells, it acted as a long-lived irritant and eventually led to the formation of a tumor. Potter simplified the procedure by injecting mice with tiny amounts of mineral oil and gained the same result. He soon had a "library" of plasmacytomas, some of which eventually found their way to Cambridge.

As the autumn of 1974 threatened to become winter, Köhler got an idea just before going to bed one evening. It was so simple, yet so grand, that he couldn't understand why no one had thought of it before. He lay awake thinking about it for most of the night:

Instead of finding the antigen that went with a given antibody, why not turn the problem around a little? Would it be possible to take a certain antigen and use it to produce large amounts of the corresponding antibody, and only that antibody? To do so meant that he would have to somehow isolate a single B-cell, or a very few, from the mixture of millions that are formed during the so-called polyclonal response. Even if he could do that, he would then have to somehow bestow longevity on the short-lived cell so that it would crank out the protein for more than a couple of days. Either task alone was overwhelming; both together seemed insurmountable. And yet, the idea of a veritable factory that produced one kind of antibody, and only one, was a fascinating one.

The idea was too different, and he wondered if he was overlooking something. The next day, he discussed it with Milstein. "One of the things about Cesar is that he listens," Köhler said, years later. "If you come to him with a crazy idea, instead of dismissing it, he will try to find out the good things about it." And skeptical though he was, Milstein did find some good things about the idea, based on his own previous work in combining rat and mouse cells. The overriding problem, he knew, was the polyclonal response that produces hundreds of thousands of B-cell families to any antigen. Like Köhler, Milstein saw dozens of reasons not to pursue the idea. Also like Köhler, he found the notion too rich to pass up.

If Köhler had joined Milstein's laboratory just a year or two earlier, there's a fair chance that the men might still be shrouded in relative obscurity. As it happened, an interesting bit of work had transpired in 1974, in which another research team had found a way of fusing two different types of cells—a yeast cell and a red blood cell from a chicken—into a single new cell.

"There was a rather intriguing question going around in immunology during the early seventies," Jarvis explained later. "It went something like this: If you create a new cell by fusing a normal cell with a cancer cell, does that new hybrid cell behave more like one parent or more like the other? Or does it have some characteristics of both? Interesting questions, right? Questions that only a basic researcher would be likely to ask, and there was little or nothing in the technical literature at the time that provided any answers. But that's the way so many things come about, including the development of the first monoclonal antibody."

Köhler started his inquiry by injecting a laboratory mouse with red blood cells taken from a sheep, a very effective antigen which had long been known to produce a powerful immune response. Within a few weeks, right on schedule, the B-cells concentrated in the mouse's spleen began to produce their defensive antibodies. The mouse was then killed and its spleen removed to chemically extract the B-cells.

The next step was to mix the lymphocytes with mouse plasmacytoma cells from one of Potter's cultures, in a ratio of about five to one. This would be the tricky part, and the basis of the idea that had kept the young German awake all night—getting the two types of cells to fuse into a single new cell. At Milstein's coaching, he added a bit of a chemical to the mixture. After a few minutes, the cells' membranes ruptured for a moment or two, just long enough for the contents of the two types of cells to flow together, like two drops of water meeting on a piece of glass, into a single gelatinous mass. Then the membranes repaired themselves.

The mixture now contained three categories of cells: some of the original unfused mouse B-cells, some of the original unfused mouse plasmacytoma cells, and a certain number of new hybrid cells containing genes from both parents. If Köhler was on the right track, at least some of these new hybrids would produce what he was looking for—antibody directed specifically against the sheep blood cells. The genes from the cancer cell, however, would bestow another feature: Like the cancer cells from which they were derived, the hybrids would continue to grow; as a matter of fact, they could theoretically live forever. So would the portion of the hybrid represented by the B-cell genes. Each hybrid was now a little antibody "factory," dedicated exclusively to producing antibodies and driven by a malignant (and thus long-lived) power plant. As a final step, Köhler added culture medium to the mixture—food on which they could multiply to many times their starting volume—then set the flasks aside.

Within a few weeks, he knew just by looking at his flasks that he had made hybrids (or hybridomas, as they came to be called—a combination of "hybrid" and "-oma," the general suffix denoting a malignancy). They had to be hybrids; they were growing. The unfused B-cells took care of themselves by simply dying after a couple of days. Unfused plasmacytoma cells were killed by a chemical called aminopterin, which Köhler had added to the culture medium. The living cells that remained had to be hybridomas; there was no other possibility. The big question was, How many of them made antibody specifically to the sheep blood cell?

To find out, Köhler set up a screening process by combining some of the original sheep cells with a dye called fluorescein. One of the nice things about fluorescein, and the thing that makes it interesting to biochemists, is that it glows a brilliant lime green when you shine an ultraviolet light on it, or on anything that contains it. The stained blood cells were then transferred in drops to a series of tiny wells molded into a large glass plate, and allowed to dry. To each reddish brown dot at the bottom of the wells, Köhler then added a drop from the hybridoma culture—each drop containing about 50,000 hybridomas—and let that dry. If any of the hybridomas were producing antigen directed specifically against the blood cells, they would bind tightly onto the blood cells in the glass plate and would remain bound after a light washing-out. And how could he identify the hybridomas that were binding? Simply by shining an ultraviolet light on the plate; any well containing the sought-after hybrid would glow with a bright green halo.

Köhler figured that his chances of success on this first try were infinitesimal. It took him almost two months to work up the courage to go back to the basement laboratory and check through the hundreds of little glass plates he'd prepared, to see what, if anything, his new cells were making. When he did return one evening just before Christmas, he took Claudia along, as much for moral support as for companionship. So he wasn't prepared for what he saw under the ultraviolet light. There they were, on the very first two plates—beautiful, tiny, shimmering halos. And in another plate. And another. And another. All signaling the presence of antibodies created against the sheep blood cells. And since the B-cells producing the antibody were all descended from one cell—they were, in other words, monoclonal—so were the antibodies. Monoclonal antibodies.

"I shouted," said Köhler. "I kissed my wife. I was all happy—it was the best result I could think of!" He had not only made hybridomas on the very first try, but he had made exactly the ones he'd wanted to make.

He had taken a million-in-one shot.

And hit the bull's-eye.

The next and final step was to isolate the hybridomas still further, then get them to multiply enough to produce a usable amount of their antibody. Successively diluting each of the wells containing the glowing complex of antibody and antigen, he finally arrived at the point at which several of the wells carried just a single hybridoma. As long as he kept the well supplied with nutrient, the cell would continue to create copies of itself, each of them a miniature factory for monoclonal antibodies. Thanks to the cancerous portion of each hybridoma, he could now count on having a steady supply of antibody that recognized only the sheep blood cell.

He probably didn't know it at the time, but there was something else he could count on. For better or for worse, he was soon to become what he said he never wanted to be: a celebrity.

In the years since Köhler and Milstein's triumph, two nagging questions remain about hybridomas: First, who really fathered the technology, Milstein or Köhler? Second, why didn't the British Government—which, as Milstein's employer, owned the new process—immediately slap a patent on the monoclonal technology? Didn't anyone realize the economic potential of the technique? Could its commercial impact possibly have been overlooked by the Cambridge overseers?

The first question is still a hot one in some laboratories. Some debaters argue that since it was Köhler who first got the idea that led to hybridomas, and since it was Köhler who did most of the work, he properly deserves most of the credit.

But there's much more to it than that. As a two-year postdoctoral fellow at Cambridge, Köhler was a scientific apprentice— bright and resourceful, but an apprentice nonetheless. He was there to take orders, to learn, to add what he could to the continuing work of Milstein's research team. Milstein himself had built the foundation for the hybridoma during the preceding ten years, had planned and executed some of the most awesomely brilliant experiments in the history of immunology. So had Milstein's 1974 coworker, Robert Cotton; and could any of that have borne fruit without the contributions of the industrious Potter in Bethesda? "It's questionable whether Köhler could have accomplished what he did anywhere else," one immunologist told me. "It's like raising flowers; it isn't enough to be a good gardener, you also need good, rich earth in which to plant. It's hard to imagine a more fertile piece of earth than Cesar Milstein's lab during the 1970s. . . ."

The second question is complicated by hindsight. The hoopla

that has been raised since 1975—"monoclonal fever," it's been called—obscures the fact that only a few scientists realized at the time what the two immunologists in Cambridge had accomplished. There had been no wild scramble to develop monoclonal antibodies. Milstein himself had often speculated about what he could do with large amounts of antibody derived from a single B-cell, but such speculation was largely academic. His real interest at the time was simply to learn more about how antibodies are programmed by the genes to recognize so many invaders. As for Köhler, he insists that he wanted only to secure a steady supply of one form of antibody to continue his studies, then get back to Switzerland.

Ask Milstein about the commercial value of monoclonal antibodies; he visibly turns off on you. He seems to be tired of thinking about the subject, and even more weary of being asked about it. Like most European scientists, he maintains that his first calling has always been to his science. Commercial matters—rather distasteful under the best circumstances—are for others to worry about.

"England may have lost some of the technology's economic benefits," he told me, "but we may also have saved some lives. We thought at the time that the most important thing was to publish our results and get the process out to where it could be used." To help speed things along, he even donated frozen samples of the plasmacytomas to other researchers around the world, in return asking only that they did not patent the resulting hybridoma.

Nevertheless, Milstein did tell his superiors about the results, and recommended that the process be patented. If they disagreed, he said, he was going to publish. Under British law, that would make hybridomas and anything described in the paper unpatentable in the United Kingdom.

Weeks went by. The bosses didn't respond to his query. Over his own and Köhler's signatures, he sent the article describing the hybridoma process to the British scientific journal *Nature*. They sent the original article back to him, he said later. While it was interesting enough, it was too long. Could he shorten it a bit so it could be run in the Correspondence column? Milstein did, and one of the most remarkable scientific advances of the twentieth century was announced as a three-page letter in *Nature*'s August

7, 1975, issue. The uncertainty with which the men regarded the process is evident in the closing lines of the article: "Such cells can be grown in vitro [outside the body] in massive cultures to provide specific antibody," they said. "Such cultures could be valuable for medical and industrial use."

Milstein's explanation regarding the patent question is, more or less, still the official story in England. "The typical European scientist wants nothing to do with commercial stuff," explained an American biologist-businessman. "There seems to be something nasty over there about making money in science, especially in the health care sciences. The attitude in many of these companies is that if you're going to do science, you should do it for the love of it, or for the good of mankind—not for money."

Another U.S. hybridoma researcher has a different, less noble explanation for the loss of the patent: "The British screwed up. Period. Milstein and Köhler had known the importance of their discovery, but the Medical Research Council apparently didn't. And once they realized it, it was too late."

Whatever the council's motivation, the United Kingdom forever lost commercial rights to Köhler and Milstein's hybridoma process. Elsewhere in the world, research laboratories and private companies determined to be a lot smarter.

CHAPTER SIX

Jack Christie waited two weeks to tell Eileen about the biopsy. During that time, he lied to her shamelessly. The results were inconclusive, he claimed; the doctors still hadn't received all the lab reports. And even while he told himself that the lies were only to spare her feelings, he knew that it wasn't her that he wanted to protect, but himself. How else could he explain the cool detachment, the stubborn conviction that the name on the lab report wasn't really his but that of one of his patients? Anyway, wasn't there even a slight chance that the pathologist had made an error?

He blurted it out to her one evening as they were drying the dinner dishes. She said nothing for a minute.

"They're absolutely sure then?"

"Yeah."

"Do they think it's fatal, or what?"

The question threw him off balance for a second. So typical of her. Direct, to the point.

"It's hard to say. There are treatments, and some of them have been pretty successful. Even without treatment, I've read about guys going years and years. Sometimes the thing goes away, all by itself. Or it could just"—how could he put it?—"just blow up on me in a couple of years. It's just too early to say."

She turned her back to him, and he thought she took an unusually long time returning the dish towel to the rack. She was smiling broadly when she at last turned around.

97

"You'll be okay," she said, then announced she was going for a bicycle ride.

In the weeks after his diagnosis, he had visited every major hospital and oncology center in Houston. To his anger and frustration, nearly every one offered a different course of action. Most of the doctors had suggested that he simply do nothing for now—he was certainly in no immediate danger, and there had been dozens of cases, just like his, that had remained almost completely dormant for years. Other specialists advised him to start immediately on a course of chemotherapy. He decided to wait, do nothing, for as long as possible—at least until he heard from Ken Foon in Maryland.

He had called Foon more out of sheer desperation than anything else. The curious coincidence was that Foon was at the time one of a team of researchers designing a new experimental NCI treatment program aimed at several types of cancers—including B-cell lymphoma. The program's most appealing feature was that it was being designed to use chemicals derived from the patient's own immune system. If the NCI men were correct, that could mean a more complete response, and without chemotherapy's nasty side effects.

The problem, Foon explained, was that it could be several months before the program was fully underway. This was April, he said; it might be November or December, maybe longer, before the patients were selected for enrollment.

"I'm just not sure what I can tell you at this point, Jack," Foon told him. "The protocol is still being written, we have to establish patient admission guidelines and set up a referral procedure, and there's even some question about what kind of budget we're going to get for this."

"Ken, I want to send you the pathology reports, alright? I know you can't tell me much right now, but would you look at this stuff? Keep me in mind for when everything gets nailed down?" Foon hesitated for a minute. He knew nothing about Jack's case; until he did, it would be cruel—barbaric—to encourage the man's hopes. And yet the voice on the other end of the phone had been so strained, so terribly urgent. . . .

"Send the paperwork, Jack. I'll be in touch as soon as I know anything."

Even at the age of nineteen, Eileen Pierce was one of the brightest and most loving women Jack had ever met. Emotionally, she was also one of the strongest. Her incredible resiliency, combined with a passionate sense of independence, often led Jack to refer to her as "one tough little Limey"; she took the title as a high compliment, a tribute to the famous English resolve with which she had determined to preserve her heritage in her new land. She made it a point to continue using some of her favorite British expressions—the bawdy ones, certainly, but also the everyday terms and phrases that unquestionably tagged her national legacy: The elevators in the downtown office buildings would always be "lifts" to her; the freeways were "carriageways"; and if she had a taste for dessert at the end of a restaurant meal, she inquired about the selection of "sweets." Hers was a unique mixture of tenderness and toughness, oddly out of place in someone so young; Jack sometimes compared it to finding a piece of barbed wire inside a delicate pastry.

She was frequently homesick during her first months in Boston, especially as they walked the beach at Swampscott during the sunset hours. But she knew how much he enjoyed those walks, how much he needed to talk out the triumphs and frustrations of the day, so she listened and laughed and asked questions about the patients, the doctors and nurses, the elderly maintenance man, the chief nurse found passed out in the supply room every Saturday night—people she had never met and probably never would.

Every new challenge was another opportunity to battle her fears and uncertainties. She had liked Boston well enough, but not Houston; she termed the summers horrid, despised the congestion and the unimaginative architecture, was oddly distressed that almost everyone seemed to be from somewhere else. ("I'm from Columbus, Ohio," a woman confided to her one day in the supermarket checkout line. "Where are *you* from, honey?") Almost everything about the region, in fact—not just its physical features, but also the frivolousness that seemed to typify so many of its residents—was completely different from her own ancient native city. Liverpool was no Eden, she said, but at least it was solid; unlike Houston, it had roots and traditions.

Yet Eileen vowed to learn everything she could about Houston's history and traditions. Returning from the library one night with six books about Texas, she shrugged that "it's my home now —we should know about where we live." On weekends she coaxed Jack to take her to the old forts and battlegrounds around the city, starting with San Jacinto on the east side. She wanted to visit Austin, San Antonio, and especially the infamous Book Depository in Dallas. She resolved to become a sports fan like Jack, faithfully tracking the fortunes of the Astros during the summer and the Oilers and Rockets during the winter.

She had never been licensed to drive in England (although like most fathers, hers had let her drive around the block occasionally, and had once allowed her to drive part of the way to Manchester on a family holiday). Once in Boston, she immediately signed up for a driving course and quickly mastered the nightmarish expressways and twisted, congested streets. Partly, it was to familiarize herself with driving on the right side of the road, and to learn the complex network of interchanges and overpasses ("flyovers," she called them, again following the British terminology). But once outside the city of Boston, it was the only feasible way of getting from one place to another in Massachusetts. Besides, it would have galled her to ask Jack to drive her anywhere.

As much as he admired Eileen's tenacious spirit, he sometimes found it utterly maddening. She fell into silence for long periods of time, for some reason unable or unwilling to share her thoughts. Usually, he didn't mind that; he too was compelled to keep something of himself private, even from her. But sometimes it seemed that she used it as a weapon, storing up her occasional angers and hurts until the reservoir became so full that it was impossible to release only one or two drops. "We were at my parents' house for Sunday dinner one day," he recalled, "and I said something that made her sore—I don't remember what it was, something minor. She trapped me in the bathroom a few minutes later and just gave me hell. Not just for what I'd said that day, but for things I'd supposedly done months before." He soon wearied of these "ambushes"—especially when they were executed in such places as his parents' bathroom. That was "dirty fighting," he told her, and she reluctantly agreed.

She also informed him, gently but surely, that although they weren't married, his bachelor days were in effect over. So was his bachelor lifestyle. Annoying little rules were set—annoying because he could find no good reason not to observe them. She was also working full-time, she explained, so they would share equally in all the household duties:

Whomever arrived home first would make the dinner. The other would clean the kitchen.

Each month, one of them would be responsible for keeping a running list of items needed from the store. The other would make sure that the items in question were secured every Saturday morning.

She didn't mind looking after the laundry and ironing, but she would not retrieve his socks and underwear from the bathroom floor, nor his shirts from the living room sofa. If he couldn't deliver these things to the laundry room, he could wash them himself.

Each would ask permission to borrow the other's personal effects. He was not permitted to appropriate the writing tablet from her desk drawer; she was forbidden to use his manicure set —a Christmas gift from an old girlfriend who had tried to break him of chomping on his fingernails—or his razor.

She didn't mind so much that he spent the warm evenings slouching around the apartment in only his underwear and baseball cap, but would he please remember to draw the window shades while he was watching the telly? "And for goodness sake, slip on a robe when you answer the front door!"

Finally, on a personal note, she would be ever so grateful if he would come with her to Saturday night Mass.

It was the last request that ruffled him most. He had been raised in the Catholic Church, had attended a Catholic grammar school; his parents were still faithful participants in parish life. As for Jack, he had not attended Mass since his undergraduate years. At first, he had blamed his heavy study load for his Saturday night absences; later, he didn't bother making excuses at all. He simply found it uninteresting and irrelevant.

Not that he had no respect for the Catholic traditions. He was often moved by the music, the lofty ideals, the glorious and colorful history. But somewhere along the way, he said, he had lost the Faith. "Or maybe I never even had it to begin with, I don't know. When you're a kid, you don't question those things so much; it's when you get older that you start to wonder about it." He wondered about the agonies and suffering over which he presided every day. So much of it, he thought, seemed to have been visited on the innocent. Children cruelly beaten, young men struck down by coronary disease, teenaged girls whose limbs had been torn from their bodies by drunken drivers who happened to cross the divider at eighty miles an hour at precisely the wrong second. What kind of a God would permit such injustices?

Eventually, he decided that there could be no God, at least not the loving, patient, forgiving God of his youth. And certainly not a God that answered prayer. Jack had prayed often as a young man—once or twice a day, and always before going to bed—but he couldn't remember a single answered prayer that couldn't be explained by chance or circumstance. He could recall plenty of unanswered prayers, though, like the dozens he had raised for Joey Haggerty, the twelve-year-old neighbor who had succumbed to his leukemia despite Jack's repeated and fervent prayers for his survival. And like those for his twenty-year-old cousin Don, who had gone off to Vietnam in 1969 and had returned in a heavy plastic bag. Eventually, Jack had convinced himself that if there was something or someone called "God"—and the evidence, such as it was, was far from persuasive—then it was nothing more than a Great Intelligence somewhere, an unknowable mentality that eight or ten billion years ago gave the signal that set all the wheels of the universe turning, then sat back to watch the fun. "When it's over, it's over," Jack told Eileen one night a few months before his diagnosis, when they had been arguing about an afterlife. "There's nothing out there, no heaven, no hell— nothing. We make our heaven and hell right here. Why do people insist that there must be something beyond this?"

Eileen disagreed, of course, and forcefully. The Church was more than an important part of her life; it was life itself. "Where I grew up in England, there were three kinds of people you always respected," she said. "The police, the nuns, and the priests. Most of the girls I knew wanted to be nuns when they grew up, and a lot of 'em did. A boy, he could have no greater ambition than to be a priest. But no more. Not here. . . ."

On the matter of church, Jack refused to budge. She attended alone.

When he finally told her about his disease, she had pedaled her bike down to the small stream that ran along the edge of their apartment complex, stood it up against a tree, then dropped down heavily in the mossy soil to cry for nearly a quarter hour. She had suspected that something was wrong—the unexplained weight loss, the sweaty tossings during the night, the unusual tiredness. And why had he waited so long to confide in her? Did he suppose she would break down in hysterics? Run off and leave him? Fly into a fit of rage, as though he had brought this awful thing on himself? Homesickness she could deal with, especially since Jack had assured her that she could visit her family as often as she pleased. She could adopt new customs and lifestyles, could learn to take part in the Texas-style entertainments, could even accept Jack's rejection of the Church. There was nothing she couldn't do, she thought, as long as it was something to be done for herself and for Jack, for them. But if there was no Jack, there could be no them. What would all this be for? What was the point of the whole exercise?

And how could she ever go on without this man?

He had looked like an embarrassed teenager earlier that evening when he had finally told her his secret, as though he had been caught doing something terribly shameful. She knew instinctively that it wasn't embarrassment, but fear. Well hidden, under control, but fear nevertheless. All the clinical terminology, the optimistic footnotes about new treatments, had been designed to take some of the sting out of the news, and to some extent it had worked. If it were anyone else under discussion, in fact, she would probably feel enormously better about the prospects. But it wasn't someone else, of course. It was him—no, it was *them;* his troubles were her troubles—and they were both terrified.

She had always reasoned that the more one knows about something frightening, the less fearsome it becomes. This thing could be no exception. Early the next morning, she called the downtown Houston chapter of the American Cancer Society and requested whatever literature they had about lymphomas. That evening, she bicycled to the library, checked out three books on cancer causes and treatment, then studded the sections on lymphoma with paper clips.

In his book *Toward the Conquest of Cancer,* Dr. Edward J. Beattie, Jr., tries to take some of the terror from the word "cancer": "We need to keep matters firmly in perspective: there is no cancer epidemic (except for lung cancer); many of the things in the scare headlines are not significant causes of cancer; the cure rate is higher than most people realize; and three out of four people never get cancer."

Beattie is right, of course. Almost every day someone, somewhere, learns something new about cancer's devious nature. The knowledge goes into an ever deepening pool of data about how it begins, how it grows, and sometimes how it can be killed, or at least controlled. For the most part, however, this knowledge has accumulated not in great dramatic leaps, but grudgingly and sometimes even unnoticed. Under such conditions, it's easy to lose sight of how much we've learned about some types of cancers, and how very far we've come in treating them.

A good example is the cancer known as acute lymphocytic leukemia, or ALL—like B-cell lymphoma, a malignancy of the lymphocytes. It is not only the most common of all the leukemias, but it is also the most tragic in that the great majority of its victims are young children. Even ten years ago, ALL claimed the lives of almost three quarters of its victims. Twenty years ago, it was a death sentence. Then researchers found a drug that seemed to slow its growth a little; another drug was even more effective, then another. It was when three or four of these new drugs were administered in combination packages that the youngsters stopped dying en masse; many of them even went on to make a complete recovery. Today, more than half of these children are able to lead normal, healthy lives five years and more after their diagnoses (assuming they are diagnosed early and receive competent treatment).

There have been other success stories, and many of them are just as heartening. For the most part, they revolve around the cruelest of the cancers, those which descend on our children. As recently as 1960, two thirds of children with the kidney cancer called Wilms' tumor died from their disease; today, thanks to a combination of chemotherapy and radiation, nine out of ten of them survive to a normal, healthy adulthood. And of the children suffering from non-Hodgkin's lymphoma, the cure rate has leaped from only about 4 percent in 1960 to more than 80 percent today.

Despite such encouraging results, however, we fear the disease we call cancer—loathe it—like none other. It's a rather odd reaction, really. Stroke and coronary artery disease kill and maim far more of us every year, yet we accept that as little more than a nuisance. Why? Probably because we have been conditioned to think that our ailing hearts are as easily repaired as broken sump pumps, as interchangeable as a worn set of heels, with a few weeks in the hospital. (After all, don't we all know someone who's had a bypass operation?) We prefer not to dwell on the fact that half of all first-time heart attack victims never make it to the hospital.

Or perhaps we reason that there are far worse ways to die than by a heart attack. It's often very quick ("Thank heavens he didn't suffer") and clean, and whether we live or die, at least we aren't disfigured or repulsed by it. Heart disease is clean. Almost heroic. There's something shameful and dirty about Big C.

We talk of cancer as though it's a solitary disease, like an intestinal virus; the truth is that it's more than a hundred different diseases. Each progresses according to its own rules, and sometimes the rules make no sense at all. Why is it that some malignancies, such as childhood leukemias and certain bone cancers, seem to respond so quickly and dramatically to drug therapy, while others defy any and all treatment? What sort of defenses are erected by tumors nestled deep within the lung? How does the malignant pancreatic cell consistently shrug off the most powerful chemical weapons we hurl at it? Why do some tumors grow slowly and in one place while others reproduce at terrifying rates, in the process shedding bits of themselves into the bloodstream with which to establish new colonies?

The tumors arrive with different histories. Some seem to arise from a hidden genetic defect that lies in wait for scores of years before springing its surprise. Oncogenes, they're called—individual links on the six-foot chain of DNA that suddenly and inexplicably seem to call out a perverse set of orders to the cell. People who study such matters now reckon that there are about thirty of them in every human cell, bearing odd names like *ras*, *myc*, and *src*, and the number of known oncogenes keeps growing. But do these renegade bits of chemistry truly cause cancer, or are they by-products of the disease? Actually, some researchers now reason that oncogenes probably account for no more than 20 percent of all human cancers; that's still a massive number of victims, of course, so it's worthwhile for researchers to keep asking questions: If oncogenes are indeed the cause of certain cancers, what switches them on? Can we identify them and permanently switch them off?

An answer of sorts may lie in the work of a group of Harvard immunologists in late 1984. Working with the oncogene named *myc* (a bit of DNA that seems to instruct the cell about when and how often to divide), Dr. Philip Leder and a group of his colleagues found a way to cause breast cancer in mice by turning the oncogene on and leaving it on.

The "on-off switch" was a piece of DNA taken from a virus called the mouse mammary tumor virus, which apparently causes cancer by responding to the chemical changes incurred by pregnancy. Using special enzymes that cut the DNA molecule only at certain places, the scientists removed a portion of the viral gene that orders the organism to reproduce itself, then spliced it into the *myc* oncogene; in a way, the process is similar to that of cutting out a leaky section of copper tubing and soldering in a replacement. Finally, a solution containing the new hybrid gene was injected into unborn mice, where the revised DNA found its way into the cell nuclei. The mice grew; the gene was reproduced millions of times over, until it was included in every one of the animals' cells. When the mice later became pregnant, their hormones apparently signaled the viral switch to turn on the oncogene. As a result, every one of the mice developed breast cancer.

But does that mean that oncogenes cause cancer? Interesting question, and for now an unanswerable one. There's only one sure way of finding out, says one investigator: Strip an oncogene from a cell, put it into a normal cell, and see how many of the cell's descendants become malignant as a result. For several complex reasons, that hasn't been done yet; until it has, the oncogene theory remains just that—a theory.

A few forms of cancers are almost certainly caused by viruses—curious bits of a chemical called ribonucleic acid, wrapped in a coat of protein, that straddle the line between living and nonliving. One of the most fascinating bits of detective work in this century was done in the 1960s by a British physician—a little white-haired dynamo named Denis Burkitt who waffled for a time between medicine and religion. He decided to do both, and discovered in his Uganda missionary hospital a lymphoma that he'd never seen before, one that was killing thousands of central Africans every year. He investigated and found that the tumor was indeed caused by a virus that thrived in the moist, hot jungles of that region. The semiliving thing later took a name, the Epstein-Barr virus, after the two researchers who went on to learn more about it than most of us will ever know about our spouses. If Burkitt's lymphoma is a viral disease, it seems reasonable to think that there are many others.

Liver cancer, the world's most common form of cancer, is almost certainly caused by the hepatitis B virus; cancer of the cervix is strongly associated with organisms called papillomaviruses, which also cause common skin warts. But warts almost never progress to cancer; what is so special about cervical cancer? The answer seems to be that another factor is needed to switch on the virus after it has wriggled its way into the cell and established residence. There is a form of papillomavirus cancer that shows up in cows, for instance—but only after the animal eats a certain kind of fern. It may be that the virus leads to cervical cancer in women in a similar way, when it is prompted to action by some other factor—venereal disease, or a multiplicity of sexual partners.

And there are substances all around and inside of us, called carcinogens, that somehow break their way into the cell and take over the genetic control booth. We all know what most of them are. Many of the components of cigarette smoke, without a doubt. Certain drugs, like diethylstilbestrol that our mothers took while we were inside, and whose cancerous effects are now appearing in our wives and sisters ("DES daughters," we call them). Of all the cancers, the ones that start this way are the ones we have a good chance of avoiding.

As with oncogenes, what we don't know about carcinogens far outweighs what we do know. What seems to happen, however, is that carcinogenesis proceeds in at least two separate stages—initiation and promotion. A carcinogenic initiator alone will not usually cause cancer, no matter how intense or prolonged the exposure. Nor will contact with a promoter alone result in the disease. Put the two together, however, and the result is cellular fireworks. The two-part process may explain the puzzling observation that most people who smoke never get cancer; while tobacco smoke is almost certainly a carcinogenic initiator, the cells of only a relatively small number of heavy smokers progress to the "promotion" stage (which might be promoted by something in the diet, or exposure to other types of chemicals).

In an age in which we seem to be under constant siege from cancer, it's surprising to learn that it really isn't all that easy to get the disease. Very rarely does it simply appear. On the contrary, a lengthy series of events must first take place that on the face of it is so complex, so unlikely, that we wonder why anyone ever develops the disease at all.

The first step in carcinogenesis appears to be a cellular assault by an active carcinogen. To do its dirty work, the substance (a few molecules of the chemical benzene, say) must first elude the macrophages and the immune system's other cells that patrol the bloodstream for invaders. The carcinogen must then chemically bind itself into the DNA at the center of the cell; if it fails in that, its effects will be felt only by that solitary cell—hardly a hazardous situation in view of the millions of other cells that make up the organ.

From time to time, of course, a carcinogenic molecule does make it into the DNA. Again, the reaction is by no means life-threatening; every cell comes equipped with a sort of chemical repair kit—the nonliving proteins called enzymes that break the abnormal DNA apart then rebuild it with spare chemical building blocks found within the cell. Most of the time, this genetic remodeling takes place very quickly, before the cell has a chance to divide into two new cells. In that case, the abnormality is again limited to just a single cell. It is only when the damage goes undetected that the mutant DNA is passed along to future generations.

Even that does not necessarily mean cancer. In many cases the carcinogen bonds itself to a piece of DNA that plays little or no important role in the life of its owner. Cancer results only when the chemical changes occur within certain "important" genes—those that produce a critical hormone, for example, or that control the cell's rate of division, or that build up into masses of solid tissue. Finally, it seems that not just one mutation is required for a malignancy, but two or three or more, and all in the same gene. Every one of these steps reduces the chances of a carcinogen ultimately leading to cancer.

Despite their variable histories, all malignant cells do have some things in common. For one, their incredible tenacity.

Even a normal cell is possessed of what might be called a fierce will to live—at least as long as it remains in its natural habitat, surrounded by its genetic relatives. Seen under a microscope, a human cell appears to be a frail and vulnerable thing, constantly open to attack by viruses, bacteria, chemicals, and physical impertinences. But the cell's seeming susceptibility is in fact a marvelous deception: Cut it open if you choose. Burn it, smash it, tear it from its moorings. Within minutes, microscopic suborganisms dwelling within its walls will spring to the site, assess the damage, and turn to its repair. If repair is impossible, other cells will rush to the scene to carry away the debris. At the same time, orders are given for the production of a replacement cell that either exactly duplicates the original or serves as the semifunctional substitute that we call scar tissue.

But such resourcefulness is almost nothing compared to the defenses launched by a clump of cancer cells. The most obvious defense is their sheer number. Normal cells divide only when replacement cells are needed, then stop for a while; cancerous cells never stop dividing for long, and are a hotbed of activity as they do so. Even the efficient, finely tuned immune system simply can't keep pace; antibodies are often formed to attack the newcomers, the surfaces of which are generally marked by unique antigens (strictly called "antigenic determinants"). And if the system of T-cells and B-cells is able to keep up with the steady growth, malignant cells have been known to adopt the insidious strategy of suddenly changing their determinants—in effect, they camouflage themselves so that they are no longer recognizable by the guardian B- and T-cells.

Cancer cells mutate in other ways, such as during an attack by cancer-killing drugs. It seems, for example, that the cells may spontaneously develop a new and special gene for producing an enzyme that breaks down the drug before it can destroy its target. In fact, there is evidence that some cancer cells even produce multiple copies of the gene—reserve ammunition, so to speak. Sound implausible? Consider the well-known case of certain bacteria—one that causes gonorrhea comes to mind—that have somehow incorporated a special segment of DNA (called a plasmid) that manufactures the enzyme called penicillinase. When confronted with an antibiotic drug based on penicillin's chemical structure, the enzyme attaches itself to the molecule at a critical point and breaks it, rendering it useless.

Another feature common to all cancers is that they all seem to arise from a single defective cell. Not uncommonly, the offspring are chemically and physically abnormal—larger than the adjacent noncancerous cells, for example, and usually much greedier for blood and nutrition. In some other cases, the cells are basically normal but too many in number; ultimately, they crowd out the cells next to them, perhaps forming a hard, unyielding mass that shuts off a vital duct or vessel, or gobbles up the nutrients that are needed by the other cells. What you don't want the mass to do is metastasize—send off little bits of itself into the blood or lymph, floating about until they land on another piece of tissue and set up a new mass.

Even the notion of genetic homogeneity is being shaken, however. Around the middle of 1984, Stanford University's Dr. Jeffrey Sklar found two genetically different lines of malignant cells in some of his twenty B-cell lymphoma patients. If a tumor arises from just one bad cell, he wondered, where was this other cell line coming from? His explanation—very iffy, he stressed—was that the malignancy may have occurred in two separate stages. The original cell probably ordered up the malignancy, but the command wasn't carried out for several more cell generations.

That interval may have accounted for one of the two malignant families Sklar found.

Spring 1981 melted into a blazing summer. Still no encouraging word from Foon. Jack Christie could no longer stand back and view his disease as a mere medical challenge. It suddenly became personal to him.

Little by little, for now painlessly, he was dying.

In the months following his diagnosis, he threw himself into his research. He spent two and three hours a day, seven days a week, in the medical libraries at Rice University and the Texas Medical Center. Wrote away for other opinions and advice. Contacted more than a dozen pharmaceutical companies, asking about their internal research on lymphomas.

By the end of July, he knew he could no longer put off his decision about a therapy. Even though the cells did not seem to be proliferating especially rapidly, there was no denying that they were growing. He spent a Saturday afternoon at the Medical Center on Houston's south side with a towering, beefy man who was not only one of the city's finest oncologists, but also a rarity in this part of Texas—a native.

"You might get along with nothing at all, Jack," the man told him. "You want my feeling, this type of cell more often'n not gets blasted pretty well with chemo. I don't think you got anything to lose. . . ." He chuckled as he revised his opinion. "Well, some of your hair, maybe, and you'll probably feel like hammered buffalo shit for a while. But maybe not—lotsa folks tolerate it very well, you know. Why don't we try it for three or four months, see what happens in there?"

Jack spotted a row of syringes in a wall cabinet, and listened as the man described the injection schedules and procedures. "I don't 'spose this stuff comes in pills, huh?"

Sorry, said the physician. Then he gave Jack an even worse bit of news: There was some chance that the drugs would leave him permanently sterile. "It ain't guaranteed, understand, but it happens enough that you should know."

That evening—a typically steamy Texas summer night, but graced by a light westerly breeze—Jack and Eileen sat on the small patio off the kitchen and shared a bottle of her favorite white wine as they reviewed the oncologist's warning. They had avoided the topic of marriage almost from the beginning; in his subtle and sometimes not-so-subtle ways, Jack had often made it clear that the subject was off-limits. Now, with the bond between them growing stronger, he confided that he found himself thinking often of marriage. Not now, perhaps, but someday.

"And children?" she asked.

"And children. Definitely children."

She smiled as she refilled their glasses; it was what she'd longed to hear from the day they'd come to Texas. The lymphoma had complicated things for him, of course. For Eileen, it wasn't complicated at all. If he was able to beat the disease, she explained (the "thing," she always called it), the children would be a glorious celebration, a tribute to themselves and to each other.

"And suppose I don't beat it?" he asked.

"Then I'll still want them," she said softly. "I'll want them every bit as much, perhaps more. They'll be a part of you I'll always have. I think I'll need that, Jack."

The following Monday, he left a small sample of fluid at a Houston sperm bank. A technician determined that the sperm was healthy, then carefully sealed, labeled, and wrapped the tube before lowering it into a container of liquid nitrogen.

A part of him was now forever safe.

Combined with the chemotherapy, the intense cramming took its toll on Christie. He was getting too close to it now. The more he learned—about how it starts, how it grows, how it resists destruction—the more he realized the sheer force of his adversary. It was no longer one of the mythical dragons he had read about as a child, no longer a multiheaded beast in a faraway land that would finally be slain by a heroic swordsman. It was he who was in the dragon's lair. He was the swordsman, and he was terrified by the power of the reptile, repelled by its foulness. "Suddenly I got burned out. I just couldn't stand to read anymore, couldn't bear the thought of talking to one more physician. Just hit the wall. . . ."

He never thought he would fear death. He had told Eileen that several times, arguing lightly that "death is nothing more than the absence of life," as though that alone were enough to take away the sting. Now he saw the words for what they were: the brave and idle sentiments of a healthy young man who fully expected to be around for forty or fifty more years. He could never bring himself to complain about the unfairness of it; that was one of the things he hated so much about cancer patients.

And yet, dammit, it *was* unfair.

The knowledge of his cancer infiltrated his whole life. There were times, lying in bed late at night, when he thought he could actually feel the malignancy multiplying in his spleen, in his bone marrow. Slight aches, once ignored, now became unbearable agonies as he imagined the maverick cells invading joints, back muscles, the base of the skull. He awoke in the middle of the night to think about it once more; the word leaped at him from every journal, every magazine article, every news report. Before long, the realization had invaded even his simplest conversations—the hot August night, for instance, when he and Eileen were reviewing the ledgers in which she kept track of the stocks, bonds, Treasury notes, and business ventures. He spotted one that he'd almost forgotten, a substantial certificate that he'd desposited early in the year.

"I think that goes for three more years," he told her, leafing through the paperwork. "You'll probably want to roll it over. . . ."

She looked up briefly, surprised.

You'll probably want to roll it over. . . .

A few months before, he would've said *"we."*

By late August, he was wondering which was worse: the emotional exhaustion or the nauseous fatigue that by now accompanied his therapy. His appetite was practically nil. Supper, when he ate at all, usually consisted of a piece of fruit, or a hard-boiled egg and a glass of beer. Most of his evenings he spent sprawled on the sofa in front of the television. Soon the subject of illness—cancer or any other kind—was off-limits for discussion with Eileen—an understandable reaction, she thought, until almost everything else was unofficially declared off-limits too. He had no interest in her career, and little in his own; he even decided that he didn't want to practice medicine anymore. He didn't need the money. More importantly, he had once promised himself that he would never become a Gomer; if he couldn't do first-rate medicine, he wouldn't do it at all. Given his state of constant preoccupation, he knew he was now far from first-rate, so that was that. They went out rarely, and he began to conjure up excuses for avoiding even their small number of close friends. Their once active sex life deteriorated, first to a weekly event and then to once a month. His withdrawal became irritability, then an open hostility that was so intense at times that Eileen found herself wondering if the malignancy had spread to his brain.

At the advice of a friend, he visited the psychiatric unit at a small community hospital; it turned out to be one of the most discouraging and humiliating experiences of his life. He had always been able to work out his difficulties by himself, had never before felt the need to unload his problems on anyone. "I just can't bring myself to open up to this guy," he complained to Eileen. "I mean, what the hell does he *want* me to say? That I'm scared of dying? That I'm lonely and depressed? What does he expect? And what can he do for me, anyway? It isn't my head that's messed up, it's my body—and there isn't a goddam thing he can do about that!" He suffered through three visits with the psychiatrist, then resolved never to return.

But he realized that his petulance still left a huge and growing emotional gap between himself and Eileen, a gap that he secretly acknowledged had to be bridged. They were hardly speaking to each other at all now; when they did speak, the words were short and little more than grunts.

She convinced him to spend the Labor Day weekend at Lake Conroe, about sixty miles north of the city—partly so they could escape the punishing Houston heat, partly to give Jack a few days of uninterrupted time to read. He always felt better in the country, she knew, and he reluctantly agreed.

By their second day in the rented cabin, he had to admit that Eileen had been right. It wasn't much cooler up here, but the air did have a fresher smell to it. Almost against his will, he quickly found that he was being revitalized by the warm southwest breezes that swept through the aromatic trees and across the lake, all the way from Laredo and Guadalajara; by Saturday night, he felt better than he had in months. That afternoon, they fished in the crisp, cool stream, then roasted marshmallows on an open fire while watching the sky turn first pink, then dark purple, and finally black. Staring into the dying coals, he started to talk—so softly that she thought at first that he was mumbling to himself.

"Christ, I don't know what to do anymore. Just out of ideas, y'know?"

"You're scared a bit, aren't you?"

He nodded, a barely perceptible nod.

"I've been thinking a lot about this the past few months," she said, pulling a sweater over her shoulders. "Maybe I don't know as much about the disease as you do, but I do know one thing you don't. . . ."

He raised his head slightly to look at her.

"I know you're a lot luckier than most people who get this kind of problem. What I don't understand is why you can't see it yourself."

His puzzled look told her that he wasn't following her logic.

"I mean, how many cancer patients have the knowledge and ability you have? You understand what's happening inside of you —don't you realize how important that is? Can't you see that understanding something like this is that first step in learning how to destroy it? I remember when my aunt died of stomach cancer a few years ago, in Liverpool. Know what I remember the most? Not that she died, but that she felt so helpless while she was dying. She never understood what was going on inside of her— the bloody doctors never told her anything, Jack, never anything at all. 'Swallow this stuff.' 'Roll over.' 'Take these things twice a day.' 'Don't eat this, don't eat that.' They never told my uncle anything either, just to follow their orders. I guess they thought they were being kind, y'know—maybe some people like that really don't want to understand. But not her. I think she needed to grasp what it was all about."

"So what are you saying? What does that have to do with me?"

"So you don't have to just come in when they tell you, follow their orders. Lord, Jack, you're a doctor too! You understand a lot of this as much as they do! You can take charge, you see what I mean?"

"What, you mean treat myself?"

"No, not treat yourself—help *them* help *you*. If you were a first-rate mechanic, would you be standing around in the garage while someone else fiddled about with your car? Wouldn't you want to get in there with them, under the bonnet—the hood—instead of sitting back following orders? Why not? What have you got to lose?"

For a few minutes as she talked, he felt his anger building again. What did she know about any of this? It wasn't *her* body that was being ravaged, cell by cell; she wasn't the one whose first and last thoughts every day were of dying.

And yet, there was something in her tone that had fired his spirit for just a moment. He had never thought about it quite in those terms. God, maybe she was right. It wasn't just his medical training that armed him with a special knowledge of his condition; all of his studying during the previous months had made him almost as much of an expert on his kind of cancer as anyone. More important yet was the fact that it was his body, his life that was under attack. Was he becoming one of those helpless, whining cancer patients he had disliked so intensely?

A few hours later, he flicked out the light in the bathroom and made his way warily across the dark room to the bed. She was there, curled up on her side, the blankets pulled all the way up to her ears. He silently slid in next to her, fitting himself against her smooth, curved back. He was suddenly reminded of how much he loved her, how desperately he needed her. She was worth fighting for, and now he was ashamed to acknowledge that he had been ready to surrender to this heartless thing that was threatening to undo them.

As they lay silently together, his arm around her, he knew from the soft sounds and trembling that she was crying. He pulled her closer. Then, after five months of damming them behind his eyes, he finally allowed his own bitter tears to flow freely.

No one knows exactly how lymphomas arise, although some speculate that a virus may be lurking somewhere about. What is known (but not why) is that it's a sexist disease: Two out of three of its victims are males. And since the disease begins in cells that are designed to circulate freely and constantly throughout the body, it comes as no surprise that more than three quarters of the cases will ultimately involve metastasized tumors.

It's gratifying, though somewhat ironic, to know that the greatest advances have been made in the most aggressive types of lymphoma, such as Hodgkin's disease and certain of the fast-growing non-Hodgkin's lymphomas; by and large, the outlook for the indolent forms of the disease remains relatively unchanged.

The aggressive forms are often limited to the nodes at first, but eventually spread to the bone marrow—where the red blood cells are formed—and sometimes to the nervous system. If the marrow is extensively infiltrated, the outlook almost automatically takes a dramatic downturn. Once the red-cell-forming ability is destroyed, the patient becomes anemic and is stricken with a condition called thrombocytopenia (a decreased number of the blood platelets that control blood clotting), or with leukopenia (an abnormally low number of leukocytes, a type of white blood cell that protects against infectious organisms).

But the outlook for many non-Hodgkin's lymphoma patients is far from bleak. Surgery is impossible, of course, since there is no solid tumor (unless the lymphoma is localized in one or more lymph nodes, or has metastasized into one of the organs). But under the best conditions, in which the malignant cells are limited to one or a very few of the lymph nodes, the disease can often be arrested simply by irradiating the lumps of tissue that harbor the malignant cells. The average NHL patient with this type of disease survives at least five years, and there have been many twenty-year survivals. In some cases, the disease regresses spontaneously—just goes away for a year or more—then reappears. This waxing and waning has been known to go on for years, regardless of the treatment.

The worst cases are called "poorly differentiated lymphocytic diffuse, nodular mixed." In patients stricken with the type of NHL called diffuse histiocytic, the malignancy often spreads to the thyroid, the bones, and the reproductive organs. And while many of these cases can be treated with X-ray therapy (especially if the disease is confined to just one or a few nodes), there are risks: For one, the radiation causes extensive and permanent damage to the bone marrow (and thus to the immune system), which in turn interferes with the chemotherapy that may later be required. Another risk is that as in the treatment of acute lymphocytic leukemia, no one is absolutely sure that radiation doesn't set into motion another form of cancer that will blossom later in life.

Marina Christie, née Capobianco, picked daintily at her salad and studied the other diners in the restaurant. She had never approved of her son's live-in relationship with Eileen—God knew she hadn't raised him to indulge himself like this—nor had she yet accepted the idea that he had chosen this Englishwoman rather than an Italian girl. Well, so be it—he might yet come to his senses, and she was a lovely young thing. Marina wouldn't allow her disappointment to ruin her first visit to Houston.

It was during the main course that she abandoned her restraint:

"So have you set a date for the wedding yet, Jack?" Across the table, he saw that his father was more engrossed than necessary in trimming the fat from his lamb chops.

"Well, Mom, I think pretty soon now. Pretty soon. We'd like to wait until our financial situation is a little more secure. . . ."

"Actually, Jack and I have been talking about it quite a bit," chirped Eileen. She was feeling good tonight, happy to see Jack's parents again and especially gratified that Jack himself had recently been in good spirits. She decided to take a chance. "I think perhaps in the early spring. Isn't that what we decided, Jack? Early spring or thereabouts?" Jack slowly placed his knife on the table and glared at her. They both knew that they'd discussed no such thing, that she was using this opportunity to once again press the point of marriage. She and her goddam dirty tricks.

"Well that's wonderful, Eileen, just wonderful! Dad and I will fly down for the wedding—just give us enough notice so we can reserve a hotel room, now. Have you told Paul and Cathy?"

Fortunately, the lights in the restaurant were dim enough that no one at the table could see the flush of crimson that was spreading across Jack Christie's face. Except Eileen.

The form of cancer treatment called chemotherapy cuts with two edges. On the one hand, as many as three quarters of NHL patients with nodular involvement can look forward to a ncar cure with combination drug therapies, especially the one called COP—cyclophosphamide, vincristine, and prednisone. (The *O* comes from vincristine's other name, oncovin.) Another regimen adds the drug hydroxyldaunorubicin—alias adriamycin—to the menu, and is called CHOP. For patients whose disease is disseminated throughout the body, a combination called BACOP is often used, standing for the drugs bleomycin, adriamycin, cyclophosphamide, vincristine, and prednisone.

But the drugs come with a fairly stiff price. They are designed to attack fast-dividing cancer cells, and they do it very well; but no drug can distinguish between the invaders and the innocent bystanders. They attack all rapidly dividing cells, including those of the digestive system; thus the nausea and loss of appetite and diarrhea. They also home in on the cells that create hair follicles, which is why most cancer patients will lose most or all of their body hair. (It will return, though perhaps with a slightly different texture, when the therapy is stopped.)

Another question: What are the long-term effects of these drugs on other parts of the body? No one knows for sure. The drugs have been in common use for too short a period of time; the effects, if any, may not have had a chance to show up yet. Nor can anyone say with certainty that, as with radiation therapy, the chemicals do not set the patient up for another form of cancer later in life. The important thing is that they have been spared, and if they have been spared only to fight another day, then at least it's reasonable to think they may be better armed than they are today.

Largely because of this cellular devastation, and because of the growing body of knowledge about the immune system, researchers began to focus on another class of therapies during the late 1970s: the group of chemicals, manufactured by our own bodies, called biological response modifiers—"biologicals" for short.

The researchers had wondered about something for years: Why didn't more people get cancer? If we are indeed surrounded by carcinogens—saccharine, pesticides, cigarette smoke, viruses —why do only about a quarter of us develop tumors? And of those of us who do develop the disease, why is it that some of us seem to be more adept than others at fighting it off? The answer seems to be that given a chance, the body often deals quite effectively with cancer. In so doing, it draws on many naturally occurring substances that defend not only against bacteria and viruses, but also against the cell that is struggling to become cancerous.

Much is still unknown about biologicals, but they seem to act in several different ways. Some of them apparently beef up the immune system so that it destroys cancer cells before they can establish a foothold; others block whatever process leads a normal cell down a cancerous path, perhaps even changing the form of an early cancer cell into a normal cell. One of their most appealing features, though, is that they are already produced in the body. They are thus known to be harmless (at least in the miniscule amounts in which they are formed within the cells), which is more than one can say for radiation and chemotherapy.

In April 1981, the same month that Jack Christie was diagnosed, the National Cancer Institute launched its own biological response modifiers program, or BRMP. Considering the seemingly impressive strides that had been made with cancer-fighting drugs during the 1960s and 1970s, biologicals were a rather novel idea. Looking back, it may have been one of the great turning points in the battle.

The group of chemicals called lymphokines and cytokines, for example, are proteins formed in small amounts by our cells to help regulate a number of cell processes. The lymphokines are produced primarily by the cells of the immune system; cytokines are secreted by several types of cells throughout the body during cell division and regulate a variety of activities. One of the best-known of the lymphokines is the protein called interferon—a drug that for a while seemed to be on every cancer researcher's wish list, until its significant limitations were later described. Other lymphokines included the molecule called interleukin-2, and a group of chemicals called thymosins. Most fascinating of all was the protein, again formed by the cells of the immune system, called tumor necrosis factor—a molecule that seemed to have the unique ability to search out and destroy cancer cells with all the deadly accuracy of a guided missile attack.

The program that eventually drew Jack Christie's interest, however, was the one that Ken Foon was helping to design during the summer of 1981—NCI's "anti-idiotype" B-cell lymphoma program. The program was, and is, based on the fortuitous fact that malignant lymphocytes are rather unique among human can-

cers: They display on their surfaces the one-of-a-kind immunoglobulin molecule that they produce. During an immunological response, the B-cell directs the production of millions of
plasma cells which produce that particular molecule and which
then secrete the molecules into the bloodstream. For some reason, malignant cells often don't secrete the protein that they
make, but retain them tightly on their surfaces.

Together with a theory developed by Neils Jerne during the
1970s, this unusual feature of malignant B-cells suggested an
interesting approach to cancer researchers. Jerne's idea—called
the "idiotype-anti-idiotype-antibody network"—hinges on the
well-known fact that the immune system forms countless antibodies against an antigen. But the response doesn't end there, nor
even with the destruction of the antigen. Rather, the new antibodies may *themselves* be perceived as antigens, thus triggering
the production of yet more antibodies—"anti-antibodies," so to
speak. These anti-antibodies go on to provoke the formation of
even more antibodies, and so on. (The process eventually stops,
of course, but exactly how and when is still something of a puzzle
to immunologists.)

If cancer cells are truly clonal—that is, all genetically identical
to the first one—then the molecules dotting the surfaces of all the
malignant B-cells should also be identical. As with all antibodies,
moreover, their variable regions (the claws of the "lobster")
should be geometrically unique, so that only cancerous cells are
dotted with these particular receptors (or "idiotypes"). If Jerne's
theory was correct, then the idiotypes should form a perfect
target: Develop an antibody to the idiotype (called the "anti-
idiotype," or simply "anti-id"), inject it into the bloodstream, and
have it seek out and attach to only the cancerous idiotype.

Not all immune system cancers respond to such an attack.
Some forms do release the immunoglobulin (which under these
conditions is called a paraprotein), which then circulates through
the blood system. If you inject antibodies into the blood to tag
onto the malignant cells, the circulating paraproteins act like
decoy missiles, binding to the anti-id and making the therapy
ineffective.

If it all sounds like a neat bit of science fiction, perhaps it is.
Conclusions that look absolutely grand on paper—or in a mouse

or a monkey, for that matter—not infrequently fall flat when applied in human patients. A decade after Köhler and Milstein produced their first hybridoma, and six years after the rest of the world leaped to build an industry around it, there is still no positive proof that antibodies alone can destroy cancer, or even slow it down for more than a few weeks or so.

Except in the curious case of a Santa Barbara cancer patient named Phil Karr.

In 1982 the sixty-one-year-old Karr made medical history of sorts by becoming the first cancer victim to be apparently cured with monoclonal antibodies. He had first arrived at Stanford's Medical Center in 1976 with most of the familiar symptoms of B-cell lymphoma—night sweats, fatigue, and enlarged lymph nodes. For the first year, his physicians—Dr. Ron Levy and Levy's colleague, Dr. Richard Miller—offered no treatment at all, preferring to just watch how the disease progressed. When it appeared to be spreading the following year, the doctors administered several doses of interferon, which reduced the symptoms to some extent. For the next three years, Karr's lymphoma followed a roller coaster course. Symptoms appeared and were treated with interferon or with COP. The symptoms disappeared, sometimes for months at a time. Then reappeared. More drugs.

The ups and downs continued until April 1980, when it seemed that the cancer had finally dug in for good. Karr's spleen and liver were enlarged, and the night sweats returned. He lost weight and was constantly fatigued. Most ominous of all, the cancerous cells had spread throughout the lymph system and now appeared as dozens of tiny, rubbery tumors—nodes packed with malignant cells—on his scalp.

Miller and Levy had been working with anti-idiotype theory for several years by the time of Karr's final relapse. They decided to try a long shot. They withdrew about fifty milliliters of Karr's blood and extracted some of the tumor cells. These they purified and injected into several laboratory mice; as expected, the animals' spleens began to turn out antibodies, many of which were aimed specifically at Karr's cancer cells. Essentially duplicating Köhler's procedure of seven years earlier, the men next created a hybridoma by combining the lymphocytes—the antibody factories—from the spleen with a plasmacytoma. Finally, hybridomas producing the specific monoclonal antibody were selected from the culture and allowed to produce large quantities of the protein.

How would they know whether or not the antibody was having the desired effects? One way, of course, was if Karr's lymphoma suddenly went away and stayed away. If the antibodies were functioning as expected, however, the amount of circulating idiotype in Karr's bloodstream (the immunoglobulin secreted by the cancerous cells) would soon start to fall. If the idiotype remained unchanged over a period of weeks—or, heaven forbid, rose—the treatment would have to be considered ineffective.

Few studies had been conducted on the possible side effects of antibody treatment. To be on the safe side, Levy and Miller started Karr's therapy by injecting only trace amounts of the monoclonal. At first, with injections of only a few milligrams, there was no reaction. They boosted it to fifteen milligrams. Karr's circulating idiotype fell, from about three micrograms per milliliter at the beginning of the treatment to less than one microgram. They kicked up the dose, eventually to seventy-five micrograms. Not only did Karr suffer no ill effects from the treatment, but the idiotype soon disappeared altogether. In fact, the more antibody that was injected, the lower the idiotype fell.

Three weeks after the start of treatment (to the admitted astonishment of his physicians, who had hoped only to see some kind of response), Phil Karr was almost literally a new man. His liver and spleen had returned to their normal size. The night sweats and the grueling fatigue disappeared. So did the nodules on his scalp. At last report, Phil Karr was still free of his lymphoma; he has received no other therapy.

Karr's story first appeared in the *New England Journal of Medicine* on March 4, 1982; the response from other physicians was overwhelming, said Miller, a smallish, mustachioed man in his mid-thirties. "People had been talking about this, about actually manipulating the human immune system, for years. As far as we know, this was the first time it was actually done." Since then, Levy and Miller have attempted to duplicate the feat on almost a dozen other lymphoma patients—with only partial success. "We've hit a few doubles and triples, but Karr is still the only home run," said Miller.

Why did Karr do so well? "That's a good question," said Miller. "We'd love to know what it was about his disease, or about his particular physiology, that made him respond so completely. We have our theories, but we still don't know."

Is Phil Karr a cured man?

"I don't know if you could say he's cured," said Miller. "But he's been in remission for four years now, with no symptoms and no therapy. We prefer to say that the lymphoma is being controlled, just like a lot of diseases are never really cured. Whichever term you use, it's pretty darn impressive. . . ."

CHAPTER SEVEN

It started out as a storybook late September morning, perfect for a sailing race. There was a slight but distinct chill in the air, a gentle whisper telling of what was soon to come. By seven o'clock the treetops along Newburyport's High Street were bathed in the warm and brilliant amber of early fall. Many of the older maples and elms were even beginning to show the autumnal tints—here a brilliant orange, there a flaming crimson—that were already bringing millions of visitors to southern New England. Word at the coffee shop along the harbor, in fact, had it that the colors were already close to peaking in New Hampshire's White Mountains, only a hundred miles to the north.

But by ten-thirty, the crisp blue to the west was giving way to a bank of pewter-colored clouds, six hundred miles across, that made up the leading edge of a massive cold front. The sky was completely overcast by noon, just as the white committee boat sounded the official start of the race. An hour later, the ninth and last boat—a Bristol 22 named Bare Pockets—rounded the second marker under light variable winds. As it did so, the skipper peered anxiously over his shoulder at the approaching army of clouds and wondered if the race would be canceled. Like most of the other contestants, he was strictly a weekend sailor. Preferably warm and sunny weekends. He had never experienced heavy-weather sailing, and in fact had little taste for such adventure.

The man at the helm of the Bristol wasn't the only worried contestant. The forecast the night before had the front reaching

Ipswich Bay during the late afternoon or early evening, carrying with it high winds and a twenty-degree temperature drop. It had obviously picked up some speed as it swept out of New York State into the Berkshires of western Massachusetts. Even the Saturday boaters now struggling to make three knots knew the look of trouble when they saw it, knew how quickly the calm sea could become a broiling, terrifying caldron of blinding foam and water. Finally, the committee boat signaled the cancellation of the race by hoisting the large pennant up the backstay—a welcome invitation to start engines, furl the sails, and head for port.

Two of the boats ignored the signal. In the Venture 21, Allan Jarvis braced a leg against the tiller while he pulled on his crew-neck sweater and hauled the yellow vinyl slicker from the ditty bag. He would probably need it. Fifty yards ahead of him, a twenty-two-foot Ensign also made ready for the front. Jarvis watched the skipper move to the windward side of the cockpit, checking to see that both jib sheets were coiled neatly on their respective benches. He turned around for a second and grinned broadly at the tall man in the Venture. Jarvis made an exaggerated display of looking around him, then shrugged as if to say, "Where'd everyone go?"

The winds increased slightly at first, then suddenly freshened to twenty-two knots. To sailors, the conditions are described by the Beaufort scale as force 6: "strong breeze, with waves averaging ten feet, extensive whitecaps, and some spray"—a combination of factors which sounds inviting enough to the novice, but which is in fact just short of a nightmare for all but the skilled helmsman. Even under force 5, halfway up the Beaufort scale, small boats trying to make port while sailing at a small angle to the wind find themselves and their crafts painfully pounded by the waves, the tips of which are snatched by the wind and hurled into the eyes as from a shotgun. The conditions dictate a quick reduction in sail area; single-handed skippers who leave the tiller in their attempt to douse the jib over the bow risk being caught in a broach—the boat is hammered lengthwise into the troughs between the waves where it is unnavigable, at the mercy of the wind and water.

Jarvis and the other sailor saw the final marker at the same time, just a few hundred yards ahead. They would round it in about five minutes, then head for home. Looking up the mast, Jarvis got the first cold spray across his face and noticed that the bright orange plastic telltales on the outer shrouds were now perfectly horizontal. He hauled in the starboard jib sheet to flatten the little sail against the wind, thus using its driving force as much as possible, then did the same with the mainsail. The boat instantly assumed a twenty-five-degree heel to leeward.

The Ensign passed the marker about thirty yards ahead of Jarvis, then started its tack to port. Shielding his face against the spray, Jarvis saw what the Ensign's skipper must have known immediately: He had turned much too wide—"overstanding the mark," sailors call it—and had given up too much of his precious forward momentum as a result. Jarvis wondered if his competitor had momentarily lost hold of the tiller because of the icy water and falling temperatures. Or maybe he had simply waited just a second too long to push the tiller across the cockpit. No matter; by the time he came on the new tack and cleated the leeward sheet, his pursuer was on top of him, then alongside to blanket the Ensign's sails for almost a full minute.

Jarvis' heart was pounding harder now that he was finally in the lead. He turned around quickly to see the fast little Ensign about two lengths astern and on the same tack. Jarvis hauled in harder on the port jib sheet, heeling the boat a few more degrees to leeward. The Ensign did the same. Jarvis heard something clattering aboard his adversary's vessel; a thermos bottle or a toolbox in the little cutty cabin, most likely. He was glad that he'd brought nothing aboard. He could devote all his attention to the sails, and to the water. His right hand was getting numb now, both from gripping the tiller so hard and from the freezing spray that had soaked his sweater and matted his long dark hair to his head. If only he could take a minute to throw on his slicker. No, that would give the Ensign the fifteen or twenty seconds that she needed to close the gap.

The rain arrived as the two sloops raced across the last thousand yards of the course. A driving, bitterly cold rain that stung the men's faces and threatened to freeze their bright red hands to the tillers. Only a mile or so from harbor, they could barely make out the forms of the buildings on shore. Under normal circumstances, Jarvis would have doused the jib long ago, and probably have taken one or two reefs in the main as well. He wasn't worried about capsizing; an experienced skipper could feel that coming, he would have time to spill the jib—just uncleat the line and let the sail blow in the wind. Dismasting was something else. It had happened to a friend of his a year before, under just these conditions. And unlike a capsize, a mast that gives way rarely provides a warning. Only the sudden explosion of a shroud bursting free of its fittings, then the roar of 30 feet of mast and boom and 150 feet of twisting steel cable as they thunder and clatter their way across the deck and over the side. Perhaps dragging the skipper with them, or leaving him broken and bleeding at the bottom of the cockpit. . . .

He could feel the temperature falling by the minute now. The howling wind drowned out every sound but its own, even the clanging of the big buoy near the mouth of the harbor until he was almost on top of it. As the bow crossed the imaginary finish line, Jarvis turned to see the Ensign just off his quarter. He had won, but by no more than a second or two.

After the vessels had been safely moored, the two men stood in the rain for a few minutes and compared notes on the race. Then they slid into their cars and headed home for hot showers and coffee. They probably didn't notice two other men who had been sitting in another car nearby, awaiting the outcome of the race. One of the men turned to his companion and shook his head.

"Allan," he said, "likes to win."

When Allan Jarvis first contacted Damon in early 1980, he was in the sort of quandary that sooner or later settles on most academics—the choice between pure and applied research, between knowing for the simple sake of knowing and knowing for the sake of doing. To the cellular biologist, pure research means the occasional thrill that goes with grasping a few of the cell's millions of mysteries; applied research means using what you've learned to make something of value—new sources of food for the world's hungry, perhaps, or novel families of drugs for treating diseases that have for centuries destroyed mind and body.

One of the things you want to make with your applied research is money.

The choice between the two is rarely simple. Most pure research labs are still bathed in a sort of esprit de corps, a sacred mission for the chosen few. For all practical purposes, commercialism is banned from within these walls. All that matters is to know; it is for others to make something of the knowledge.

But many academics learn that there's much to be said for applied research, especially since most of it is performed by companies in the private sector. "University labs and foundations are wonderfully cerebral places," said Jarvis. "The problem is that you're always wondering where the next check is coming from, so you spend half your time writing proposals and looking for research grants." And since many such laboratories are funded at least in part by government agencies, there's another hazard: "It can be very, very political," another laboratory director told me. "A new President, a new Congress can suddenly change everything. I remember periods when I spent two thirds of my time running back and forth to Washington, trying to justify what we were doing for them. And the people heading up the agencies were spending two thirds of their time trying to justify what they were doing before Congressional committees. How can you work like that?"

Almost any reasonably well-to-do company suffers none of these indignities. What's more, even a single commercial success can bring in enough new dollars to carry the staff through half a dozen more research projects.

There was thus much more to Jarvis' inquiry at Damon than learning about the company's unusual little capsules. In fact, he had been torn between the two worlds of research for several years. He loved the environment that surrounded basic molecular biology research and had acquired an impressive professional history by early 1980—a recognized expert in the genetic control of interferon and a variety of other biological proteins. And he had worked with two of the nation's most prestigious research institutions—Memorial Sloan-Kettering Cancer Center on New York's Upper East Side, and the Worcester Foundation.

Still, he was curious about what he called "the real world." What happened, he wondered, to the thousands of research articles and reports that he and hundreds of others published in obscure journals every year? How does a company select from among these millions of words, home in on one or two specific subjects, then nurse it and care for it and bring it to the market-place? What would it be like to work in a well-funded laboratory, where he could hire the right people and buy the right equipment and run the right experiments? And what could he and his wife Marty do with a real salary? Now there's an interesting question. As a postdoctoral fellow at Worcester, he earned the grand sum of $15,000 a year; not bad for a postdoc, and since Marty held down her own job with New England Telephone in Arlington, they were able to meet the bills every month. Sometimes even have a little left over. But he was almost thirty-two now; he was beginning to weary of the meager paychecks and the tight budgets. Along with his other wonderings, he asked himself if he really did have the makings of a corporate researcher.

So Vasington didn't have to argue too hard to convince Jarvis to add his resumé to the hundred or so others that had arrived as the result of the company's ad in *Science*. Within a few weeks, the field was narrowed to three. With his youthful, clean-cut good looks, softspoken manner, and the natural ease with which he explained complex technical matters, Vasington and Lurier agreed that he was the man for the $25,000-a-year spot.

Until Allan Jarvis joined the company, Dr. Paul J. Vasington was probably the only person at Damon who was in a position to recognize the potential impact of Milstein and Köhler's work. The problem was that he'd had few chances to tap the technology during the intervening four years. Now, with Jarvis chasing down the elusive interferon molecule, Vasington began to wonder about the curious cells called hybridomas.

The stocky, middle-aged Vasington had come to New England in 1976, lured away from Lederle Laboratories in Pearl River, New York, as part of Damon's assault on the diagnostics market. Reporting to Ed Lurier, his responsibilities were outlined in terms that were at once fuzzy and sharply defined: to create new business opportunities for Damon Diagnostics. It was under this broad umbrella of a job description that he had urged Lim to follow through on Lurier's obsession with diabetes treatment that night in San Francisco. Besides, he had developed a genuine liking for "Eddie," and was almost as intent as Lurier on finding a new way to attack the disease.

By Vasington's account, Damon's diagnostics division was beset with problems almost from the beginning. Although the company had been licensed by a large Swedish firm to distribute a laboratory test for TPA—tumor polypeptide antigen, a chemical marker present on some types of cancer cells—Vasington recalled that "the business just wasn't doing well, partly because no one at Damon had any experience in this kind of technology."

Nor was he convinced that Damon could establish itself as a first-rate diagnostics company by offering technology that had been conceived elsewhere, such as the TPA test. The company had to create its own. "But in order to do that well, you must be able to grow cells," he told me. "That wasn't so easy in 1976; cell culture simply wasn't at the point it is today."

By the late 1970s, however, Lim's LiquiSol technique had provided Damon with a solid foothold in proprietary diagnostics. But Vasington suspected that Köhler and Milstein's hybridoma offered another opportunity for the diagnostics division. Simple, easily reproducible, inexpensive, and virtually unprotected by patents or licensing constraints, monoclonal antibodies represented a completely new method of creating diagnostic kits on demand. In theory, an antibody could be raised against any antigen, and could be used as the basis for cheap, reliable diagnostic kits—kits that the company could develop in-house and sell for fantastic profits. The cost of producing one of the kits was only about fifteen cents or so, but they could be sold for about ten dollars. And if Damon didn't want to make the things itself, there was always the alternative of licensing the technology to other companies for production.

By 1980 there was yet another wild card in Damon's deck: Lim's new encapsulation technology. Even before Jarvis' arrival, Vasington had a powerful hunch that Damon had in its grasp a simple, almost foolproof way of doing what a growing number of other companies were still struggling mightily to do: turn out huge amounts of antibody, and do it cheaply and efficiently.

None of this would have been possible before the late 1970s, before the advent of the New Biotechnology. By 1981, barely seven years after Cohen and Boyer's gene transfer experiment, more than a hundred biotech firms—sporting names like Genentech, Cetus, Biogen, and Genex—had been created to tap into the new technology called genetic engineering. Everyone claimed to see opportunities around every corner: Once-rare drugs, like insulin and growth hormone and interferon, could now be made almost in bucketfuls, they said, falling back on the inflated terminology of the times. All that was necessary was to isolate the appropriate gene from humans or animals (not a very difficult step, as it turned out) and place it into fast-growing bacteria, such as *E. coli*. The organisms grew at incredible rates, and they didn't require much in the way of special attention. When they reached a certain density (their implanted new genes all the while producing the drug), all the scientists had to do was scoop up the bugs and run them through a couple of extraction and purification steps, sell the drug, and watch the money pour in.

But there were many factors that the scientist-businessmen of the late 1970s and early 1980s didn't reckon with until it was too late. Looking back, it seems that most of the entrepreneurs had taken their own press releases too seriously, truly believing that biotechnology was practically guaranteed to do for the eighties what computers had done for the seventies. Too many of them failed to appreciate the enormous differences between printed circuits and living organisms. "The computer industry started out with a handful of engineers working evenings in their garages and basements," one veteran biologist told me. "You could do that with computers—all you needed was some silicon, maybe a few chemicals, and a soldering iron. Hell, you didn't even need much money at first, just enough to buy a couple of oscilloscopes and voltmeters." Once the bright young engineers had a crude working prototype, it wasn't all that hard to scrape together the million dollars or so needed to build a small production line. The rest, as they say, is history.

For the clever young biotechnologists, money proved to be the least of the obstacles. Lurking around the corner were headaches far greater than they had imagined. The problem of scaleup, for example—methods and equipment for increasing the amount of product they could make from a milliliter or so (barely enough to cover the bottom of a thimble) to batches thousands of times bigger. Even knowledgeable and experienced biochemists were discouraged to find that scaleup is more complex than simply making bigger pieces of equipment and tossing in larger quantities of chemicals. They learned that things that go wrong inside a hundred-milliliter flask—slight temperature variations, contamination, the sudden uncoupling of an oxygen hose—are disastrous in a batch of one hundred liters; the effects are multiplied not a thousand times, but millions of times.

In fact, many of the most serious problems were equipment-related—not so surprising when one considers that much of the equipment being installed in the sparkling new laboratories had never been used before. There simply was no precedent for growing large amounts of engineered living cells and keeping them happy. Not a few of the big stainless steel fermenters of the time—looking much like oversized tin cans and typically measuring about two feet high and eighteen inches across, their top lids studded with ports and gauges and valves for introducing gases and the sweet-smelling nutrients—were made not by high-tech bioequipment companies, but by local machine shops as researchers tried to determine the best designs. And as they struggled, hoses continued to pop off (usually in the middle of the night), mechanical stirrers seized up and ground to a stop, temperature regulators went haywire, contaminating organisms stole into the fermenters to turn thirty liters of custom-made nutrient into the biological equivalent of so much dishwater.

Nor did many of the new companies recognize soon enough the unique people problems that still characterize the biotechnology industry, or that biological researchers are something of a breed apart from researchers in most other disciplines. Almost from the very beginning of the New Biotechnology, corporate progress suffered in hundreds of little ways because of the silent clashes between research and management. Anthropologist Frank A. Dubinskas, among others, has written on the subject:

"Start-up biotechnology companies often show two public faces—one of academic science, and the other of financial entrepreneurship. And like the Janus of Roman mythology, the two faces frequently look in opposite directions. The practical outcome is intramural conflict. Bench scientists and executives clash over what goals the company's researchers should pursue, whether the firm's direction should change, and how the choices should be made. Such conflicts can portend problems for either the short-term products that guarantee cash flow or the long-term research projects that offer hope for a future big success."

Oddly enough, the grass-roots differences between management and research never seemed to surface to any extent in the computer industry. By and large, everyone in the business was there for just one reason: to make a lot of money, and perhaps have some fun in the process. The men and women who ran the early biotechnology laboratories very often had other goals in mind: the service of mankind, for one—after all, didn't they hold in their hands the very secrets of the cell?—and the joy of pure science for another. Financial compensation was very often of secondary importance, and sometimes of no importance at all.

Even the casual visitor to a modern biotechnology company quickly becomes aware of the fact that the building houses two very different civilizations, populated by two very different tribes. The executive offices are usually plushly carpeted, silent except for the *rappety-rap* of a secretary on the word processor and the occasional muffled ring of a phone behind a closed door. The walls are often paneled in a dignified walnut and decorated with limited-edition posters or in some cases original art. Within the offices are plants taller than the occupant, more original art, journals and reports stacked neatly on mahogany credenzas, gold-framed portraits of the family.

There's another world just a few hundred feet away. The typical bench scientist arrives for work every morning looking like he's on his way to a weekend camping trip. No Brooks Brothers here, no Gucci shoes or thirty-dollar silk ties. Even the Ph.D.s who run most laboratories day to day are more likely to show up in blue jeans, old tennis shoes, and a sweatshirt. The walls are decorated not with framed posters taken from *The New Yorker,* but with glass-and-enamel cabinets, fire extinguishers, steam lines. (At one of Damon's laboratories, the sole piece of art is a hand-lettered sign above the sink: "Your mother doesn't work here. You'll have to clean up after yourself.") Instead of framed family pictures, there are snapshots from the company Christmas party and months-old newspaper comic strips. ("Garfield" is the most popular, with "Doonesbury" running a close second.) More often than not, there's a radio in the corner tuned to a soft rock station.

And the divisions between management and research go much deeper than outward appearances. The tribes never forget that there's a constant tug-of-war here between those who need to make money for the company and those who are committed to doing good science. The result is an "us-and-them" atmosphere, an ambience that too often becomes "us-versus-them." Lunching one day at a Chinese restaurant—a local favorite of the lab workers because of its low prices and fast service—I asked a group of biotechnologists if the company tried to foster a sense of camaraderie among its employees.

"Well, yes and no," one of them replied, spearing another chunk of green pepper from a large bowl. "Management is always trying to get everyone to go out to picnics, form bowling teams, and so on. What usually happens is that the guys in the lab socialize from time to time among ourselves, but very rarely with the big shots. I think everyone's more comfortable that way."

For their part, executives are convinced that in matters of business, lab types are at best naive and at worst obstructive. What do molecular biologists know about how the venture capital market works? Have they ever had to explain yet another two-cents-per-share loss to a board of directors? Where do geneticists think the money comes from to run just one more series of studies for a skeptical would-be client?

The doubts and the grousings run in both directions. Lab workers are just as sure they are being unfairly put upon by the front office, especially if its occupant lacks a scientific background (which has increasingly become the case in the past few years). In the never ending need to come up with results for the investors, executives tend to lean on their lab personnel for results. CEOs are unsympathetic with the notion that some kinds of science take more time than others, that living cells can't be rushed into production as though they were so many pieces of silicon. "I recognize the fact that the company has to make money to stay in business," one bioengineer told me. "But there's a perception up there"—he nods his head in the general direction of the company's marketing department—"that all they have to do to get results is push us a little harder. Down here, success is getting a tenth of a gram of antibody out of one of those pots over there. . . ."

Too many of the new biotechnology companies grossly under-estimated yet another problem that was unique to their industry: the difficulties of dealing with the Holy of Holies in Washington, the Food and Drug Administration. They would learn all too soon.

The FDA has exercised almost complete control over the New Biotechnology almost since its inception. That came as no sur-prise to anyone, of course; what did startle some of the business-men was the FDA's decision regarding new products that were identical to products already on the market, or to products such as human growth hormone that were made in the human body. Those new chemicals, said FDA, would still have to undergo the new product approval process—a series of steps and forms and trials that could take up to ten years and cost upwards of $70 million before the new drug ever got to the marketplace.

But the dozens of processes that together were called "genetic engineering" made up only one of the New Biotechnology's two faces. The other was, and is, represented by the hybridoma. Al-most immediately after Köhler and Milstein published their re-port in *Nature*, scientists and businessmen all over the world saw what they perceived as hybridomas' enormous commercial po-tential, a potential that rested on what is often called the "exqui-site sensitivity" of monoclonal antibodies—their ability to zero in on and bind to just one molecular target out of millions of decoys. Here at last were the fabulous "magic bullets"—the drugs envisioned late in the nineteenth century by Paul Ehrlich, the frail, cigar-chomping man who is still called the "father of modern immunology."

The businessmen found themselves asking the same question that Milstein had asked almost a decade earlier: What could be done with large amounts of these bullets? How might they use a steady stream of antibody that could be designed to recognize virtually any antigen?

One answer was found in the emerging technology called drug delivery systems—methods of sending molecules of powerful drugs only to where they were needed in the body, thus sparing the rest of the body's cells from their toxic effects. If a company chose to produce a new drug delivery system to reach only a particular infectious bacterium, for instance, the biologists would first secure a culture of the bacteria and inject them into a few laboratory mice. After a couple of weeks, the mouse is killed; B-cells are gathered by chopping up the animal's spleen. Among the cells so acquired will be hundreds of thousands that produce only the antibody specific to the bacterium. These can be separated by any of several fairly simple methods.

Once separated and purified, the next step is to combine the B-cell with a plasmacytoma cell that has been specially engineered so that it doesn't produce any antibodies of its own. The resulting hybridoma is then injected into another mouse (or some other cell culture method), where it will multiply and produce millions of antibodies against the original bacterium. Since everyone who is infected with this organism has the same organism, you have a custom-made antibiotic that anyone can use. And the antibodies that don't bind to the bacterium won't affect any other cell; they will drift about harmlessly in the body until they are finally destroyed by other members of the patient's immune system.

Another use for monoclonal antibodies: imaging agents that help physicians determine whether a patient has a specific disorder. Heart disease, for example.

A surprisingly large number of Americans suffer "small" heart attacks every year without realizing it. The pain is usually minor enough to be passed off as indigestion or a pulled muscle. But while these miniattacks are rarely fatal, they are warnings and they must be spotted if the next attack is to be averted.

How can you know whether you've had a heart attack? Monoclonal antibodies provide one way of knowing. When a portion of the heart muscle dies as the result of a coronary, the cells around the affected area burst open to release a protein, called myosin, which lingers in the area for three or four days, then is cleared by the body's scavenger service. In the same way that antibodies are produced (or "raised") against bacteria—or sheep red blood cells, as Köhler used—it is relatively simple to raise them against myosin.

In a process developed in 1983 at Massachusetts General Hospital, the antibodies are combined with a mixture of radioisotopes so that each antibody now carries a cargo of one or two radioactive molecules—not enough to be hazardous, and very short-lived so that it's completely out of the system within a few hours. The doctor injects a bit of this radioactive antibody, waits a few minutes for it to reach the heart muscle, then slides the patient under a camera that takes unusual kinds of pictures: It records only gamma rays emitted by the antibody. If the patient has suffered a heart attack within the previous few days, the antibody will cluster around the myosin in the heart muscle and show up as a bright spot on the developed film. It will also tell the doctor where the attack took place, how big it was, and even how much damage it did.

There are other kinds of diagnostics, used by doctors and technicians in their laboratories—the devastating (and sometimes fatal) venereal disease called chlamydia, for example, which has recently reached near epidemic proportions in the United States. Until 1984 a woman who suspected that she might be infected had to wait several days to find out—days during which small tissue samples were grown in special cultures in the laboratory, then tested with various chemicals. Days during which the microbe continued to multiply and spread throughout the body. In 1984 a young Seattle company named Genetic Systems found an easier, faster, and less expensive chlamydia diagnostic. Based on monoclonal antibodies specific to the infecting organism and "tagged" with a fluorescent dye, the reagent is simply mixed for a minute or so with a few drops of fluid taken from the woman, then studied under a microscope equipped with a special light that excites the dye. If the chlamydia is present, the antibodies are easily seen as clumps of glowing particles under the microscope; treatment can now be started immediately, rather than after several days.

The idea of binding monoclonal antibodies to other chemicals quickly led to another, even more fascinating idea: If the antibodies could be chemically attached to harmless molecules for producing an image, why not also to death-dealing isotopes and drugs? Today the principle goes by the name "immunoconjugation"—the marriage of an antibody to any of dozens of deadly chemical partners. Injected into the body, the antibody portion of this two-part missile (called a conjugate) seeks out its target antigen—a malignant tumor buried deep within the lung or the pancreas, for example. Once attached, the conjugate releases its lethal payload into the mass of cells. The beauty of the method is that the drug or the isotope is released only to the target cells; unlike chemotherapy, healthy tissues are spared the toxin's effects.

Far out? Not at all. As of early 1986, several major companies in the U.S. and Europe were readying their custom-tailored immunoconjugates for trials on cancer patients. "Many of these patients really have no other alternative," said one pharmaceuticals expert. "If these conjugates get results in even a few cases, the implications are absolutely staggering."

The techniques were not lost on aggressive biologist-businessmen; within a couple of years of the *Nature* article, more than a dozen new companies had been formed to bring the technology to market. In Hayward, California, Bio-Response was convinced that they had the key to making large amounts of monoclonals: cows. Calling their system the Mass Culturing Technique, the company first removed lymph from the cow and filtered it to remove bovine cells and other components that could interfere with hybridoma growth. The lymph was then filtered again to remove the hybridomas that had multiplied, and returned to the cow. In effect, the company claimed that they had developed a never ending supply of growth medium, and was soon producing several grams of antibodies a month. (Bio-Response has since dropped the system, and now makes antibodies in large vessels.)

Another example can be found on the western outskirts of London, England. The official story in Great Britain is that the company called Celltech was founded in 1980 (largely with government funds) to bring the United Kingdom's expertise in molecular biology up on a par with the rest of the West. To many foreigners, it seemed more likely that the United Kingdom had too late realized its blunder in not patenting Köhler and Milstein's hybridoma technology; in a belated move to catch up with other countries (especially the United States), the British Government pressed Celltech into formation, then gave the new company virtually exclusive rights to technology developed in government laboratories—including Milstein's Cambridge lab. Granted this running head start on its competition, Celltech's charter was to bring the technology to commercialization and little by little buy itself back from the government.

By 1985, Celltech was doing just that. With a vengeance.

The visitor to Damon Biotech soon becomes aware that there are at least two versions of what happened in Needham Heights during the early 1980s: Paul Vasington's and the "official" corporate account. There's plenty of bad blood here, and it flows in both directions. Both sides have their loyal supporters. As a result, many of the recollections—recounted by seemingly responsible and fair-minded men and women—vary so widely that it's almost impossible to distinguish fact from wishful thinking from outright fabrication.

One thing is certain: Paul Vasington could not have been unaware of the potential impact of monoclonal antibodies on his division. By 1981 all one had to do was glance through any of the dozens of monthly biotechnology trade journals to realize that the proteins had become one of the hottest topics the diagnostics industry had seen in decades. The names of several monoclonals companies, often at the bottom of brightly colored full-page ads, appeared in every issue; barely a month passed without another hybridoma conference or seminar. It was plainly impossible for anyone even remotely connected with medicine or biotechnology to have missed the message.

Nor could Vasington easily have overlooked the importance of Frank Lim's little capsules in all of this. He knew as well as anyone that what separated one new monoclonals company from another was the proven ability to make the proteins cheaply and in large volumes.

By early 1981 there were just two ways of growing hybridomas: you could do it in cell culture or you could do it in mice. Neither was very appealing. Like any other living cell, hybridomas were persistently unhappy in culture—they couldn't reach the high densities craved by all cells, nor could many cell culturists consistently devise the best combinations of culture media. And even if a culture proved itself in small glass dishes, the results could rarely be transferred to the big steel vessels that were needed for commercial antibody quantities. Problems that could easily be spotted in a glass vessel—a foreign organism, say, or a mechanical stirrer that suddenly refuses to stir—might go undetected for several hours inside a forty-liter tank, long enough to wipe out two weeks' labor.

And so many companies turned to the idea of growing the proteins in mice. The hybridomas were injected into the animals' abdominal cavities; bathed in the natural fluids called ascites, they often grow nicely and rather naturally to very large volumes. As many researchers have learned, though, the method is not without its problems. One is that the animals are not blessed with what manufacturers like to call "economy of scale"—that is, if it costs ten dollars to grow cells in one mouse, it costs a thousand dollars to grow the same product in a hundred mice.

And you need lots of mice—thousands—to make just a few drops of purified antibody. The animals are surprisingly expensive to maintain, to feed, to watch over, and ultimately to kill. And what happens if just one of them gets sick? A fast-spreading infection could wipe out hundreds of thousands of dollars worth of research in less than a day.

Vasington eventually realized that Lim's capsules offered a third alternative. If pancreatic cells survived inside the things, and red blood cells, why not hybridomas? What's still in question is how or whether he followed up on the hunch, and how or whether his response was backed by Damon management.

Ask Vasington and he'll tell you that he quickly understood that monoclonals were a "hand-in-glove" fit with the company's diagnostics business. At one point, in fact, he had asked Lim to create a new test method that would wed monoclonals and the capsules. Lim obediently worked on the project for a few months, but apparently without success. "He worked in the lab as if he was wearing boxing gloves," someone recalled later.

But Vasington wasn't going to give up the idea that easily. Drawing on his $750,000 special-projects budget, he and Lurier soon decided to organize their own hybridoma team in Needham Heights, headed by a cell biologist named George Koch. The men also agreed that until they had something to bring to Kosowsky, the project would stay under wraps.

They seemed unaware that along with his other activities, the Damon chairman had also been tracking the hybridoma's progress during the preceding year. Admittedly no expert on the subject, he still wondered if the technology was right for his company. Too many of the hybridoma's interesting angles had already been snatched up by other companies, he thought, and anyone wanting to seriously chase down the business would have to generate a unique application or processing twist. What would be Damon's twist?

"All I really knew at this point was that we had this interesting encapsulation process," Kosowsky recalled later. "But I don't think anyone in the company really knew what to do with it."

By early 1981, though, he was getting some clues. One was the growing conviction by his staff that practically any living cell could be grown inside the capsules; in fact, Jarvis was excitedly reporting that he'd not come up against a single cell line that he couldn't get to grow. At the very least, said Jarvis, Damon seemed to have on its hands a dazzling new method for growing cells (including those that Jarvis suspected might yield a previously unknown form of interferon, called epsilon-interferon). In the meanwhile, Koch and others had already turned to the possibility of growing hybridomas in the capsules, some of which might result in commercially important antibodies.

Kosowsky might logically have asked why the company wanted to grow antibodies. He'd have his answer within a few months. Damon Corporation was about to step off in a startling new direction.

The Damon press release, dated April 7, 1981, described "the formation of a new subsidiary, Damon Biotech, Inc., to engage in the research, development and production of a broad range of products in cellular and molecular biology, genetics and immunology. . . . These techniques will be employed to produce interferon, monoclonal antibodies, cancer diagnostics, vaccines and other biological products."

To help Damon Biotech achieve these objectives, a scientific board was named—five men to begin with who would provide the company with their special insights into the murky and uncharted waters that were swirling about its feet:

Dr. Herman Eisen, professor of immunology at MIT;

Dr. Harvey Lodish, professor of biology at MIT and a consulting scientist at Children's Hospital;

Dr. Irving London, director of the Harvard-MIT division of health sciences;

Dr. George Whitesides, professor of chemistry at MIT;

Dr. Howard Green, chairman of the department of physiology at Harvard Medical School.

Vasington didn't like the name of the new company, he said: "Damon wasn't all that well thought-of at that time; people still remembered how the venture into the hospital labs had turned out. Under those circumstances, I didn't think it made sense to saddle the subsidiary with the name of the parent company."

He was overruled. And not for the last time.

Any company needs two things: products to sell (either goods or services) and customers to buy those products. As it approached its six-month anniversary, the new Damon Biotech had neither.

The most important reason was that for most of its first year, the company still had only vague ideas of what it wanted to become. The word "Biotech" provided a hint, of course, but that could have meant anything: interferon, growth hormones, immunological testing, agricultural genetics, monoclonal antibodies.

In order for the company to grow antibodies, however, it needed to secure small amounts of the corresponding hybridoma. And there's the rub, explained Tibbie Posillico, a tall, slender woman in her mid-thirties who now heads one of the production facilities at Needham Heights: "A lot of clients, or people we'd like to have as clients, don't like to let these cells out of their own labs. Part of the reason is simple security—some of these hybrids could become very valuable financially, and no one wants to take a chance on their getting into the hands of a competing company."

But there's another reason, she said, and it probably doesn't make much sense to anyone who doesn't grow cells for a living: Few cell culturists like to see the cells they grew and nurtured—for months, in some cases—pass into the unsympathetic hands of others. Terri Grdina isn't the only one who forges an affection for her "children," said Posillico. "It really is like watching your kids leave home."

Damon Biotech today is considered a monoclonals company only because another company—Hoffmann-La Roche in Nutley, New Jersey—decided to produce the anticancer chemical interferon. From that seemingly unrelated decision emerged two pivotal outcomes for the young New England company. First, it provided Jarvis and his colleagues with a priceless opportunity to put their capsules to work not on the limited scale of a laboratory benchtop, but in a massive industrial project that might later capture the attention of the medical world. The second outcome was the birth of a new business concept, now known in the monoclonals community as "contract production"—the large-volume production of antibody from the client's proprietary hybridoma.

There is still some disagreement about how the contract agreement actually came about; the important thing is that, in 1981, Roche (as it is usually called) was in the early stages of producing alpha-interferon in genetically engineered bacteria. The problem was that once the bacteria had manufactured the interferon with its transplanted new genes, the chemical had to be separated from the dozens of other cellular products within the mixture. For that, Roche had decided to use monoclonal antibodies. Roche researchers were already gearing up to use the interferon as an antigen, just as Köhler had used sheep red blood cells: The chemical would be injected into mice to stimulate antibody production, and the B-cells fused with cancer cells to form the anti-interferon hybridoma. The next step would be to inject the hybridomas into mice, where they would grow in the ascites fluid. When the finished antibodies were mixed with the contaminated interferon, the proteins would bind only to the interferon; everything else could be rinsed away. Roche had already installed a thousand mice at Nutley; if the animals proved to be reasonably efficient hybridoma factories, the company would scale up by adding several thousand more.

It didn't take much argument by Damon Biotech to persuade the Roche men that capsules made infinitely more sense.

The exact details of the Roche-Biotech agreement are still confidential. What is known is that it provided for an up-front payment of $2 million to Biotech, spread over three production stages; Damon agreed to produce ten milligrams of anti-interferon antibody in the first stage, a gram during the second, and ten grams during the third.

It was clearly the major turning point for the new company, the first opportunity to demonstrate the feasibility of the encapsulation process (which Kosowsky had dubbed "Encapcel"). Not for making micrograms of antibody—*lots* of people could do that—but batches thousands of times larger.

But there were some who realized that the agreement could sink the new company before it ever left the dock. Suppose that Damon Biotech actually couldn't make the antibodies?

No academic question, this. "In truth, we didn't really have all the necessary technology in place at that time," said Vasington. "But we just couldn't afford to let an opportunity like this go by. Here we'd been making all this noise about our encapsulation technology; Roche was basically telling us to put up or shut up. Sometime you have to stick your neck out, do something that forces you to push ahead in the laboratory."

At the beginning, the Roche work was envisioned by some as a model of simplicity. Following the procedures developed by Jarvis and his staff, the production of the anti-interferon would go something like this:

Once the biologists in New Jersey had made the appropriate hybridoma, the cells would be frozen and shipped to Damon Biotech. There they would be expanded several times in the company's cell culture lab, coated with the sodium alginate, then mixed with calcium chloride. These two steps would put a rubbery coating around the hybridomas, after which they would finally be encapsulated.

The encapsulated hybridomas would then be placed into large fermentation vessels (referred to simply as "pots" in the lab) for several weeks as they multiplied to thousands of times their unencapsulated volume. In the last step, the capsules would be broken up to release the anti-interferon antibodies, which would then be shipped back to Nutley for purification. Hoffmann-La Roche scientists would then chemically attach the pure antibodies to millions of small inert beads mounted inside a glass column. When the impure interferon was poured into the column, the drug molecules would bind to the antibodies while everything poured out the bottom. Pure interferon would be obtained simply by chemically unhooking the antibody-interferon complex.

The nightmares started almost immediately, said Kevin Gilligan, the amiable, curly-haired young graduate student who from certain angles bears a remarkable resemblance to Warren Beatty. They continued for more than a year. And while no single technical problem proved insurmountable, each was complicated by the fact that every variable in the process—polymer, reaction times, temperature, nutrient, wash steps—had to be isolated, one at a time. Each corresponding test required a week or more to run; each test put the team further behind schedule. "We had Frank Lim come up to Needham a couple of times to help us," said one of the scientists. "But he wanted to change everything at once, just throw all these possible solutions into the problem and hope that one of them worked. We couldn't do that, of course—even if you solved the problem, you could never know how you did it. I think Frank was just involved in too many other things in Virginia at the time; it seemed as though he'd lost interest in the encapsulation work."

One problem was that the anti-interferon antibody was leaking out of the capsules; large amounts of it—four or five times the desired amount—could be detected in the surrounding medium. "It had probably been a problem from the beginning," said Gilligan later, "but some of the early antibodies may have been held on to the capsule by electrostatic charge, so no one ever noticed it. Only when very sensitive assays were developed did the problem become noticeable. Naturally, leakage decreased the yield of the antibody—if you're losing 20 percent of the protein into the surrounding fluid, that means that you've got to run another batch to make up the loss."

It took Jarvis and his group almost a year to track down the cause of the leakage: the hybridomas were being allowed to sit in the alginate for too long before encapsulation. "The longer they sat there, the more tightly they were being compressed," Gilligan explained, flexing his hand as though he were squeezing a tennis ball. "When we put the membrane on top of that, the diameter of the gel stayed the same; but when we liquefied the alginate inside with the citrate, all of a sudden"—he popped his hand open—"the thing expanded and stretched out the membrane." The stretching, of course, also widened many of the pores, providing an easy escape for the contents.

There was another glitch, but to see it you had to look at the alginate-coated cells under a microscope. They should be perfectly spherical, said Gilligan, because such a shape provides the most uniform polymer coverage. But some of them were a little lopsided, or had noticeable dimples in them. When the membrane was applied over the spheres, the dimple formed a weak spot at which the polymer might crack.

Over a period of several months, Jarvis and Gilligan traced the cause to trace contamination within the 20-gauge hypodermic needles they were using to drop the spheres into the calcium chloride solution. Most of the time, the droplets formed perfect microspheres as they emerged from the tip of the needle and dropped into the chloride; occasionally, however, the semiliquid picked up an invisible speck of dust, just enough to distort the sphere into an ellipse. The dimple was probably coming from the dust being carried into the coating. The only solution was to scrupulously clean all the equipment before making the spheres.

Dimpled cells turned out to be one of the least of the problems. Within a few weeks, the researchers found that poly-L-lysine, the polymer that Lim had used in his original encapsulations, worked for some of the hybridomas, but not all. The quality of the finished capsule was too irregular, said Gilligan. "So we ran through a long series of different polymers—that put us further behind schedule, of course. We finally arrived at a combination of two polymers, one of which is called polyvinyl amine. That worked fine; then the company that made it found out that some of the materials used in its manufacture were hazardous, so they just stopped making it altogether."

The biggest problem came during the critical third stage scaleup, when Damon was required to produce ten grams of the anti-interferon antibody—a phenomenal amount of protein at the time. In fact, this is the point at which most biotechnology laboratories trip up even today, assuming that what works in small amounts will also work in large volumes. To help solve the problems (and thus strengthen the program, by Jarvis' reasoning), Dr. Randy Rupp was hired in late 1981.

The bearded, soft-spoken Rupp was to scaleup technology

what Terri Grdina had been to cell culture. He had a sort of sixth sense about the business, Vasington said later; he knew instinctively how to stroke the delicate cells into doing in large pots what they were known to do in tiny glass vessels.

To accomplish that, Rupp and his young staff found themselves practically living in the laboratory for weeks at a time. For a while, in fact, Rupp had a cot for himself in the corner so that he could spend several nights a week baby-sitting the cells, keeping a practiced ear tuned to the hoses that tended to pop noisily from their fittings in the middle of the night, peering into the smelly broth in which the cells struggled to survive, looking for early symptoms of disorder. "If you got there in the morning and found something had shut off, you were just too late," he said.

The schedule raised havoc with their home lives, of course. Rupp considered himself fortunate that his wife was also a cell biologist—even more fortunately, an understanding one. Little Joshua Rupp wasn't quite so comprehending, however; the boy became depressed when his father went off to work on Sunday evenings, knowing that it might be another week before he returned. Others in the lab were somewhat less dedicated. Many resigned, weary after months of fatigue-induced short tempers and the seemingly endless string of sixteen-hour days and seven-day weeks; a larger number stayed, determined to see that their wayward children in the glass and steel pots were properly raised.

Slowly, the problems were resolved, thanks largely to Rupp's resourcefulness. At one point he wanted to buy a large industrial fermenter for the program—one of the massive hundred-liter stainless steel pots fitted with ports and inlets and gauges and fittings. His request was turned down; Vasington explained sheepishly that the company simply couldn't afford the fifteen thousand dollars. Rupp drove to a restaurant supply company in Newton, wrote a personal check for an eighty-five-dollar stainless steel soup pot, then took it home to install the fittings himself. To his delight, the pot worked like a charm.

Today the anti-interferon antibodies are produced in Needham Heights almost exactly as they were in mid-1982 (although several steps have been altered, added, or dropped over the years in the interest of quality assurance and more efficient production).

On a warm day in July, I was escorted into Damon's ground-floor laboratories, where I donned a nylon gown, jammed a gauzy elasticized cap on the top of my head, and stood back to watch a bit of magic.

At first glance, the small laboratory seems cluttered, overrun with people, hopelessly disorganized. There is a steady stream of chitchat between the green-gowned chemists and biologists, this day revolving mostly around an upcoming softball game between Damon and another local biotechnology company.

The unobservant visitor cannot move more than a few feet across the tiled floor without bumping into a huge glass vessel or stainless steel cart; the bench tops are almost entirely covered with microscopes, small electronic instruments, and miniforests of laboratory glassware (which is more often than not fashioned of unbreakable, chemical-resistant plastic). In one corner of the room, a portable radio is tuned to WBCN, a Boston soft rock station; the average age of the workers appears to be about twenty-six.

The visitor soon learns that there's a method to this seeming madness. It would be much neater to keep the flasks and beakers tucked into the wall cabinets, but that would mean hundreds of extra steps every day. The carts are where they are to minimize the distance the heavy vessels must be carried to reach them. The instruments are used several times a day and so occupy the most convenient locations.

Hoffmann-La Roche ships their anti-interferon hybridomas at regular intervals to Needham, where they are received in small glass vials, each containing about forty thousand cells, packed in dry ice. Like all incoming cells at practically every laboratory in the world, they are first quarantined—kept under close observation for two weeks in a separate room to be sure that the vials do not also contain some unwelcome stowaways. Certain viruses have been known to survive for several days, even at these low shipping temperatures. So have the common bugs known as the Mycoplasmas—a hardy and extremely infectious group of organisms that can survive for two weeks in some laboratories and wipe out entire colonies of cells with astonishing speed. These particular organisms do their dirty work by robbing the host cells of arginine and other vital amino acids.

After the quarantine period, the tiny plug of frozen hybridomas must be grown to a much larger volume before encapsulation. That's where the cell culture team comes in, headed by a miniscule blonde in her late twenties named Ellen Mullaney. The cells are thawed and placed in a seventy-five-milliliter T-flask —a flat, pentagon-shaped clear plastic bottle with a bright orange screw-on cap—partially filled with a clear red liquid called EMA (a mixture of amino acids, minerals, and other nutrients needed) that will keep the hybridomas growing happily. The flasks are stored in large steel-and-glass cabinets kept at 37° C—about the same temperature as the interior of the human body. A few weeks later, Mullaney transfers the growing body of cells to a larger T-flask and adds some more EMA. Two weeks later, the hybridomas and nutrients are transferred once more, this time to a two-liter spinner flask—a large glass jar with two short arms sticking out at angles from the sides; the arms can be used as inlets for gases, special supplements, or for sampling. The spinner flask is then set on a magnetic surface in another cabinet, and Mullaney carefully drops into it a Teflon-coated magnetic bar, about three inches long. When the power to the magnetic surface is switched on, the two fields oppose each other, forcing the bar to spin rapidly on the bottom of the flask and stirring the liquid. This continual stirring action not only assures that the cells are distributed evenly through the liquid, but also prevents them from drifting to the bottom of the flask, where most of them would be crushed to death by their neighbors.

After about four weeks in the spinner flask, the volume of the hybridomas is large enough for encapsulation. The man doing the work today is Ken Fontaine, a thin young chemical engineer of about twenty-seven. Besides holding degrees in both engineering and biology, Fontaine fancies himself something of a singer, and likes to accompany Linda Ronstadt and Billy Joel as they hold forth from the radio in the corner. Fontaine's opinion of his musical talents, unfortunately, is not widely shared in this laboratory; trooper that he is, he sings nevertheless.

Fontaine lifts the spinner flasks from the cabinets onto a steel cart, which he then wheels into his little rat's nest of a room—a six- by twelve-foot area which has been walled off from the rest of the laboratory. Along one side of the room is a large glass-doored hood equipped with a negative pressure device; that is, any organism that might find its way into the cubicle will be swept up and out through the hood instead of hanging about the premises.

Fontaine washes the cells in sodium chloride, then transfers them into a large glass beaker containing a solution of sodium alginate. From here, the alginate-coated clusters of cells are pumped through a plastic tube to a jethead—a plastic-and-metal device, about eight inches across, shaped like a tuna fish can. The flat surface of the jethead has been drilled with twenty-four tiny, perfectly round holes; an air hose feeds in from the side. The coated cells emerge from the holes and are simultaneously hit by a stream of air that forms the droplets into perfect spheres as they fall into a beaker of calcium chloride. The reaction between the alginate and the chloride results in a semisolid coating around the cells; each cluster contains anywhere from one or two to hundreds of thousands of hybridomas. Most of the time, Fontaine tries to regulate the flow so that each cluster contains about 150 cells.

"Wanna feel?" asks Fontaine. He scoops up a few drops of the grayish mixture on the edge of a glass slide and wipes it on my fingertips. The glob of particles feels gritty and slimy, as though someone had dropped a teaspoon of sand into a cup of warm gravy.

The cells still have to be encapsulated. Fontaine does this by carefully pouring the coated cells into a stainless steel pot, about two feet high and eighteen inches across, which is covered by a thick clear-plastic lid. Before encapsulating, however, Fontaine has to make one more check: He dribbles a small sample of the alginate spheres on a glass slide and measures their diameter under the microscope.

"We try for a diameter of seven hundred to nine hundred microns," he explains as he focuses the scope. He steps back to let me look. There is a scale etched into one of the lenses inside the scope; peering down, I can easily compare the clear clumps of cells against the scale, and so get a very close approximation of their diameter.

"You have to remember that the amount of the polymer we use for the coating is held constant," Fontaine explains. "So is the volume of the cells. So if a lot of the clusters are too big, they'll have only a very thin, weak layer of polymer; if the clusters are too small, they'll have too much polymer. We have to avoid that, because then it might take too long for the nutrients to get in and for the cells' waste products to get out—too many channels and pores."

Today Fontaine is satisfied that the cells' diameter is in the acceptable range, so he proceeds with the encapsulation. He starts to pump a solution of the polymer (a chemical called poly-L-ornithine, or PLO) into the steel pot.

"Now each one of those gritty little things you felt is being surrounded by a layer of the PLO," he announces. "Just flows around the particle, and it should be forming pretty much of a perfect sphere." As the mixture agitates, Fontaine discusses another, more pressing issue with one of the other biologists: The second man has just discovered that the keel on his eighteen-foot boat is warped and is wondering what he can do about it.

When the mixture has agitated enough, Fontaine completes the final step by adding some citrate solution to the pot. "This partially liquefies the alginate inside the capsule, and most of it flows out. But we want to keep a little of it inside—it's sort of a nutrient for the cells. So what you've got now are these perfectly round polymer capsules, and inside each one is a little of the alginate and the hybridomas. Over the next couple of months, those hybridomas are going to just crank out their antibodies for us."

"And we'll all be filthy rich," someone pipes up from the next room.

"Get my keel straightened out, maybe," adds the unhappy sailor.

From here the encapsulated cells are transferred to a forty-liter pot and wheeled down the hall to the fermenter room. There, sitting on a shelf with a half dozen other pots, the hybridomas will continue to reproduce inside the capsules, turning out up to four grams of antibody per pot.

As Fontaine finishes his batch of hybridomas—the "run"—Ellen Mullaney is checking on the progress of some other recent encapsulations, a task that is performed every three or four days. She takes a few drops from fermenters in the other room, places them in small T-flasks, and lays the flasks under the microscope.

She's looking to see how the cells are growing, and whether some unwanted garbage has crept into the medium.

There are several ways of doing this. The easiest is to simply look at the color of the EMA; if the cells are growing properly, the nutrient will be turning from its beautiful crimson to a bright and gaudy orange—the result of a reaction between one of the nutrient's ingredients and the lactic acid that is produced and ejected by the growing cells.

Mullaney also wants to peek inside the capsules. She spreads a few drops from the T-flask onto a glass slide called a hemacytometer, then adds a drop of blue dye. Under the scope, the capsules are transparent; they look like large clear-glass bowls with the hybridomas clearly visible inside. Using a mechanical counter with her left hand, Mullaney can easily tally the hybridomas inside a capsule, then extrapolate the count with the help of the grid etched into the glass slide. Dead cells will appear dark blue under the scope. "Healthy cells can eject the dye from their cytoplasm," she explains. "Dead ones can't, and so show up dark blue." Also under the scope, she can see how the hybridomas inside the capsules are growing. Individual cells are beginning to cluster together inside the spheres after a few days; after twelve days, the clusters are much larger and fill more than half the capsule. After three weeks, the capsules are so fully packed they appear ready to burst.

Today, Mullaney finds something else in the flasks—an organism of some kind, although she can't easily identify it. "Look down there," she says, "just to the right of center. See that thing? Looks like a speck of dust? It's probably pseudomonas, a bacterium that pops up here and there. In people too. We'll give it a shot of something and see what happens."

Mullaney and Cathy Brooks, another cell culturist, decide to give the speck not one, but two shots. Brooks goes to a bench drawer and withdraws two 10-milliliter plastic syringes, one prepackaged with penicillin and the other with streptomycin. These she brings down the hallway into the warm and humid fermenter room. Climbing a stepladder to reach the top of the pot, she first injects one needle into a rubber tube feeding into the fermenter, then the other. "That should kill whatever's growing in there, but we'll take another look in a day or two to be sure.

For in vitro applications—if it's something that won't be used inside somebody—things like this aren't such a big deal, as long as the client knows about it. If it's going to be used in vivo, injected into a patient, that's something else altogether. Absolutely, no way. . . ."

A few weeks after encapsulation, the antibody is "harvested" in another room—a large, noisy place with a drain in the center of the floor. (The noise, I see, comes from the loudly hissing steam lines that are used to sterilize each pot before it receives its next cargo of encapsulated cells.) The fermenter is wheeled here from the fermentation room and its contents poured into a two-hundred-liter plastic jug. Practically all the capsules are soon sitting on the bottom of the jug; the fluid above them is siphoned off, and the capsules are pumped from the jug to the homogenizer—an industrial version of an ordinary kitchen blender—sitting on the floor near the drain. As the capsules pass through the homogenizer, they are broken up by the steel blades; the antibodies are unaffected.

The final step is the purification of the antibodies—separating them from the mixture of alginate, medium, and capsule fragments. They will then be tested for activity and contamination, packaged, and shipped to New Jersey.

The New Biotechnology meant more than brilliant science and the promises of corporate prestige. It also provided a milieu in which even the most obscure young geneticist could rise to the top of his field in a matter of months, and in some cases make a tremendous amount of money in the process. At the new company called Damon Biotech, it soon became apparent that one of the rising stars was none other than Allan Jarvis.

From the beginning, Jarvis seemed to possess all the technical qualities that Kosowsky needed to help get the new company off the runway. He was an accomplished researcher who seemed to enjoy the respect and affection of his laboratory subordinates; he and Marty frequently entertained the lab workers in the Jarvises' antique Newburyport home, and Gilligan often sought out the older man's advice about graduate studies; he could explain the most complex principles of biotechnology with a few simple phrases and diagrams—a talent perhaps inherited from his father, a high school principal in Haverhill. He was also one of the men who had overseen the formulation of the Roche program—the most important bit of work the company had performed thus far, the one that had ushered Damon Biotech once and for all into the privileged ranks of serious-business monoclonals producers. Moreover, he clearly enjoyed his expanding role as an articulate spokesman for the company, often representing management in complicated presentations to prospective customers and investment analysts. "David thought that this kid could do just about anything," Vasington complained later.

Along with several other workers, Vasington wondered if Jarvis' star might be rising a little too quickly. There was that whopping salary raise that Allan received in 1981, with Vasington's approval. When another big increase came through in 1982, though, Vasington objected. Kosowsky and Lurier listened carefully to his qualms, then overruled him.

"I liked Allan very much, and still do," Vasington said, years later. "He was a good scientist, and an excellent spokesman for Biotech." Here he swiveled about in his chair to stare out the window while he chose his words. "But I didn't think he'd had the time to build all the skills he needed to move into a top management spot. I'm not sure he had the universal respect of his subordinates, for example. You don't build a corporate leader in two years."

By itself the salary incident was a small one, and might have been quickly forgotten had it not been just one in a series of such events. In fact, tensions between Vasington and Kosowsky had been mounting for months. Vasington learned that the chairman was spending several hours a week in Jarvis' laboratory reviewing the day's results and even planning new experiments, despite his lack of training in biology. Worst of all was Vasington's growing suspicion—fueled by months of real or imagined humiliations—that Jarvis was in effect sidestepping him by quietly reporting directly to the front office.

The growing chasm between Vasington and Kosowsky is still a ticklish subject at Damon Biotech. For his part, Kosowsky refuses to comment on the matter, saying only that "Paul was and is an excellent scientist, and a good businessman. My perceptions at the time were simply that he wasn't moving quickly enough to develop some of the new business we wanted to pursue. I felt that he was too involved with a large number of small projects; we'd committed ourselves to pushing ahead with a small number of much larger projects, and I think Paul had some problems with that."

Another Damon researcher, now working elsewhere, thought that "David liked the aggressive, go-getting type of executive. That wasn't Paul. He was smart, efficient, hardworking but sorta laid-back. At least, that's the impression he seemed to give to David."

Lurier acted as a go-between for the two men for a while, advising Vasington to "just pay attention to the diagnostics business; we'll look around for someone else to handle the hybridoma end. Besides, you don't really need this crap with David, do you?" Returning to his Norwood home every night, Vasington complained to his wife that "no one knows who's giving the orders in the lab anymore." Key people, people who would be hard to replace, were turning in their notices rather than struggling through the embarrassing confusion.

Even the hard-driving Kosowsky seemed to recognize from time to time that chairman or not, he had occasionally stepped too close to the bounds of propriety. Vasington recalls that following a tense meeting one day, Kosowsky softened for a minute and offered a halfhearted apology: "This is just the way I am, Paul. You're gonna have to deal with my personality."

Personality Vasington could put up with. He would not tolerate what he considered blatant professional insults. He had been invited to give a paper at the prestigious Gordon Conference in New Hampshire during the summer of 1982, and had spent several weeks in its preparation. A few days before the meeting, he was informed that Kosowsky wanted Jarvis, not Vasington, to give a paper for Damon Biotech. Lurier made it official over lunch one day: Let Jarvis do the technical presentations, and Kosowsky will give the business talks.

Vasington, in other words, essentially had nothing to do.

It could mean only one thing: A dream team was being assembled at Damon Biotech, and he clearly was not to be part of it. There were rumors, in fact, that the front office had already put

Vasington on ice as far as the company was concerned—because of his precarious health, according to one story.

Vasington had suffered his heart attack in late 1976 while dashing across New York City's upper Park Avenue, dodging a taxi on his way to a business meeting. It was a doozy, he said later. Half an hour later, he was being bundled into the back of an ambulance. "You remember the damnedest things about these incidents," he said later. "I don't recall anything about the paramedics arriving, but I do remember that they couldn't get the stretcher secured in the rear of the ambulance. So I bounced around the back of that thing—this is in the middle of rush hour traffic, siren going like crazy—all the way to Lenox Hill Hospital."

He spent three weeks in Lenox Hill. He had indeed suffered a heart attack, the cardiologists told him; they showed him the angiogram. One of the arteries supplying his heart muscle was almost completely blocked off. A second was nearly 50 percent blocked.

The experience had not discouraged the hopes he still carried of moving up the ladder of the new company, however. After all, he reasoned, it was he and Ed Lurier who had laid the foundations for Damon Biotech. They'd built the company's diagnostics division to a million-dollar-a-year business, had avidly supported Frank Lim's encapsulation work, and had brought Damon Biotech to the threshold of becoming one of the most intriguing of the new biotechnology companies. If anyone deserved the recognition that goes with the front office, he thought, it was he.

And so he wasn't quite prepared to learn that the company had been advertising for a new president for more than a month before he'd felt himself squeezed out of the daily operations. In fact, the company had hired an executive recruitment firm to find the right man to handle both the technology and the business. When Vasington later came across a paper detailing the new man's responsibilities and qualifications, he said, he found himself described almost perfectly. "What they wanted was a Paul Vasington," he said later.

Instead, they got Dr. Nigel L. Webb, a thirty-five-year-old molecular biologist via Cambridge and King's College in London.

As Webb settled into his new position during the closing months of 1982, he pored over the company's records and correspondence files. Among the papers was a two-page letter to Vasington from an NCI physician named Abrams in Frederick, Maryland. The letter suggested several ways in which Abrams and Damon Biotech might collaborate on the anti-idiotype program.

CHAPTER EIGHT

Kenneth A. Foon, M.D., is full of surprises.

For one, he's delightfully undoctorly. No intimidating white coat with a stethoscope dangling rakishly from one pocket, but knit shirt, chinos, jogging shoes, and the most infectious grin you're ever likely to see. He's about thirty-five or so, and so slender that when he turns sideways most of his six-foot frame disappears, except for the shaggy brown hair and mustache.

In a field populated with some of the world's most colossal egos, Foon ("Ken," he insists) is almost a heretic. Discussing a prominent West Coast immunologist, Foon can't resist noting that "he's really a brilliant guy, but so bloody arrogant you can barely stand to talk with him." Another superstar researcher gets a somewhat more positive review: "I'm one of his greatest fans; I worship the water he walks on . . ."

At first, all of this seems to be a mere putdown of one's professional rivals—an example of the catty, gossipy comments that in some medical circles use up almost as much time every week as clinical work. But the visitor soon realizes that while Foon takes his work very seriously, he doesn't mind poking a bit of fun at himself and his colleagues from time to time. Among the framed degrees on his office wall—including the one awarded in 1972 "With High Distinction" from Wayne State University Medical School—is a send-up of Rembrandt's famous painting *Doctor Nicolaas Tulp Demonstrating the Anatomy of the Arm,* in which some of the doctors wield carpenters' hammers and saws as they prepare to examine the cadaver before them. And when asked why he entered medicine, he explains that "my mother told me to—I didn't dare argue." (Later, he elaborated that "like so many second-generation Jewish families, there are enormous pressures to achieve excellence. It never occurred to me to fight it.")

He has a bizarre sense of humor which at one time revealed itself in outrageously colored ties, or bounding into a patient's room at Frederick wearing a pair of comic glasses with spring-mounted plastic eyeballs. Describing a case history one day at a stuffy medical conference, he concluded his slide presentation by claiming to have developed a remarkable treatment for skin cancers:

"Here is the patient when she first entered our program," he intoned in his most somber voice. At that point, a slide of a gauze-wrapped mummy flashed on the screen, courtesy of an old Hollywood horror film. The image was quickly replaced with one of Marilyn Monroe in one of her most alluring poses. "And here is the patient after three months' treatment!"

Like Jack Christie, Foon had struggled with the decision about a specialty while in medical school. For the next few years, he leapfrogged around the country—from Detroit to San Diego to Bethesda, then back to Southern California. "I guess that my decision to go into cancer treatment was partly by chance," he said in one of his sedate, calm moments. "But I was also fortunate, really fortunate, in that a lot of my professors became role models. By the time I got to UCLA in 1977, I knew that I wanted to go into oncology and hematology."

Foon had been on the job at Frederick for only a few weeks when he received Jack Christie's phone call. It took him a few minutes to place the younger man; what was it—a year? two years?—since they had seen each other in California? Since that first call, he had reviewed the reports from Houston as he'd promised, and had concluded that Christie might qualify for admission to the anti-idiotype program later in the year. Maybe. He and the others would have to see Jack, of course; for now, he refused to hold out promises that he might not be able to fulfill.

The two men spoke by telephone two and three times a month during the summer of 1981, with Jack describing any changes in his condition and Ken relaying information on the status of the developing Frederick program. By the time he returned from the Labor Day weekend in the mountains, Christie was getting exasperated. He understood that the program was slow in coming up, that it still might be months before the tests and treatments got underway, but he was increasingly anxious to explore this alternative to the disagreeable chemotherapy. "I feel like I'm just sitting around doing nothing," he complained to Eileen.

"Listen, Ken. I've been through the literature twenty times over the past couple of months. You know what's going on in the field. If you were me, where would you go for some advice on this?"

Seated in his beige cinder block office in the basement, Foon leaned back in his chair and hooked one bony leg over the corner of his desk. A small air conditioner mounted in the window struggled against the stifling Maryland heat, all but drowning out the voice on the other end of the line. Foon thought about Christie's question for a moment. As he did so, he absently wiped a few spects of dust from the top of the ceramic statue of Groucho Marx that presided over his littered desk.

"I always thought that Stanford was on top of this better than most other places," Foon finally replied.

"You mean Levy and Miller."

"Yeah, Levy and Miller and a few others. You know about that guy last year, the anti-id guy." Christie grunted an acknowledgment; it was the Levy and Miller work, in fact, that had led to Foon's anti-id program in Frederick.

"Now you gotta remember, Jack," Foon said. "He's still the only one. That guy's the only one. *Ever.* No one knows why he responded as well as he did, and there's no guarantee that those guys are gonna be able to do it again. Coulda been just a lucky shot in the dark. You know the way those things go."

Jack thanked Foon for his time and promised to keep in touch. He hung up the phone, then immediately picked it up again to dial the information operator for Area Code 415.

Not everyone was taken with Ken Foon's occasional zaniness. Some of his coworkers were irritated at what seemed to be his need to be at the center of attention. Were those outrageous ties really necessary? What about that picture he had taken of himself in boxing getup, under the words "The Fight Against Cancer"? And would he ever stop talking about the fact that he had for two years treated Nathan Pritikin, the famous proponent of the low-cholesterol diet, until Pritikin's leukemia had finally led him to take his own life?

It was during his two years in Bethesda that Foon became fascinated with cancer cell surface markers, then a relatively novel idea in oncology. While it was clear that all cancers shared various characteristics, it was becoming just as clear that they were also very different from each other. One of the most intriguing differences were those which made up the cell surface markers—millions of microscopic strings of fat and protein and carbohydrate that decorated the outer surface of each and every cell. What tugged at Foon and others during the late 1970s was the fact that every cancer cell arising from a single original malignant cell exhibited the very same pattern of markers; at the same time, the patterns on one cancer cell were nothing at all like those that dotted the cells of another cancer patient, even one with the same kind of cancer. Those markers had to be an important clue of some kind—a target, perhaps. If a drug could be devised that recognized only that marker, then bound itself to it, the result could be a revolutionary new cancer therapy.

Foon quickly realized that monoclonals technology provided precisely that opportunity. If antibodies could in fact be designed against any antigen—including cell markers—then grown in large quantities . . . "There were a lot of us thinking about that kind of thing back in the late seventies," Foon recalled. "God, the possibilities just blew us away."

So he was receptive to NCI's job offer in 1981. His job, he was told, was simple: Find new, safe, effective ways to kill cancer cells. And oh yes, please try to do so within the budget.

The second part of his job description didn't seem so tough. With the institute seemingly sloshing in a billion dollars a year, Foon was sure that this was his chance to do things no one had ever done before. The budget also meant that he would be relieved of the dreary, time-consuming chore of writing the grant proposals that are so important to most researchers. And like so many other cancer academicians, he couldn't help but realize that a stint with NCI would be an especially colorful feather in his professional cap.

Stanford University Medical Center, about thirty-five miles south of San Francisco, consists not of one building, but several. Like much of the Bay area, the architecture here hints strongly of the Spanish influence that is still so prevalent in the region. And unlike Los Angeles, the area has by and large retained a rich sense of its identity, whether in the cheerfully colored gingerbread homes along Union Street near downtown San Francisco or in the distinctive high-tech region popularly known as Silicon Valley.

The visitor enters the multiacre Stanford complex by way of a winding road that soon brings him to the administration building —a three-story, sand-colored structure graced with a large fountain near the entrance. The towering trees and huge hanging plants near the entrance provide a welcome relief from the harsh geometric design that makes up the building's facade.

Impressive as the exterior is, it pales to insignificance against the activity inside the complex. In fact, it's hard to name another medical institution in the country with a broader, more colorful history of health research than Stanford. (Harvard comes close, and Columbia in New York.) During any given year, major programs are being conducted in every conceivable area of medicine: cancer, infectious diseases, immunology, coronary disease, genetic defects, nervous system injuries and disorders, diabetes, molecular biology. And of the university's ten Nobel Prize winners since 1901, two still labor on the Medical Center's research, clinical, or teaching staffs.

If medicine were a god, Stanford would be its western Mecca.

Jack arrived at Stanford early one afternoon in September 1981. He felt instantly at ease at the center, and even more so with Levy and Miller. He said later that it was like working with a team, not just two physicians—a team that was still cautiously basking in the afterglow of their recent success with Phil Karr, the man who remained free of his lymphoma more than a year after his anti-idiotype treatment with Stanford's monoclonals.

Richard Miller was thirty years old at the time of Jack's visit. He had interned at Stanford in 1975, then decided to specialize in oncology. Four years later, his postdoctoral work brought him into the laboratory of the bearded, balding Ronald Levy.

Unlike some other cancer researchers, the forty-year-old Levy had completely divorced himself from the rising tide of business concerns that now attended his work in monoclonal antibodies. He was, in fact, repelled by the public relations hyperbole being churned out by so many companies (often in an effort to hike their stock values) while issuing what Levy regarded as premature, and often cruelly false, hopes of a new "cancer cure." Levy decided that while he could not control corporate public relations, he could refuse to contribute to it. He soon adopted an almost fanatical avoidance of the media.

The first thing that Levy did was to give Christie a complete physical examination and review the medical reports and lymphangiograms that Jack had brought with him. He didn't want a hopelessly ill patient, but one who stood at least a fair chance of responding to the anti-id treatment. To use the therapy on a patient who was clearly beyond help would at the very least be needlessly insensitive by raising unwarranted hopes for a remission.

The most important part of the exam was the determination of how much paraprotein was circulating in Christie's bloodstream. Levy and Miller both knew very well one of the operating principles of the anti-id therapy: that high levels of this cellular flotsam could make the antibody useless by acting as decoys in the bloodstream. Each therapeutic antibody would be seized and tied up by a paraprotein molecule, leaving untouched the real targets—the lymphoma cells that were generating the paraprotein. Christie's chances of being accepted into Levy's program, therefore, were indirectly proportional to the paraprotein count.

There are several methods for counting the various molecules that are carried in our bloodstreams; which one is used depends largely on the degree of accuracy that is required. If an extremely precise number is needed, the analyst may choose to chemically react the proteins with isotopes such as iodine-131, then tally the number of radioactive molecules in an instrument called a gamma counter. If a less precise figure is needed, the method called electrophoresis can often be used. It was this technique—called serum protein electrophoresis, or SPEP (pronounced "ess-

pep")—that Levy used to measure Christie's circulating paraprotein.

Ess-pep is based on the fact that protein molecules (and many
other particles within the body) are electrically charged; the
strength of the charge varies from one molecule to another, but
each has a distinctive electrical character. To run the analysis, a
blood or serum sample is prepared with a combination of chemicals, then placed on a special surface between two electrodes.
When the current is switched on, the protein particles actually
begin to migrate slowly toward one electrode or the other, depending on their respective charges. When the migration is complete, a distinctive pattern is formed across the surface, from
which the analyst can readily separate one protein from another.
More important, the pattern can be translated into a series of
curves, one for each protein being measured. The higher the
curve, the more protein in the sample.

Most such curves resemble so many low hills off in the distance.

The portrait of Jack Christie's paraprotein looked more like the
Matterhorn. Rich Miller later said that he'd never seen anything
like it.

Jack's official paraprotein count was entered on his report at
1900 micrograms per milliliter of serum. (By contrast, Phil Karr's
paraprotein two years before had been less than 5 micrograms.)
Christie's malignant cells were throwing off idiotype at a phenomenal rate.

Both men knew instantly what the number meant: There was
no chance of treating Christie with the antibodies. The circulating idiotype would snatch the injected proteins out of the bloodstream long before they could ever reach the parent cells. The
next day, Miller apologized to the dejected Christie and sent him
back to Texas.

That night, Jack got disgustingly drunk for the first time since
he'd graduated from medical school.

The following day, a somewhat under-the-weather Jack Christie was on the phone again, this time with Foon: Having read the
Karr case several times and studied the work being conducted
elsewhere, he was convinced that his type of cancer made him the
perfect candidate for the Frederick anti-id program when it got

underway. "Set aside Levy's results for a moment," he pleaded into the phone. "I know we can make this work, Ken, I know it will work. . . ."

If Foon knew then what he knows now, he said later, he might well have hesitated—and for the same reason that Levy and Miller had refused Christie as a patient. There was no way in heaven that the antibodies could penetrate such a massive network of circulating paraprotein; sooner could a rifleman at the forest's edge hit a tree that stands a thousand yards inside the woods.

The simple fact is that neither Foon nor his associate, Dr. Paul Abrams, fully appreciated the significance of the paraprotein at the time. The anti-id therapy was an intriguing concept, but still little *more* than a concept; only Levy and Miller had used it to score a true kill on a cancer cell (and then in just one of several patients). Still inexperienced with the anti-id therapy, Foon saw no good medical reason why he couldn't duplicate that one success. Near the end of 1981, Foon enrolled Christie in the Frederick program, thus bringing the number of anti-id patients to three.

"But I think there were two other reasons for Ken's decision," said a Stanford physician who had watched the process from the sidelines. "One was the growing personal friendship between the two men, and that would be a powerful argument for anyone. But second, Jack Christie is a very persuasive man—when he wants something, he'll do whatever he has to do to get it. And Jack wanted desperately to live . . ."

Question: Are we winning the war against cancer?
Answers: Yes. No.
It depends on who you ask.
In 1981 NCI published a slick and colorful magazine called *Decade of Discovery*. At first glance, the booklet is an informative report on the institute's progress in understanding and treating cancer. There are inspirational articles on breast cancer and childhood malignancies, helpful stories on chemical carcinogenesis and drug therapy. Most readers will close the cover with confidence that yes, we have cancer on the run. The Beast is yielding to the assault.

In fact, the NCI publication was little more than yet another impressive public relations effort by a federal agency that finds itself increasingly under the public gun.

The question of whether or not we're winning the cancer battle is a point of contention among educated and totally guileless men. Roughly half of them argue, convincingly, that there are thousands of cancer survivors who would have been dead had their tumors been diagnosed ten or fifteen years earlier. Victims of breast cancer, Hodgkin's disease, lymphoma and leukemia, intestinal tumors. These men and women are alive today, the argument goes, not only because of better treatments, but because their diseases are being diagnosed earlier than they could have been two decades ago.

Therein lies one of the problems surrounding the statistics of cancer. It is easy—valid, even—to claim that even if cancer patients cannot be cured, they are surviving longer than ever before. At first that sounds encouraging enough, until we spot the fallacy: If a tumor is found in its very early stages and treatment is initiated, it's logical that the patient is surviving longer; it's simply a matter of starting the clock earlier. A more pertinent question is whether or not that patient stands a better chance of living a normal life than he once would have. Put that way, the answer—with a few notable exceptions—appears to be no. For the victim of lung cancer, liver cancer, bone cancer, prostate cancer, and several other malignancies, the outlook in 1986 isn't much more encouraging than it was in 1966.

Yet ten years after the National Cancer Act of 1971, the NCI was receiving a billion dollars a year from the government, almost five times the funding provided during the Nixon Administration. Now, like a startled diner after a disappointing meal, the nation was studying the bill and asking questions: "What are we getting for our money?" "How close are we to a cure for cancer?" "Where are the new drugs we were promised?" "What is cancer, anyway?"

Unfair questions, one might argue. During the early 1970s, Americans had been warned by a special government study panel that if cancer ever yielded all its secrets, it would be only in small bits and pieces. A few years later, that warning was echoed by Sir Peter Medawar, one of the patriarchs of twentieth-century immunology, in his book, *The Life Science:* "The cure for cancer is never going to be found. It is far more likely that each tumor in each patient is going to present a unique research problem for which laboratory workers and clinicians between them will have to work out a unique solution."

Until that point is reached, most oncologists are content to simply strike a sort of truce with cancer—an agreement in which the cancer neither kills nor is itself completely killed. There's plenty of precedent for such a goal: Diabetes is never cured, but it can often be controlled for long periods of time. The same can be said for epilepsy, severe arthritis, allergies, even alcoholism and other forms of drug dependency.

There's a man near Nashville—in the town of Franklin, to be precise—named Dr. Robert K. Oldham, who has thought a great deal about cancer during the past two decades or so. He's so caught up in the subject, in fact, that he normally puts in sixteen or eighteen hours a day, six days a week, grappling with it and trying to unravel some of its mysteries. He was two days shy of his forty-fourth birthday when we first met; at various times during eighteen of those years, he had served as the chief of oncology at Vanderbilt University, had sown the seeds of revolution in cancer treatment, had made a goodly number of enemies at the National Cancer Institute ("and a lot of friends," he insists), and had written eight books and more than 250 technical articles about the nature and treatment of cancer.

With that kind of work schedule, one is tempted to ask him how he and his wife got together long enough to arrange for the conceptions of their five sons. ("Two of 'em were twins," one of his colleagues explained, "so that saved them a little time.")

From some angles, his thin face and droopy eyelids make Oldham look at least five years older than he is, except when he smiles, which he does often. His blondish hair is still almost untouched by gray, and he slouches his slim frame deep into his chair as he talks.

"The usual question everyone asks is 'If we can put a man on the moon, why can't we cure cancer?' " he said in his soft, rumbly drawl. "The answer is that the moon shots utilized good, existing technology. In cancer research, the technology has been much less clearly defined, at least until recently. It's only been during the past couple of years that we've started to get a good handle on cancer; now I think we're about to see some real progress."

Even Oldham admits that no one really knows whether cancer cure rates are rising, falling, or holding steady. He's written on more than one occasion that the overall cure rates remained basically unchanged between 1980 and 1985. But he doesn't dispute the possibility, posed by another medical writer, that while some cancers are clearly yielding to new treatments, the overall rate of occurrence is as much as 10 percent higher than during the late 1970s. Specifically, the nation can expect to see about 910,000 new cases of cancer during 1985, up from 870,000 in 1984. One common explanation is that more of us are living long enough for slow-acting carcinogens to finally become activated; others maintain that the real problem is that certain types of intractable cancers—especially of the lung, the liver, the pancreas—are striking down new victims faster than we can respond. Regardless of which factor is most prevalent, the statistics boil down to an unhappy conclusion: Unless cancer cure rates climb more than 10 percent, malignant tumors could surpass heart disease as the number one killer of Americans by the end of the century.

It was against this background that NCI tapped Oldham in late 1980 to design its BRMP program in Frederick, Maryland. In the beginning, it was a reluctant decision for the agency. Biologicals were unproven alternatives to the conventional chemotherapies that dominated cancer treatment. True, chemotherapy often ravaged the patient's digestive system to such an extent that many cancer victims seriously considered dropping out of the therapy and taking their chances with gentler, albeit less effective, treatments. But dammit, chemotherapy worked. The drugs called methotrexate, vincristine, adriamycin, and cisplatin killed cancer—that was the important thing.

But even the most dedicated proponent of chemotherapy had to admit that the biologicals idea was a fascinating one. And so the NCI program sputtered to life, fueled by a rising interest in the concepts of immunomodulation (the techniques by which a patient's immune system could be "tuned" to fight off a disease). It was one of the first organized examples of the intriguing concept of customized cancer treatment; that is, one patient's disease might be treated in a way somewhat different than some other patient, even though they both had the same disease.

There was almost certainly another motivation for the BRMP, said a medical researcher in Boston: "There's no doubt that the NCI had to get something going to justify that $20 billion it had spent since '71. Something highly visible, something that stood a good chance of working.

"The biologicals program was just the ticket, since all the patients who were to be enrolled were basically terminal patients. They might survive for two or four or ten years, but these people had nothing to lose by going to Frederick, and everything to gain."

Once Oldham had accepted the BRMP position, he and his wife decided that he would have to spend most of his time in Maryland, at least until the program was well underway. She and the boys would remain within the strong and comfortable social fabric they enjoyed in Franklin, about twenty miles south of Nashville; he would commute home every three weeks or so. Accordingly, Oldham arrived at Frederick driving a thirty-five-foot motor home, which he parked near his office. "I've always worked long hours," he explained, "and didn't want to spend a lot of time going back and forth to an apartment in town."

Like Ken Foon, Oldham is not your conventional doctor. He prefers "Bob" to "Dr. Oldham," and enjoys telling stories on himself, like the one about how he happened to be pumping gas at a local service station the night one of his patients drove in. He chuckles as he recalls the tale:

"Well, for several years I owned this station in Nashville that was run by my parents and sons. I thought it would be nice to hold on to it to give the folks a little extra financial security; also, it gave my boys the chance to make a few bucks two or three nights a week.

"One night I stopped in at the station to talk to my teenaged son for a few minutes. He's busy with two or three other cars, so when this Buick pulls in, I walk over and grab the nozzle and start filling. Suddenly, this woman sticks her head out the window, her eyes big as pumpkins—it's a woman I've been treating for a couple of months for breast cancer. She was pretty calm about the situation, but I know damn well that she's still trying to figure out why the chief of oncology at Vanderbilt had to spend his spare time pumping gas. . . ."

Why was the idea of biological response modifiers—"biologicals"—so slow in developing? The existence of these chemicals in the body has been known or at least suspected for more than twenty-five years, and many of them have been under intensive study for more than a decade.

There are at least two reasons why biologicals are just now moving to the forefront of cancer research, becoming what Oldham calls "the fourth modality" of cancer treatment (along with surgery, radiation, and chemical drugs). First, it has only been since the late 1970s that immunologists have learned enough about their science to detect these molecules and study their effects in living systems. Second, biologicals are present in the body in only the tiniest amounts; it has been estimated that all the interferon in the human body would barely fill the eye of a large needle. Until the advent of new genetic engineering processes since 1980, there simply was no way of obtaining enough of these materials to study in the laboratory.

Even with these advances, much is still unknown about biologicals—only that each of them acts in its own way to repel infection and devastation. Some of them apparently beef up the immune system so that it destroys cancer cells before they can establish a foothold; others block whatever process leads a normal cell down a cancerous path, perhaps even changing the form of an early cancer cell into that of a normal cell.

One group of biologicals are the so-called thymic factors—proteins made by the thymus gland to help the immune system's immature lymphoid cells grow and develop, an essential step before the cells can participate in the immune process. The hormones called thymosins, for example, somehow boost the activity of the T-cells made by the thymus gland. Some cancer patients, such as those with certain forms of lung cancer, are known to have T-cell defects; for them, the thymosins may one day play an important therapeutic role.

Other molecules are called retinoids, and include retinol or vitamin A, a natural chemical found in some foods and hundreds of the vitamin's artificial cousins. In some experiments, these chemicals seem to halt or reverse the growth of precancerous cells—and in some cases appear to block the conversion of a chemical into a carcinogen—and so fall into the general category of "carcinopreventive" agents.

Probably the most interesting of all the biologicals are the lymphokines (made by the lymphoid cells in the immune system) and cytokines—natural chemicals that are able to attack and destroy cancer cells in the body, apparently by binding to the cells and punching fatal holes in the membranes. The biological called tumor necrosis factor, or TNF, is an example of this latter class of molecules. TNF was the subject of intense research in the United States for a while—and still is at some sites—after it was discovered that it utterly destroys cancer cells in the laboratory. In the excitement that followed, some researchers even suggested that a mere 25 pounds of the biological could cure cancer worldwide. (It was later conceded, however, that malignant cells in vitro bear little resemblance to the same cells growing in the body. Spread out on the shallow flat petri dish, in fact, they are easily killed by ordinary steam. Coca-Cola would probably do the same thing.)

One of the best-known of the lymphokines, and the subject of one of the hottest controversies yet to surround the infant science of biotechnology, is the protein called interferon. Actually, the human genes code for at least three distinct forms of interferon, called alpha, beta, and gamma, and there are several varieties of each of these. The alpha variety is produced by certain white blood cells during viral attack; beta-interferon is produced by cells called fibroblasts, which make up the connective tissue of the muscles and ligaments. Gamma-interferon, meanwhile, is secreted during an immune response by white blood cells in the spleen and elsewhere.

Interferon's intriguing biological activities were discovered in 1957 in a laboratory near London by virologist Alick Isaacs and his young associate, the shy, soft-spoken Jean Lindenmann, who were trying to learn why human cells become infected by only one virus at a time. As part of their research, they injected influenza virus into chick embryo cells and saw that the cells soon released a substance into the surrounding fluid that protected healthy cells from infection. The men called the substance interferon, since it seemed to interfere with the virus's reproduction.

Even today, one is awed by both the potency of these biologicals and by the incredible complexity of the cells' defense system. Once the material is released by an infected cell, a few molecules drift through the intracellular fluid, quickly locating and binding to the receptor of a neighboring cell. At this point, the second cell is activated to release its own molecules of interferon, or some other chemical—a process called cascading.

Interferon apparently does not inactivate viruses directly, however; rather, it renders the invaded cells resistant to viral multiplication. And since the interference process occurred within hours (instead of days, as with antibody production), interferon appeared to be a first line of defense against viruses. It now seems that interferon also affects a cancer patient's immune reaction to invading cancer cells, as well as working directly against existing tumors. No one is yet sure how interferon works against cancer— or why, apparently, it sometimes doesn't. One explanation is that it directly exerts some kind of growth-inhibiting effect on malignant cells; another is that the interferon molecules activate certain other cells to resist or retard the rates at which their cancerous neighbors divide. It might even alter the cancer cell's chemistry so that it becomes more vulnerable to attack by other components of the immune system.

Most researchers suspect that the interferons function in at least one of three ways: by preventing the virus from producing the nucleic acids needed for replication, by chemically breaking down the nucleic acids that the virus does manage to form, or by inhibiting the virus's formation of essential proteins. There is also evidence that two types of interferons acting together have a potent multiplier effect—this is probably how they work together in the body, in fact. In 1984 researchers at the University of Texas showed that alpha- and gamma-interferon added together are more than ten times more effective against viral infection than alpha-interferon alone.

Thanks largely to the media (and to the public's relentless thirst for a single cure for cancer), interferon was catapulted to "wonder drug" status during the late 1970s. In the closing weeks of 1985, another biological—the lymphokine called interleukin-2, or IL-2—stirred the same kind of public response. The excitement arose from a report by NCI's chief of surgery, Steven A. Rosenberg, describing how he had obtained tumor remissions in fifteen of thirty cancer patients who no longer responded to conventional therapy. (By comparison, most researchers allow themselves to get excited if only 10 or 15 percent of patients respond to a new treatment.)

Rosenberg's procedure, which seemed to back up the findings of a group of Italian physicians the year before, went like this: He withdrew about 10 percent of the patients' white blood cells and mixed them with IL-2. He then injected the treated cells back into the patients, along with large additional doses of the lymphokine. Nine months after the treatment, two of the patients remained entirely free of cancer; in thirteen other recipients, the tumors shrank by more than half and remained that way for at least a month.

No one claims to know precisely how IL-2 destroys cancerous cells, though some immunologists speculate that it somehow activates the body's natural killer cells to fight the tumor. And while the therapy is not without side effects—including fever, chills, and fluid retention—they disappear shortly after treatment and are in any event less severe than those of chemotherapy.

Is IL-2 the "wonder drug" of the 1980s? Understandably, Rosenberg and his colleagues are cautious about the results. They emphasize the small number of patients in the study, and the fact that fifteen other patients showed little or no response to the treatment. Furthermore, it may be several years before anyone knows whether the effects are permanent.

Interesting possibilities, say researchers, but none of this means that these chemicals can be injected at random into cancer patients. There remains a huge gap in our knowledge of the interferons, a gap which will require years of animal testing, followed by several more years of human tests, to close. (Which explains why the government now classifies interferon, TNF, and most other biologicals as "experimental drugs." Neither you nor your physician can obtain them; they are available only to qualified researchers in tightly controlled experimental settings.)

Jack Christie adjusted his pillow, kicked off his shoes, and tried to forget that he was six miles above the ground.

He had always disliked flying. Sitting in one place even for a half hour or so was difficult for him. His legs cramped. His neck, shoulders, and buttocks hurt. The processed air in the cabin was too dry. The seats were uncomfortable. These four-hour cross-country flights were almost unbearable, even in the first-class section that on this trip had cost him two hundred of his own dollars.

When air travel was unavoidable, he packed along as many papers and journals as he could stuff into his shoulder bag, reasoning that the flight would be a good chance to catch up on his reading. On this flight, the papers remained under the seat in front of him. He was distracted by the smallest bumps and jolts and by the occasional changes in pitch from the engines. Even worse, he found himself seated next to an elderly woman who had to use the restroom every fifteen minutes, forcing Jack to scoop up his papers and step into the aisle.

He didn't even try to read on this flight. Just put his head back and relax, maybe page through a couple of magazines. Think, mostly. He'd been terribly tired for the past few weeks, and had made up his mind that he would try to sleep through most of the flight. The weird, disturbing dreams arrived as soon as he dozed off, infiltrated with the sounds of the plane cabin. One dream had him on the ferry that runs between Fisherman's Wharf in San Francisco and Alcatraz Island. The drone of the DC-10's engines became the soft roar of the ferry's diesels; the conversation across the aisle became the questions posed to him by an elderly couple on the ferry. The old man was wearing a top hat and a large bow tie, and repeatedly asked him, "But why are you going to Alcatraz, young man?"

He didn't know what to tell the old man. Why was he asking all these questions, anyway? As he groped for an answer, the ferry tour guide announced that they were passing over Charlotte, North Carolina.

Christie shook himself awake.

". . . and we don't expect any delays between here and Washington. Should have you folks at the gate at National Airport just about on schedule." Jack caught the attention of a flight attendant and asked for a cup of coffee.

It would be good to see Ken Foon again, he thought. He had always liked Ken personally, and had admired the man's energy and witty intelligence. He wouldn't mind at all if they were able to establish a personal relationship. Most important, though, was the fact that Foon seemed to be on his way to becoming one of the most knowledgeable men in the country about Christie's type of cancer and its treatment. If Foon couldn't help him, and Levy and Miller wouldn't help him, then what? Sloan-Kettering Center in New York? Dana-Farber in Boston? Anderson in Houston? He would have to think about that. . . .

He thought too, as he had every day since April, about how his life had suddenly been revised. It wasn't as though he were in imminent danger of dying; he had every reason to think that even if he chose to take no treatment at all, he would probably be around for at least another three or four years, perhaps six or eight. Maybe his cancer was one of those which ebbed and flowed over the years, like a bursitis or a migraine. At any rate, there was no need to rush about and put his life in order; there would be no bitter realizations that he'd already enjoyed his last Christmas party or Thanksgiving dinner with the family. Not like the young man he had met the year before, the liver cancer patient who suddenly found himself with less than six months. Christie wondered if he could take something like that.

How and why did such things happen, he wondered. Was it just a roll of the cosmic dice, like he had often said? What had happened inside of him, among his cells, that had led to this? And yes, why him? Why Jack Christie? He had always lived a clean life; he had never smoked or drunk excessively and had usually observed a sensible diet. Until a few months ago, in fact, he had considered himself healthier than most men his age. He remembered reading stories in the paper about how the ten millionth customer at a department store was suddenly showered with gift certificates. The customer had nothing to do with it. It had to happen to somebody, and that somebody was Joe So-and-So, a fifty-year-old appliance salesman from Bellaire.

Looked at in that way, why not Jack Christie? If the salesman from Bellaire can stumble into the store at the right time, why couldn't Christie stumble onto the tables of cancer statistics?

For more than thirty years he had had almost everything fall into place for him, and not because he had planned it that way. Why had he been born into an intelligent and hardworking family? Why had he been able to acquire significant personal wealth, and a medical education, and a loving Eileen, when all around him he saw men and women and children who would never taste any of it? There had never been any promises that it would last forever, not even the threescore and ten years that most of us are granted. The whole thing was nothing more than a crazy crap game, that's all, and if you can't accept that, brother, then you might as well dig in for hard times ahead. . . .

He remembered the day, several years before, when he was driving through a slum on the outskirts of Boston. That's where you saw how most of the world lives. Run-down shanties, children playing in the littered gutters, or just sitting on the front stair staring vacantly at the trash piled along the curb. Once he had seen a man fall over on the sidewalk in front of a small corner tavern—just topple over, like a felled tree, as he tipped his brown paper bag to his mouth. Sitting at the stop light, Jack had heard the man's head hit the sidewalk with a startling *crack!*, and had seen the blood spread like a bucket of spilled paint across the concrete and into the weedy lawn. For a moment, Jack thought about jumping out of his car to help the man. There were other cars behind him, though. And he was running late. And there were plenty of people on the street who would call for an ambulance. . . .

Someone had told him once that the problem with being well-off is that you're never well-off enough; there's always more. For people like the guy sprawled on the sidewalk, maybe death was a handy way out. Intellectually, Jack knew that even if he had only another year or two, he could hardly complain. Emotionally? Yes, he wanted more. Another chance. Another chance to . . . To do what? Make more money? Chase more women?

He'd never had reason to think about such questions before, and now he was confused. Just what was it that he was trying to accomplish with his life? Was he trying to accomplish anything at all, or just drifting through? Almost everyone he knew was committed to something; for his father, it was his career and the family's security. For his mother, it was the home and its comforts for her husband and children. Most of his colleagues had committed themselves to their professions, to the health of their patients. What was Jack committed to?

Deep down, he was often nagged by the knowledge that he had never made any such commitments. Medicine? For all practical purposes, he had given that up. His bankroll? The money itself had never meant all that much to him; it was the making of it that was fun—the primal excitement of rolling a few dollars into an intriguing business opportunity, then watching it grow. He didn't really even know how much he was worth, and didn't care. And besides, what kind of commitment is that? He had long ago ruled out a commitment to religious principles, so that took care of that. His fellowman? Too vague. Besides, he often quoted the "Peanuts" comic strip that had Charlie Brown saying, "I love mankind; it's *people* I can't stand!"

Eileen. Now there's someone who gets into life. At first, he thought that her grating enthusiasm was just part of being nineteen, that she would get over it. It soon became apparent that her zest for living was as much a part of her as the mole on her shoulder. He remembered her excitement when she first arrived in the States—the rush to learn everything at once, to see it all, to experience all the new traditions and lifestyles, first in Boston and later in Texas. "Don't act like such a tourist!" he told her once. Yet he envied that boundless curiosity, the need to drink it all in before it's gone forever.

Peering out the window, he could see that the plane was nearing Washington. It was snowing. He suddenly felt more lonely than he'd ever felt in his life.

Frederick, Maryland, is an attractive, mostly residential town of about twenty thousand, plunked off to the side of Interstate 270 some forty-five miles northwest of Washington, D.C. Nearby is Fort Detrick, which once served as a major biological warfare research center for the government. It was fairly natural that Fort Detrick would thus become the forerunner of the National Cancer Institute's Frederick Cancer Research Center ("the Facility," as it's known at NCI).

An important part of the Facility is housed in the Medical Pavilion—an unstylish three-story red brick building that once served as a nurses' dorm—adjacent to Frederick Memorial Hospital near the center of town. One of my guides for the tour of the Facility is Pamela Holmes, R.N. Like a few other BRMP nurses, she's salaried by Frederick Hospital but works for NCI a few days a week under a special contract between the two institutions.

There should be a rule somewhere requiring all nurses to look and behave like Pam Holmes. She was probably in her late twenties and seven months pregnant at the time of my visit, so her pleasant features were probably slightly more rounded than usual. She speaks with the slight southern accent so characteristic of this part-Yankee, part-Dixie region. Her full face, framed in thick brown hair, is dotted with leftover freckles, and she is blessed with an engaging, almost giggly personality. As we tour the hospital next door, one of the center's outpatients—a man of about sixty in a plaid flannel shirt and gabardine slacks—catches up to her to show off his new silhouette.

"That's fantastic, John! How much weight have you lost?"

"Twenty-five, thirty pounds. How do I look?"

"Just great, John, just great. You were getting pretty chubby there for a while, y'know. Keep up the good work."

It isn't easy for a cancer patient to be admitted to the BRMP, she explained later. The patient usually must be referred to the Facility by his or her own physician. (Most oncologists, in turn, learn of the program through the media, NCI publications, or, less often, the American Cancer Society's "information hotline.") The patient must also be fairly healthy (his malignancy notwithstanding), meaning that he must be at least 60 percent functional —that is, stand a pretty good chance of responding to the therapy —and have no other treatments available to him; in other words, the patient will otherwise sooner or later almost certainly die of his disease. "Yet, they're not desperately sick in the usual sense of the word," Foon told me. "If we take people who are really bad off into the program, it's basically a humanitarian gesture."

Patients who do gain admittance to the NCI program find that Frederick is a very special kind of place, said Holmes: "They spend a lot of time together while they're here. One reason is that many of them thought they were the only ones with their disease;

that's a common reaction among cancer patients. Once they find that there are others going through this, they seek each other out —they have lunch together, they talk about their disease, and exchange information about their therapies." Meanwhile, closer-than-usual relationships often develop between the patients and the nurses. Many of the stricken now understand (often for the first time) why certain tests are performed and what the results mean.

Once a patient is accepted into the Frederick BRMP, he or she is first admitted as an inpatient in the four-bed ward held aside on the second floor of Frederick Memorial Hospital. There they undergo a complete physical and chemical examination by the NCI staff to determine precisely their type of cancer, its stage, its cell characteristics, and the overall suitability of the patient for one of the Frederick programs. On later visits, which usually last less than a day, the patients receive therapy in the Pavilion's outpatient ward and learn how to administer their own medication. They are examined again to determine their progress, then sent home to Texas or California.

Ordinarily, it would be an expensive process. In these cases, the patient's insurance company is billed by the NCI, which might also arrange to pick up whatever the carrier doesn't cover. "The only thing I ever paid for was the headset on the plane," said Christie.

Frederick is the last resort for many cancer patients, Holmes told me. "But those who take the trouble to seek out this treatment are usually the survivor types," she added. The BRMP is an experimental program; it uses treatments never before administered on a large scale, the results of which are still largely unknown. At the time of my visit, there were several subprograms under way; in one, about seventy cancer victims were receiving interferon supplied on an investigational basis by two large companies, Hoffmann-La Roche and Schering-Plough.

Within twenty-four hours of his arrival at Frederick, Christie learned the ground rules of the program: He would have to spend a day or two in Maryland roughly every six weeks. Once his condition stabilized—that is, once the circulating paraprotein was brought under control—the Frederick team would prepare the anti-id in their Fort Detrick laboratory. And like the other patients, he would be examined by Foon and the other physicians for signs of metastases, as well as for his general physical condition.

Most blood-cancer patients, including Jack Christie, agree that the worst part of the examination is the bone marrow aspirate. The test is absolutely essential, however, to determine whether the blood-forming marrow is harboring cancer cells. The answer usually suggests not only the most appropriate therapy, but will also later determine how efficiently it is doing its job.

The marrow is withdrawn by quickly plunging a short, stout needle into the bone. The pelvis is the most common site, just above the buttock, where the broad, flat section of bone provides an easy target for a fast, nonglancing puncture. Within a few seconds, the marksman withdraws a few milliliters of the gritty-looking marrow into the barrel of the syringe, then quickly removes the needle. Later, a few drops of the marrow are placed on a microscope slide to be explored for malignant cells. "Oh, it can hurt like hell," said one physician. "Fortunately, the pain is very brief. A lot of patients compare it to the pain of an electrical shock, or when the dentist hits a nerve."

A close personal friendship developed between Foon and Christie almost from the beginning. Jack often brought Eileen with him on the flights to Washington, usually checking her into the Sheraton on I-270 while he spent the day in Frederick. They would usually linger in the area for a few days, staying with Foon and his wife, Rebecca Garrett—also a physician, with a private practice in Hagerstown—and their two young girls at Foon's hundred-year-old farmhouse in Frederick.

Ken had changed since Jack met him in California. The most obvious change was that he was thinner than Jack remembered. In fact, Ken had become something of a "health nut." If he ate lunch at all, it was a piece of fresh fruit; more often, he ate nothing during the day. He arose early every morning to work out with his weights, and had adopted a stringent dietary plan that prohibited fats of any kind. He kept two refrigerators in his home, one of them just to hold a steady supply of grapefruit, oranges, and other fruits. His wife and children opted not to join his regimen, however, choosing instead a more conventional low-calorie reduced-fat diet.

Christie was grateful that Foon never donned the mantle of the obnoxious crusader. Still, he now and then expressed a silent displeasure over Jack's eating habits—the horrified grimace as Christie spread a paper-thin layer of margarine across a slice of bread at lunch one day, for instance, and the casual but pointed comment that his, Foon's, cholesterol level was only about 90. Most cardiologists are content to measure serum cholesterol at around 175, and Christie himself had been delighted to learn earlier that month that his own cholesterol was just around 180. Strolling across the small patch of lawn that separates the Cancer Center from Frederick Hospital, Foon glanced at the visible softness around Jack's midsection. "I used to be heavier than this, too," Foon said, pitching his apple core into a dumpster, "but I was always sorta uncomfortable. Always thought there had to be a better way. . . ."

Dr. Paul Abrams absently stroked his heavy black beard as he strode to the front of the conference room. Reaching the easel, he turned to the small group of men seated around the long table.

Like hundreds of other oncologists, Abrams had been fascinated with the anti-idiotype work being reported by Levy and Miller at Stanford. As a key member of the Frederick NCI team, he was convinced that the technique could be used successfully with some of his and Foon's patients. By late 1982, however, the men had run into a serious technical problem; if what Abrams had heard about Encapcel was true, the answer could be in this room.

"What we hope to do in the anti-id program, basically, is this," he began, turning to the chart and picking up the felt marker. "Once a patient is selected, we'll withdraw a small amount of blood, or biopsy one of the lymph nodes. One of the components, of course, is the malignant B-cell that bears this unique immunoglobulin molecule." Here he drew a large circle and added several scribblings on the circumference to represent the paraprotein marker. "We want then to use those cells to create a hybridoma that secretes this antibody. We then use the purified antibody to immunize mice, which react by making the anti-ids . . ."

It took Abrams less than ten minutes to explain the concepts of the NCI anti-id program to Jarvis, Vasington, and the other men in the room. Most of them jotted down notes and questions as he talked.

"Now here's the problem we've been running into," Abrams continued. "We've had only partial success in growing these particular human hybridomas. It seems that they grow to a certain density, begin secreting the antibody, then stop. We're having trouble getting even the milligram of purified idiotype antibody we need to immunize the mice to generate the anti-ids."

"What are you using to grow the hybridomas, Paul?" asked Vasington. Abrams explained that he was growing the cells in fetal calf serum, a standard nutrient-rich medium used by many researchers for growing various types of cells.

"My idea," he continued, "is to use Damon's capsules in a different way than you've been using them. Let's say we encapsulate the hybridomas to improve the yield after purification. Or maybe adjust the capsule pore size so the antibodies can leak out slowly. Then we inject the capsules into the mouse; I think that this leakage will provide a steady stream of immunogens. Either way, we can use the capsules to solve our initial hybridoma problems. And those problems are now our major technical obstacle."

"So in other words, Paul, all you need is that milligram or so of idiotype antibody?" asked Jarvis. "But at some point you're still going to have to grow the mouse hybridomas that produce the anti-idiotype antibody, correct? And you're going to grow these in ascites?"

Abrams nodded.

"How much of the anti-id do you think you're going to need per patient?" asked Jarvis. Abrams thought that about eight or ten grams would be required. Jarvis did a quick bit of arithmetic on his yellow pad.

"That means about four hundred mice per patient, assuming you get fifteen milligrams per milliliter of ascites. I could see that wouldn't be too difficult for a couple of patients, but don't I understand that you want to have twenty, twenty-five patients?

That's more than eight thousand mice, right? And that's if each mouse is an average producer."

Abrams nodded again, and saw the next question coming:

"The way I understand it," said one of the other men, "is that antibodies grown in mouse ascites are going to be contaminated. I mean, the animal contributes his own immunoglobulin to the antibodies, is that right? So that some small fraction of the antibody you finally collect . . ."

"Will be just mouse antibody, not anti-id, you're right," Abrams finished.

Precious little data had been gathered about how the human immune system might react to large doses of mouse antibody. It was almost beside the point, however; for now, there was no realistic alternative way to make the things. One reason is that human hybridomas are for some reason notoriously hard to grow, in any kind of culture; even Jarvis had been disappointed with the antibody output when he and Terri Grdina had encapsulated some experimental hybrids made from a culture of human cells obtained from a Boston hospital. A second reason was based in simple ethics: Almost by definition, hybridomas must be created by first immunizing an animal against a specific antigen, then capturing the B-cells from the spleen. Even if it were possible to collect large numbers of human B-cells easily, it was unthinkable to consider immunizing a human being with a cancer cell or a bacterium or any other kind of potentially harmful antigen.

And so like everyone else, NCI was hooked into mouse antibodies, reaction or no reaction. "But when you consider the alternative for these patients, a possible severe reaction—and we don't know that there will be such a reaction—is by far the lesser of two risks," Abrams told the men around the table.

Jarvis did have a solution for Abrams' problem with antibody output, however. He opened his folder and extracted an inch-thick sheaf of lab reports and time-versus-density graphs.

"You can take copies of these with you, Paul, but let me just say that we can do a lot better in this respect." Abrams had heard about the encapsulation process; in fact, it was the reason he'd called Vasington the month before. Jarvis continued.

"You take any usual cell culture method, and you can get your mouse hybridomas to grow pretty well—probably ten to the sixth per mil." (Here he used the common lab jargon for "a million—ten to the sixth power—cells per milliliter of ascites fluid.") "And that will yield perhaps twenty micrograms of antibody per mil. Not bad.

"What we've found is that you can take that same cell line, put it into our capsules, and grow them to a density of ten to the eighth—a hundred times higher—for an antibody output of up to a milligram per mil. And we've done it enough times to think that we can do it every time, with just about any hybrid line."

As the meeting ended an hour later, Jarvis put a question to Abrams: Why not have Damon Biotech make *all* the anti-idiotype antibody, rather than just the trace amounts of human idiotype needed for immunizing the mice? That is, have NCI send Damon the patients' hybridomas—each made up of the mouse B-cell and the plasmacytoma—and the anti-ids as well. Then Damon would simply encapsulate the hybrids, let them grow for a few weeks, and send the purified antibodies back to Frederick. To Abrams, Jarvis was thus offering much more than the oncologist had hoped for; it would answer problems both of development and scaleup.

Abrams promised to discuss the idea with Oldham and Foon as soon as he returned to Frederick.

On Jack's first visit to Frederick in January 1982, Ken Foon offered him the best news he'd heard in nine months: The chemotherapy had dramatically reduced the paraprotein levels since summer, from 1900 to about 500. Presumably, that meant that the number of cancerous B-cells had also been cut by almost 75 percent, a prospect that made the drug-associated nausea and partial baldness seem relatively minor. (He had been only faintly amused when Eileen brought him a Harpo Marx wig from a downtown gag shop.) With the paraprotein level stabilized, Foon and Abrams decided to end the COP treatment and switch to alpha-interferon until the paraprotein dropped to below the 200 mark; at that point, Ken explained, they could begin to consider the anti-id protocol.

"When you get back home, you're going to be taking three interferon injections a week," Foon told him. Skittish as always about piercing himself, Christie would have Eileen perform the injections.

There are several problems associated with even the most exciting new or experimental therapies. One of them is to determine the most effective dosage, what some researchers call the "therapeutic window"—enough to wage fair battle against the target cells, but not enough to provoke unacceptable side effects or counterreactions by healthy cells. Fortunately, most common drugs (aspirin, for example) have relatively wide windows; in the case of interferon, there was little previous human experience for Foon and Abrams to draw on. The men decided to start Christie at the high end of what was considered to be an accepted dosage scale and watch him carefully for reactions.

For Christie, the worst part of that decision was the needle that Eileen would have to use—a stout, wicked-looking device with a business end almost four inches in length. Because of the large doses, said Foon, he wanted the interferon to be injected deep into the large muscle beneath the buttocks; there, the rich supply of veins and tiny capillaries would transport it rapidly into the bloodstream where it was needed.

(Patients receiving interferon today are more fortunate, Foon said later: "Intramuscular injection made sense at the time because of the big doses some researchers were using. Most of us are using smaller doses now, and it doesn't seem to matter much how you give it." As a result, most patients now take the injection under the skin, using a smaller and more comfortable needle.)

Even after twelve weeks on interferon, though, the paraprotein was stubbornly hanging at around the 250 level.

"What now?" asked Christie.

"Ever seen a plasmapheresis?"

Basically, plasmapheresis is a fairly simple way of cleaning the blood by removing certain unwanted proteins from the bloodstream (or more specifically, from the yellowish plasma in which the solid blood components are suspended). In that sense, it's similar to hemodialysis, in which a kidney patient's blood is routed outside his body through a series of filters to remove potentially fatal wastes, then returned to the patient. Christie's plasmapheresis was designed to remove not waste products, but the paraprotein that was still holding up the anti-id therapy.

This was done on a balmy day in April 1982 in a smallish room on the second floor of the Frederick center. There Jack Christie was bedded down next to a machine about the size of a large office typewriter. A needle was inserted into his arm, permitting the blood to flow through a plastic tube into the machine. Inside, it was routed into several large glass tubes arranged in a centrifuge. As the centrifuge spun the tubes, the relatively heavy solid blood components—red and white cells, platelets, various proteins—were packed against the bottoms of the tubes, leaving the lightweight paraprotein in solution. After a few minutes, a pump inside the machine automatically withdrew the plasma from each tube, discarded it, then added a few ounces of plasma substitute (albumin and saline, usually) to the hard-packed pellet of cells which remained; another tube then returned this "new blood," minus the paraprotein, to Christie's other arm. At any given time, only about 15 percent of his blood was outside his body; the entire process took about two and a half hours.

The procedure immediately cut the paraprotein in half, to less than 100. Within a few weeks, the level was over 200 again.

"You're turning the stuff out like crazy, Jack," Foon said. "We're sucking it out alright, but the B-cells in the bone marrow keep manufacturing more. It's like when you wring out a sponge and put it on a paper towel, you can watch the water seeping out." Despite their disappointment, the men at least were provided with a quantitative measure of the cells' activity—"a picture of the enemy," as Foon put it.

Like many other patients on high dosages of interferon, Christie found that while the biological isn't quite as harsh on the system as the traditional chemotherapies, neither is it completely without unpleasant side effects. Besides the permanently sore buttocks, he found himself uncharacteristically lethargic after a couple of weeks and had to force himself to finish even the smallest task. Also, there would be little or no alcohol while taking the drug: The combination produced symptoms that resembled the flu, only worse—severe nausea, achy joints and muscles, and sometimes dangerously high temperatures. Reluctantly at first, he abandoned his nightly bottle of beer.

More alarming was the fact that large amounts of interferon somehow disrupt the central nervous system, starting with the brain and working outward to the peripheral system. He was haunted almost every night with bizarre dreams and nightmares, and distressed to find that his memory was slipping badly; he began to write himself notes—"Pick up cleaning"; "Stop at library"; "Need shaving cream"—which he posted all around the apartment. From time to time, he lost the sensation in his hands and had to give up tennis for a while. For the same reason, he took to watching himself in the mirror as he brushed his teeth, lest he scrub so hard that his gums started to bleed.

He was especially troubled by the decline of his sexual abilities, due partly to the interferon-induced lethargy and partly to the drug's effects on the nervous system. He was impotent for the first time in his life, and was unconsoled by Foon's assurances that the condition was almost certainly temporary.

One of interferon's strangest effects, however, was on the top of his head. His hair started coming back almost immediately after he was taken off the COP, but it didn't look the same. Christie was startled to see that at first it was coming in much curlier than it had ever been; a little later it turned almost straight, then curly again.

Nor was Christie the only cancer victim to experience the treatment's odd effects on hair growth. There was a story going around Frederick about another interferon patient whose eyelashes suddenly and inexplicably began to grow at incredible rates, curling up into his eyebrows or down across the iris so that he was forced to cut them once or twice a week. "It's like looking through a spiderweb," the poor man complained. "And I'm getting sick and tired of the nurses telling me how much they just *love* my eyelashes, and could I please get some interferon for them . . ."

Nigel Webb set several priorities of business for himself after arriving at Damon Biotech in late 1982. One of the very first was to find out what had come of Paul Abrams' visit to Needham Heights a few weeks before Webb's arrival. The answer was, nothing.

Abrams and Jarvis had talked informally about the anti-id program several times, and Jarvis was clearly excited about the prospect of supplying Frederick with anti-id antibodies. The problem was that NCI wasn't offering to *buy* the proteins—just *use* them, and reimburse Damon for its production costs. Hardly a profitable arrangement for a company in need of more paying customers.

Still, Webb and Jarvis were entranced with the idea. Profits or not, they told Kosowsky, the agreement could become a model application for the company's antibodies, not to mention the humanitarian element. It might also be possible for Damon to arrange a contract agreement with NCI, he continued, under which the company would retain commercial rights to any new technology developed in Needham Heights.

Webb's first contract proposal was sent to Bob Oldham a few days before Christmas 1982.

CHAPTER NINE

Every new industry, especially the ones that sally forth under the banner of high technology, boasts a contingent of what are popularly known as the young Turks. They're not necessarily Turkish, of course, and many of them are no longer young. In general, they are the men (and occasionally women) who have managed to combine two difficult careers into one that is practically impossible: Turn good science into good (that is, profitable) business. By most accounts, Nigel L. Webb was Damon Biotech's leading young Turk.

He found that there were certain advantages to being a newcomer to Needham. One was that while others in the company had made heavy emotional and intellectual investments in the past (with many of them becoming wedded to a single corporate project or strategy as a result), Webb carried no such baggage, and so could view the company with a fresh and unjaundiced eye. And what he saw both thrilled and unsettled him.

The thrill came from the fact that Damon Biotech had in its possession all the physical ingredients of a first-rate biotechnology company: an exciting and truly innovative new process for growing antibodies, some of the brightest men and women in the industry, and a massive financial commitment from the parent corporation. What unsettled him was that no one had yet managed to pull all these ingredients together. Like a finely fitted but rudderless vessel, Damon Biotech was adrift.

Not that Damon Biotech was the only company in such circumstances. By early 1983, there were only a handful of biotechnology firms that had been able to pull off the alchemy that turned sound scientific principles into an organized, self-sustaining enterprise. Most still hadn't yet grappled with the familiar temptation to splash about in basic research. For the young biologists and cell culture professionals in the glittering high-priced new laboratories, it was interesting. Sometimes it was great fun. Moreover, such dabblings promised heaping shares of personal and professional rewards further down the road. The problem was that it wasn't making money, and woe to the man at the helm when the stockholders finally decided that enough was enough.

And so Webb, Kosowsky, and dozens of other corporate officers and research directors sat up late at night asking themselves some knotty questions. Mostly, the queries came down to just two:

Where have we been?

Where in the world are we trying to go?

For the first several weeks of his command, Webb pondered the answers.

With just a few exceptions, no one doubted that Nigel Webb had been the perfect choice for Damon Biotech. His slender frame, topped with a stylishly unruly shock of blond hair, neatly complemented the company's new image of youth and vigor. Even the voice—a pleasing contrast to the harsh accents of New York and New England—hinted that something new was about to happen. True, he seemed too young to have had much experience in biotechnology; but it was after all a young business, and even its aging veterans were still little more than newcomers. If some folks at Damon remained uneasy about the way in which Paul Vasington had ostensibly been ushered into corporate obscurity, others would concede that perhaps the man really hadn't carried out his mission of directing the company into fertile new fields. If anyone could do that, it appeared that Webb was the man.

Once he had determined to make the leap from science to business, Webb had swept like a comet through the heavens of biotechnology. And he came well equipped: He had been a student in the first cell biology course ever offered at Cambridge, and had spent more than ten years refining both his technical and business skills, beginning with six years at Searle in Europe and in the United States. Shortly after arriving in the states, he had moved up quickly at Searle to become product manager of one of the company's major divisions, and then had spent two years at Sherwood Medical Industries. His next stint was for two years as director of marketing for Johnson & Johnson's Ortho division (during which the company became the first to sell monoclonal antibodies).

Now, only thirty-five years old, he was the president of what stood to become one of the hottest companies in the field. And while the responsibilities of the position were enormous, so were the rewards: more than a hundred thousand dollars a year (plus stocks and bonuses), plus a generous severance agreement to aid his departure if and when he left Damon.

He looked and acted like the president of a successful company, barreling his sporty silver-gray Mercedes between Needham Heights and fashionable Weston, where he lived with his Rhodesia-born wife and their three children. And even though his was often the last car out of the company parking lot at night, he determined that he would not become a prisoner of his work. He separated his business and private lives as often as possible by playing classical piano at home, or working at his cabinetmaking.

Whereas Kosowsky was widely regarded as the company's "idea person"—implying a certain discomfort in dealing with individuals—Webb was also an ideal "people person." Most of his colleagues were quickly taken with his seemingly unflappable nature and his droll, low-key British humor. An example of the latter was the day he introduced the company's new personnel director, Kathy Fay (once a teacher of autistic children) to a meeting of Biotech employees. "Kathy will fit right in with us," he grinned. "She's quite accustomed to dealing with troubled children."

As 1982 crystallized into the frigid January of '83, David Kosowsky and Nigel Webb agreed on one fact: Damon Biotech had to get moving, and quickly. It could no longer enjoy the luxury of moving at its own pace; there were too many other companies trying to bring monoclonal antibodies to market. Companies like Centocor, Celltech, Bio-Response, and especially the booming

Hybritech out in San Diego. An article in the April 1983 issue of *Bio/Technology* magazine lionized Hybritech as "a recognized leader in commercializing hybridoma technology," and called it "a model of rapid growth" for other biotechnology firms. Damon's competition was coming up fast, and in the meanwhile was capturing too many headlines in the trade press. By contrast, Damon Biotech had scored just two major accomplishments in the preceding two years: the Lim-Sun pancreatic islets paper in late 1980 (which had appeared to prove, for the first time, the technical viability of growing cells inside capsules) and the Hoffmann-La Roche program, which had demonstrated that the company could indeed do what many of its competitors couldn't—grow large quantities of pure monoclonals. There was the possibility of an NCI agreement, of course, but that was still under discussion. In fact, it wouldn't be formalized until late in the year.

And so one of Webb's top priorities after joining Damon Biotech was to write a detailed business plan for the company. Most small companies write such a plan, for two reasons: One is that writing the plan is itself a valuable exercise in self-discipline and helps the writers identify the company's goals, strengths, and weaknesses. The second reason is that the report can in some cases later be used as an effective fund-raising tool by distributing it to selected investment companies, government agencies, and others with a legitimate interest in the company's capabilities. With all its appendices, the Damon Biotech business plan, bound in a handsome metallic blue cover, came in at a hefty 116 pages.

The message between the lines was clear: The company had invented and proven the efficiency of an entirely new way of growing large quantities of living cells—a feat that few other companies had been able to match. As such, Damon Biotech had sole possession of one of the most important keys to biotechnology's commercial future. Not just in hybridomas, mind you, but eventually also in gene-splicing, drug-delivery systems, and medical diagnostics.

Moreover, Damon Biotech had something else not shared by most of its competitors: experience. In a sense, it had existed for six years as Damon Diagnostics, and had therefore acquired a wealth of priceless experience in financing, fund-raising, budgeting, strategy planning, recruitment and training programs—difficult, time-consuming, often costly chores and responsibilities that still had many of the younger companies running in circles.

Damon Biotech, suggested Webb, thus found itself on the very doorstep of greatness in the adolescent industry. The previous two or three years had merely been a period of basic training, during which time Kosowsky had allowed his team to forge its technology into a crack research and production unit. Now, for the first time, the company had a specific direction in which to move; the growing recognition of the hybridoma called for an organized and aggressive move into the national marketplace.

But there would be an important difference between Damon and its competitors: While the others were describing themselves as innovators in monoclonal antibody technology, Webb recognized that Damon's real talent lay not in designing hybridomas or antibodies against a specific antigen (although some of Damon's staff had long since acquired such skills), but in growing those that had been created elsewhere. In effect, Damon Biotech was to become a provider of contract services, not of proprietary products—at least not now; if and when the company later decided to expand into other, much riskier technologies (genetic engineering, for example), the contract work would furnish a financial "safety net."

The important thing now was to get Damon's name and unusual capabilities out among the prospective customers. By mid-1983, Damon Biotech had already become a familiar fixture at American and European biotechnology conferences, at which Damon researchers often delivered speeches on growing hybridomas in capsules while their colleagues from sales and marketing hawked the company from the costly and colorful booths in the exhibit areas.

Not everyone was comfortable with Webb's new emphasis on marketing, nor with his pursuit of the NCI work. "I didn't think we were ready to push our technology into the marketplace," one researcher told me later, after he'd left the company. "I could understand that Biotech was probably in a sticky position: We couldn't afford to sit still any longer. There were too many other companies who had already made their name, and Nigel knew how important it was for us that our name was running alongside theirs. Things move so quickly in this business—all of a sudden people are asking, 'Damon who?' "

Here the biologist paused for a minute, wanting to choose his words carefully.

"At the same time, we'd had a lot of trouble with the Hoffmann-La Roche anti-interferon contract. I mean, not many people know how much trouble we had, how close we'd come to wiping ourselves out on that one. It finally worked out alright, and Biotech can be damn proud of what we'd accomplished during that period. But the main reason we were successful was that some of us were there fourteen and eighteen hours a day, six days a week, baby-sitting the pots. Now here it was a year later with the NCI thing coming up, and some of us weren't sure we were able to handle it. We figured it would be Roche all over again, and maybe this time we wouldn't be so lucky."

The Frederick anti-idiotype protocol (a step-by-step procedure for conducting an experiment or for treating a specific condition or disease) was written in early 1983, largely by Ken Foon working under Oldham's supervision. The jaw-breaking official title read: "BRMP Protocol 8301, Treatment of Patients with Immunoglobulin-Bearing Malignancies (Chronic Lymphocytic Leukemia and Lymphomas) with Monoclonal Antibodies Recognizing Idiotypic Determinants." Foon was listed as the principal investigator on the twenty-five-page document, with Oldham, Paul Abrams, and several others as associate investigators.

The paper began with a review of the theory behind anti-idiotype therapy—how certain malignant lymphoid cells do not release their immunoglobulin molecules, but retain them on their surfaces, thus creating a target for an injected monoclonal antibody. There followed a discussion of the technical feasibility of creating this anti-idiotype antibody to this surface protein, as Levy and Miller had reported the year before. Foon proposed to select ten to twenty B-cell lymphoma patients from the BRMP— patients who had not responded to any other form of therapy and who were thus regarded as terminally ill—engineer anti-idiotype antibodies specifically against their malignant cells, then see what effect, if any, the antibodies would have on the disease.

The process by which the anti-ids were produced was a dazzling application of Jerne's "idiotype-anti-idiotype" theory and generated not one hybridoma, but two. The first was made by fusing the patient's malignant B-cells to myeloma cells; as expected, the hybridomas that resulted turned out large amounts of antibody—that is, the B-cell idiotype.

These idiotype antibodies were then purified and injected into a laboratory mouse, which soon began to manufacture antibodies against the B-cell idiotype. After about ten days, the animal was killed and the spleen removed. The organ was chopped up and forced through a fine stainless steel screen to expose as many of the cells as possible to the chemical extraction step that will yield the antibody-producing lymphocytes. The final step, making the anti-id-producing hybridoma, was made by fusing these lymphocytes with another batch of myeloma cells for about three minutes, then setting the mixture aside. If all goes well, these new hybrids will produce only anti-idiotype antibody.

Damon's part in the program would be to receive the hybridomas—frozen in tiny glass vials, packed in dry ice—and encapsulate them. After a few weeks, when the hybridomas had grown to a certain volume, the capsules would be broken up to retrieve and purify the anti-ids for shipment back to Frederick. As a control and backup system, Frederick would also grow its own anti-id in mouse ascites.

Damon Biotech would receive no payment for their work, only cost reimbursement. For Webb, the agreement provided infinitely more than that. Thanks to a then-new White House order concerning government research agreements with small businesses, Damon would retain certain patent and licensing rights to much of the technology arising from their work—in effect, rights to later develop the technology into an entirely new category of proprietary antibodies. If the first patients showed a positive response to the anti-id therapy, the company would negotiate the next step with the NCI.

Webb was now convinced that the agreement was one of Damon's missing links. It stood to at last make the company a serious contender in monoclonal production; by lending NCI's credence to its technology, Damon Biotech would now come to the attention of the skeptical financial and technical communities. Never mind that for now there would be no financial rewards; by hooking itself to the prestige of the NCI, the company stood to gain far more than financial rewards. It would be an enormous feather in the cap. More importantly for both Damon and NCI was the very real possibility of taking part in a genuine break-through in cancer therapy—the first in more than two decades. And the business opportunities that lay beyond that were truly staggering.

Eileen and Jack were married in March 1983, in the small Catholic church in Houston that Eileen had joined a year earlier. His brother Paul was best man; Eileen's sister Pam was maid of honor.

He had always known that he wanted to marry her. For her part, she never disguised her enthusiasm about the prospect; even aside from the fact that she loved him and wanted him as her husband, the live-in arrangement they had shared for almost three years still jabbed at her fierce Roman Catholicism.

He had always found a reason to delay the marriage. When they had first arrived in Boston, he had admitted to his emotional hesitancy about marriage, and she had accepted that. Then there was his schedule at school and at the hospital, which he character-ized as too hectic to accommodate a traditional family life. Later, of course, it was the disease. How could he expect Eileen to marry him when he might be gone within the next year or two? How does one suggest marriage to a woman who is in line to soon become a widow? It was not only unfair to her, it struck him as rather macabre.

Every time he went to Maryland, he discussed the dilemma with Foon, who at first gave no opinion on the matter. Finally, he couldn't stand to hear the waffling any longer:

"Listen, you love Eileen, don't you?" asked Ken.

"Yeah, of course. I mean, we get along great, you know that."

"So why don't you knock off the bullshit?"

"What bullshit?"

"This stuff about 'It isn't the right time yet,' or 'Houston isn't the right place for my kids,' or 'I'm not a well man,' or whatever. So you have no guarantees. Neither have I; neither does anyone. If we all refused to get married because we might be dead in a couple of years, the race woulda died out thousands of years ago."

Later, Jack noted that "one of Ken's greatest talents is the way in which he cuts through the crap. . . ."

Although the NCI contract wasn't actually signed until late 1983—a year after Paul Abrams' first contact with Vasington and Jarvis—the need for the new laboratory had become a top priority by early in the year. To finance the construction and equipment of the new facility, Webb and Kosowsky decided that Damon Biotech needed a massive dose of money, the kind of money that could be raised only by a public stock offering.

They first of all made sure that the Roche program was in good working order; it would be not only embarrassing but outrightly suicidal for the company to issue a prospectus based on a solitary unhappy customer. Randy Rupp's staff had made sure that the customer was happy—so happy that Roche had signed a ten-year agreement for Damon Biotech to produce its anti-interferon antibodies.

Damon Biotech became a public company in June 1983 by issuing 2.4 million shares of stock, for a total of $38 million. Completion of the new lab was scheduled for May 1984.

Robert Oldham hadn't been at Frederick very long before he decided that the NCI's support for the biologicals program was actually considerably less than he'd been led to believe. While his $21-million budget at first seemed like a windfall, he later calculated that it was only about 2 percent of the NCI's total annual billion-dollar budget.

The growing public pressure on the institute to start showing some tangible results didn't help the budget situation a bit. One of the most vocal critics was Senator Paula Hawkins, the Florida Republican, who had been quoted as calling the NCI budget a prime example of government profligacy. When Oldham heard that, he snorted to an assistant that "they don't seem to realize that a billion dollars—our whole budget at NCI—is only about the price of a new Trident submarine. And what are we spending for biologicals? Twenty million a year, more or less? Hell, that's about the same as the cost overruns by the military every day! If they're looking for inefficiency, why don't they run across the river and take a look at the Pentagon?"

He often reflected that in the previous twenty years, something like half a million new drugs—that is, synthetic chemicals, many of them produced at huge profits by the major pharmaceutical companies—had been screened for cancer effectiveness. To the general public, that sounded like a massive effort; Oldham knew that no more than forty or forty-five of those had ever been approved for clinical trials (that is, actually tried out on cancer patients on an experimental, controlled basis). And of those, only about ten are now considered to be at least moderately effective against tumors.

Yet the institute, in Oldham's opinion, was still irreversibly wedded to the idea of more drug research. Biologicals, he said, were being treated like a bastard stepchild. "About 10 percent of cancer patients have some response to interferon, but only about 1 or 2 percent of the patients respond to the new chemicals."

The problem, he complained, was that like all government bureaucracies the NCI was a hotbed of empire building, special interests, political intrigue, and a general commitment to risk-avoidance—the mentality that asks first, "How did we do it last year?" On an individual basis, he said, you couldn't find a group of brighter, harder-working, more innovative scientists than the men and women at NCI. Too many of them were being tethered by conservatism and government politics.

On the morning of June 27, 1984—about a month late—Damon Biotech celebrated its new laboratory by erecting a huge yellow-and-white tent in the front parking lot. A small stage equipped with folding chairs was erected at one end of the tent; at the other, several large tables were set up to hold the buffet lunch that was scheduled for early afternoon. In between, a dozen or so large round tables were arranged to accommodate the two hundred guests—the press and investment analysts, mostly—who had been invited to the opening of the cell culture facility. As it turned out, the tent wasn't even necessary. It was a perfect early summer New England day—breezy and sunny, with a temperature in the upper sixties.

Franklin Lim was there, of course, looking ill at ease as he wandered aimlessly among the three-piece suits and television cameras. But he was one of the most important guests of all; in a way, he was the one who had made it all possible. MIT immunologist Herman Eisen, looking like everyone's favorite uncle, gave a brief keynote address on the importance of monoclonal antibodies to the medical industry, and the special importance of this particular laboratory. Evelyn Murphy, the Secretary of Economic Affairs for the Commonwealth of Massachusetts, delivered a routine speech on the importance of the biotechnology industry to the future growth of the Bay State. Lunch was served after the talks, with the guests filing past the tables in the rear. Beginning at one-thirty, small groups of visitors formed in front of the building for guided tours of the new facility.

To reach the new laboratories, you must enter the building's main lobby—a bright, breezy-looking area equipped with mustard-colored walls, plants, one or two modern paintings, and two vinyl sofas. Off to the side is a stylish staircase leading to the second floor. Following your guide, you walk past the receptionist's desk down a corridor, make a few turns, and arrive at a door with a push-button combination lock. This brings you to a small gowning room. Before going any further, you must don a light green nylon gown, slip some flimsy white covers over your shoes, and pull a silly-looking gauzy white cap over your hair. To leave the gowning room into the main laboratory complex, you need a plastic card with a magnetic strip.

The gowning room is one of the features that makes the laboratory a GMP facility in the eyes of the Food and Drug Administration; the lab is reportedly the first such U.S. facility geared to pharmaceutical-quality monoclonals. Such a designation does not mean that the company is officially blessed by the FDA, however, only that it conforms to minimal standards set by the agency. Put another way, being a GMP lab does not assure that your products are accepted or in any way endorsed by the government; if your lab doesn't meet GMP standards, however, you don't stand a chance.

And what makes a lab GMP? Sterilization facilities. Air locks and other barriers that prevent nonqualified passersby from wandering in from outside, and that even discourage employees from passing freely from one side of the building to another. Special product purification equipment. New cell quarantine facilities. Features that make it easy to disinfect the rooms, such as the way in which the walls languidly flow into the floor, to minimize the number of cracks and crevices in which stray organisms can hide and grow.

In a small and surprisingly seedy-looking laboratory on the grounds of Fort Detrick, you might find a man named Steve Giardina, Ph.D. He appears to be in his late twenties or early thirties, and like so many people in this business, he defies the common perception of what a Ph.D. should look like. He's rather short and stocky, has a wild head of thick curly black hair and a bushy mustache, and wears a yellow T-shirt under his white coat. His fingernails are closely nibbled. At first, he reminds you of the man who came to repair your washing machine last week. After spending a little time with Giardina, however, you soon realize that he is very good at what he does. And what he does is grow hybridomas.

It is Giardina's laboratory that receives the idiotype antibodies —the ones produced by the first hybridoma, the ones that bear the unmistakable molecular markings of the patients' malignant B-cells. When the proteins arrive, Giardina and his lab assistants proceed with what by now has become the standard method of producing the anti-id in mice:

Approximately one hundred micrograms (one ten thousandth of a gram) of the antibodies are injected into white laboratory mice. The animals are officially designated as BALB/c (signifying a certain carefully controlled genetic strain); in most labs, they go by such names as "Sloopy," "Mighty Mouse," and other such endearments. After about ten days, the animals are killed, their spleens removed, and the new lymphocytes fused to myeloma cells to create the critical second hybridoma.

"After a week or so, you can start to see the hybridomas," said Giardina, looking down into the covered glass petri dish on his bench. "See the way they're beginning to cluster together? That's hybridomas starting to form. Now we just let 'em grow for a while, then sort through them to find the ones that are secreting the anti-id antibody. Those are the only ones we want."

Giardina finds the hybridomas of interest with a simple analyti-

cal test called ELISA (standing for "enzyme-linked immu-
nosorbent assay"). Once they're identified and confirmed as being the only hybridomas secreting the anti-id, he places some of
the cells into a separate vial, caps it, labels it, and puts it into the
refrigerator against one wall of the lab. "You always gotta remember to stash some of the hybridoma, in case something goes
wrong," he explained, as if everyone knew that. "Otherwise you
have to start all over again—that's another month down the
drain."

His stash secured, he sets the rest of the cells aside to grow in
culture for about two weeks, finally reaching a volume of about
10 million cells. Some of these are then injected into a second set
of mice. There, sheltered among the animals' natural cells and
fluids (the ascites), the hybridomas are allowed to divide for
another ten days; by this time, each animal has become a factory
for producing antibody against the idiotype component of the
hybridoma. Each will generate approximately twelve milliliters of
ascites fluid, each milliliter containing up to fifteen milligrams of
anti-idiotype antibody. Finally, the fluid is removed from the
animal, purified, and the antibody tested for activity against the
patient's original idiotype.

Giardina doesn't inject all of this final batch of hybridomas into
his mice. Some he freezes and sends to Damon Biotech to be
grown in capsules. There the 1.8-milliliter vials are received by
his counterpart—another Ph.D., named Kevin Gilbride. The first
few times I met with Gilbride, I was struck by his resemblance to
Gene Wilder, although Gilbride was somewhat more rounded
than the comedian. He was probably in his mid-thirties at the
time, and ran the laboratory responsible for the NCI program.

Gilbride often wondered about the patients from whom the
cells had been drawn. Studying the encapsulated hybrids growing in the T-flask, he was curious about where these living things
had been just a few weeks before. What made them so dangerous? How did they become that way? Was the patient a man or a
woman? Did he or she have a family? Where? How old was the
patient? Gilbride would never know; the hybridomas arrived in
his laboratory bearing only the cryptic label identifying them as
"BL-1" (the first clone produced in the B-cell lymphoma program) or "BL-3," the third clone.

Making the Anti-Idiotype for B-Cell Lymphoma

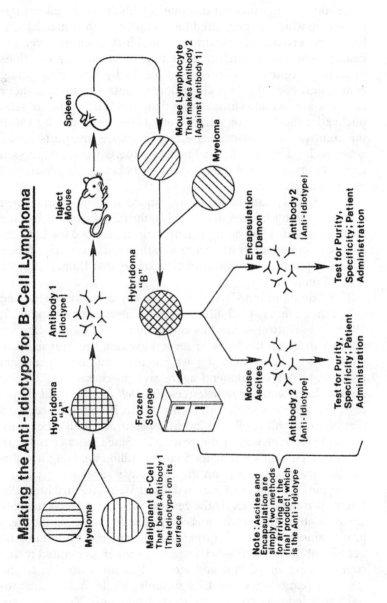

Myeloma

Malignant B-Cell
That bears Antibody 1
[The Idiotype] on its
surface

Hybridoma "A"

Antibody 1
[Idiotype]

Inject Mouse

Spleen

Mouse Lymphocyte
That makes Antibody 2
[Against Antibody 1]

Myeloma

Hybridoma "B"

Frozen Storage

Encapsulation at Damon

Antibody 2
[Anti-Idiotype]

Test for Purity,
Specificity; Patient
Administration

Mouse Ascites
Antibody 2
[Anti-Idiotype]

Test for Purity,
Specificity; Patient
Administration

Note: Ascites and
Encapsulation are
simply two methods
for arriving at the
final product, which
is the Anti-Idiotype

It soon became apparent that one of Webb's special talents was the way in which he presented the company to the financial analysts—the groups of investment specialists from all over the country who spent much of their time at formal presentations (usually preceded or followed by lunch) by promising young companies. For all practical purposes, these two-to-three-hour sessions are actually little more than carefully polished sales pitches by the host companies—organized programs by which the company sells its expertise and its future prospects to the analysts. If all goes well, the financial experts will be impressed enough to recommend the company's stocks to their private and corporate investors.

Webb's presentations were much more articulate and refined than Vasington's had been, and he had the distinctive touch of the born salesman. This was especially important, since the financial analysts were the ones who were so influential in deciding where investors put their money. And God knows that Damon Biotech needed money.

The "dog-and-pony" shows, as Vasington and others had called them, finally paid off. In its client newsletter of August 1, 1983, E. F. Hutton advised its subscribers that "Damon Biotech appears to be on the brink of several exciting breakthroughs in commercial applications for its patented microencapsulation technology. We recommend aggressive purchase. . . ." A few months later, another newsletter—the *Holt Investment Advisory*—reviewed Damon's work with Hoffmann-La Roche and predicted that "Damon will enter into industrial contracts with other companies before the end of the year. . . . Since monoclonal antibodies are currently selling for $3 to $5 million per kilogram, this would have a big impact on the company's revenues. . . ."

The personal styles of Kosowsky and Webb are strikingly different. Kosowsky is clearly the restless innovator, Webb the cool and cautious manager who was charged with translating the ideas into business. One can't dispel the feeling that there must be occasional clashes here—brief sparks, perhaps, generated by the coming together of flint and stone—that are traceable to the men's disparate ages and backgrounds. While Webb tends toward guarded understatement, the tell-it-like-it-is Kosowsky rapidly strips away the verbal frosting. At the same time, the men appear to complement each other nicely; they share their ideas often, and one or the other can usually explain why a particular idea can or cannot be made to work.

Even if the NCI's anti-id program proved to be a great success, Webb and Kosowsky knew that Biotech's collaboration must be regarded not only as an end in itself, but also as an important opportunity. Down at Frederick, Foon and Abrams had signed up only four patients by the middle of 1984, and would probably never enroll more than two dozen; such numbers meant that even if the NCI contract provided for payments over and above costs, the program could hardly serve as a commercial vehicle. Rather, its primary value lay first in the prestige that accompanied the partnership—the fact that Damon Biotech's antibodies were being tested in a vital new cancer therapy.

There was another feature of the collaboration, and it would later prove to be just as important: The program could become the company's gateway to what analysts were already describing as essential to long-term success: the development of proprietary, one-of-a-kind antibodies for patients like Jack Christie. And not just a couple of dozen, but tens of thousands.

Webb spent much of the summer working out the precise numbers. When he had finished, he tucked them under his arm one afternoon and bolted up the stairs to the second-floor conference room. There he was joined by Kosowsky, Jarvis, and a half dozen other officers and technical consultants of the company.

Webb got right down to business.

"We know that there are something like 350,000 cases of B-cell lymphoma here in the States, in Western Europe, and in Japan; those are government figures, and they agree pretty well with estimates by other researchers. We also know that the number of cases is rising by a couple of percent every year, though no one's really sure why that's so. But if it is so, we'd expect more like 400,000 patients in those three areas by 1989.

"Now let's say that Levy and Miller and the people at Frederick are on the right track. Let's say that this disease really does respond to monoclonals, or can somehow be made to respond. Based on the Stanford report last year, that certainly seems to be the case. That means we can consider each one of these patients as a potential recipient. From a practical standpoint, of course, we're not going to reach all of them; suppose we aim for just 1 percent of the market, alright? One percent, that's about four thousand patients, worldwide, by 1989.

"The current thinking is that a full therapy of anti-idiotype antibody will come to approximately ten grams of pure antibody, perhaps given in ten dosages of one gram each. I look about and I don't see any other company that can grow those volumes, certainly not at our costs. If we move along, I believe we can own that market within five to eight years."

"What about pricing, Nigel?" asked Kosowsky.

"To begin with, forty thousand dollars per patient—ten one-gram doses at four thousand per. Later, as we move along the learning curve and scale up the processes, we could reduce it to three or maybe two thousand. If that sounds steep, consider that today it costs an average of a hundred thousand to fully treat a lymphoma patient."

"And that's just direct costs," added one of the consultants. "That doesn't count lost wages, productivity, and so on."

"Okay," murmured Kosowsky. "Four thousand cases, forty thousand each. That's . . ."

"A hundred and sixty million dollars," Webb finished. "And by 1992, I think we could easily estimate thirty-five thousand patients—less than 10 percent of the patient population—at twenty-two thousand dollars each. That would bring revenues to $770 million. And even aside from cancer therapy, the anti-id antibody could also be used as a monitoring tool, to follow the progress of the treatment and during regular checkups to see if the malignancy is growing or going into regression."

One of the men in the room sat forward and wanted to know how the Food and Drug Administration approval process would be expected to affect all this. It was well known that FDA could be notoriously slow-moving in such matters. How could Damon Biotech expect to have the therapy into the nation's hospitals and clinics in only five years? The average new drug takes eight or ten years to move through the FDA approval process. Webb had the answer for that one too.

"We have every reason to believe that FDA is ready to grant this therapy a fast-track treatment," said Webb. "You have to remember that there's a very poor prognosis for these patients. Even if only a few of them respond to the anti-id, that result is much better than nothing. And we're confident that the government wants to see some of these new treatments out where they can be used.

"Gentlemen, I think we could look for the FDA to approve this therapy in less than one year after we submit the test data . . ."

CHAPTER TEN

Ken Foon was trying very hard to control his temper.

"I just wish they wouldn't BS me," he muttered, chugging down the cluttered hallway toward his office. "If they're having problems with the damn thing, I wish they'd just say so. . . ."

The people at Damon Biotech had promised Foon that Jack Christie's antibody would be delivered during the summer of 1984, shortly after the opening of their cell culture facility. Looking out his window, Foon watched the red and gold leaves drift lazily to the ground. Still no antibody, and still no word from Damon. He had called the company several times to ask about the delay; every time, he had been assured that the clone was growing nicely and that purification and delivery were just a few days away. Were they getting a runaround, he asked Abrams—the old "check is in the mail" routine?

By early 1984, Jack Christie and three other B-cell lymphoma patients had been screened for enrollment in Frederick's anti-idiotype program. It was a far cry from the dozen or more participants which Foon had envisioned for the program, but it was surprisingly difficult to find people who satisfied all the entry requirements set down in the protocol. Giardina had already grown hybridomas for two of the four, and the fused cells were sent to Damon Biotech for encapsulation.

As for the other two hybrids, problems had developed partway through the procedure. One patient had died of his disease before the anti-id could be grown. The other had inexplicably developed a multiple clone—that is, his malignant cells suddenly started to display not one idiotype, but two. It was the very same phenomenon that Jeffrey Sklar at Stanford would later confirm in his own research, and it now posed a knotty question for the future not only of the NCI anti-id program, but of the whole concept of anti-idiotypic therapy: If the malignant B-cells could spontaneously mutate—just assume an altogether different cellular configuration—how could an antibody ever be developed against it? It would be like trying to hit a target that not only moved around constantly, but also changed its size and shape.

By the time autumn of 1984 arrived, that left only two patients in the anti-id program: Christie and a fifty-two-year-old salesman from Minneapolis.

Bob Oldham was worrying about his future in "official" cancer research; less and less did it seem that that future would be inside the National Cancer Institute. He frequently found himself thinking about joining a private company where he presumably would enjoy a looser rein to put his medical ideas to work.

What really bugged him, he said, was the fact that most of his day-in, day-out problems weren't those of cancer treatment—he could handle those—but of NCI politics. He complained to his wife that it was becoming all too clear that the biologicals program at Frederick wasn't getting nearly the financial or conceptual support he'd been promised at the beginning. He was convinced that he'd been abandoned by the very men (some of them at the very top of the NCI pyramid) who had urged him to return to the agency. And if that weren't bad enough, he sensed that the little clout he'd retained at Bethesda was now being turned over to researchers—vocal advocates of drug therapy, mostly—who hadn't a fraction of his experience in biologicals.

He was developing an intense dislike for many of them, especially the ones he considered marginally competent or mere political lackeys. There was one researcher in particular who galled him, a middle-aged man whose specialty at technical presentations was to review the published findings of other researchers. "He just sorta stood up there and pontificated about what this meant and what that implied," Oldham chuckled. "That gave some people the impression that he himself was really up on all this. Actually, he didn't know beans about any of it."

Many of his colleagues, at NCI and elsewhere, returned his hostility. He was arrogant, they said to each other (but almost never to Oldham himself), and abrasive. Self-righteous. Oh, there was no doubt about the man's intelligence; positively brilliant, but impossible to work with. As long as such assessments stayed within the NCI, Oldham let them roll off him. The problem was that they were getting around. . . .

Foon had been right: All was not well up in Needham Heights. Some of the delays were unavoidable, especially those incurred in the FDA approval process. "Physicians sometimes get very impatient during this stage," explained one biologist. "They have sick people awaiting treatment; government paperwork is often seen as a damned nuisance."

One of Gilbride's problems was that the opening of the cell culture facility had been more than a month late because of last-minute changes in FDA-ordered designs and materials. The delivery of much of the cell culture equipment had been delayed by several weeks; Rupp and Gilbride had even had to send away to France for some of it—the fermenter pots, for example—when it turned out that no American producer would guarantee compliance with all their quality control requirements.

The hang-ups continued even after the hybridomas had been grown, said Gilbride. Especially with the contamination of the antibody with pyrogens: minute cellular by-products—garbage, in a way—that are released by the hybridoma into the surrounding fluid, and which may cause high fever if injected into a patient (hence the name). To remove the contaminants, Gilbride poured the liquid containing the antibody over what is called an anion-exchange column—a tall glass cylinder filled with a chemically reactive material. As the proteins flow over the material and out the bottom of the cylinder, the electrically charged pyrogens are seized and tightly held inside the column. "Actually, there's been some evidence lately that a high fever in some cases isn't such a bad thing," Gilbride said later. "It sorta charges up the body's whole defense system. But the FDA specifies that there can be no pyrogens in these products, so we had to get them out. And that took a lot of extra time."

Still, Gilbride had successfully generated several grams each of BL-1 and BL-2, and had shipped them to Frederick for administration to the Minnesota salesman. There, Foon and Abrams ran a series of tests in which they pitted the antibodies against malignant cells from five other patients. To be acceptable, the monoclonal had to bind specifically against only the original cell, and none of the others. The salesman was then given a small quantity of the antibody intravenously, Foon dribbling it in at the rate of about half a gram an hour. The two physicians then watched for twenty-four hours, waiting for any possible reactions to the injection. Some patients who had received the antibody at other locations had developed temporary fever and nausea; a much more serious reaction would be anaphylactic shock—in effect, a powerful and potentially fatal allergic reaction in which the patient's own antibodies attack the injected antibodies and form a life-threatening complex of new molecules in the bloodstream. To Foon's knowledge, that had never happened to any patient, but in theory it was a very real threat.

While Christie was waiting in Houston for word that his anti-id had arrived from Damon, he made a decision: He wanted to resume practicing medicine. He had watched and worked with Foon and Abrams for almost two years, on and off, and was slowly gripped by a new sensation: He was jealous. Jealous of the men's intensity in their work, envious of the special camaraderie that so obviously existed between them. They were doing what he had set out to do—they were using their skills and education to make some important changes in the lives of sick and dying men.

He began to study the medical journal want ads, and found a small group practice on the north side of the city that was looking for an internist. "It looks like I'm gonna play doctor again," he told Eileen. "Wanna play with me . . . ?"

The Minneapolis salesman had shown some remarkable progress as the result of his treatment. The lymph nodes were shrinking, and the amount of circulating id had dropped significantly.

Foon decided to halt the antibody treatment for a while and put the patient on standard therapy.

Robert Oldham resigned as the director of the BRMP in October 1983; a few months later, he also resigned from the National Cancer Institute. He refused to discuss publicly the reasons for his departure, or to speculate on his replacement. A medical newsletter at the time, however, noted that "it is no secret that he has been dissatisfied with what he felt was the lack of emphasis his program has been getting from the NCI. . . ."

The first batch of Jack Christie's anti-idiotype arrived by Federal Express at the Frederick Cancer Research Center in late September 1984. The package consisted of ten glass vials full of clear liquid. Dissolved in each was one gram of pure monoclonal antibody.

Rather than starting the therapy immediately, however, Ken Foon decided to hold back for a few weeks. The circulating paraprotein was still too high.

For the year following Oldham's resignation, the Frederick program was in a palpable state of disquiet. "When the top man leaves a program like this, it's usually just a matter of time before his staffers start to think about moving on as well," Webb said later. "Even though the number-one man will sooner or later be replaced, the men on the line know it won't be the same. And at Frederick, I think it was easy for Foon and Abrams and the others to perceive that they'd also heard a message from Bethesda."

Actually, Ken Foon had already been negotiating details concerning a job offer that had come to him during the hot, sticky summer of 1984, from the University of Michigan Medical Center. Unlike Oldham, he had never had any interest in entering the commercial world; the salary wasn't bad, and he loved the academic environment. In fact, Christie had often tried to sell Foon on the financial and intellectual joys of the business world; Ken had just laughed, shaken his woolly head, and walked off as though Jack had been trying to sell him the Fourteenth Street Bridge.

While Foon was discussing the Michigan offer, Paul Abrams

had been sitting in on some interesting conversations of his own. Like Foon, he had seen Oldham's departure coming—the man had simply been too much of a maverick for Bethesda—and was looking into the idea of teaming up with several other physicians and researchers to start a new company.

Even from six hundred miles away, it was obvious to Webb and Kosowsky that the Frederick biologicals program was in deep trouble in the wake of Oldham's departure. There was still no way of knowing who, if anyone, would replace Oldham, nor whether any of the other men at Frederick would even remain with NCI. Nor was it yet clear whether or not Oldham's complaints about the "stepchild" nature of the program had been justified. But if his perceptions had been only partly correct, that meant massive implications for the future of Damon's B-cell lymphoma program; none of them was encouraging. There would be influential observers who would interpret the events in Frederick as an official discreditation not just of Oldham, but of his work and his ideas. That in turn would cast a deep shadow over the whole concept of anti-idiotype therapy for years to come. With Oldham out of the picture, and with Foon and Abrams also hinting at their departure, it fell to Webb, Kosowsky, and Jarvis to search out a new opportunity to plug the encapsulation process into cancer therapy.

The most logical new alliance for the company, Webb insisted, was none other than Ron Levy—the "king of the hybridoma," as some monoclonal experts were already calling him—and Rich Miller, the Stanford team that had presided over the only apparent cure attributable to monoclonal antibodies. In fact, Webb later recalled, Damon had been following Stanford's progress for two years, ever since they published their work in the *New England Journal of Medicine.* There were even stories that wealthy patients were actually trying to buy their way into the laboratory, in some cases offering tens of thousands of dollars. The two physicians sympathized with the desperate men and women; they had set rigid entry requirements for their studies, and no amount of money could change that.

After several phone conversations, Webb phoned Levy in March 1984 for an appointment, then flew with Allan Jarvis to

San Francisco. They arrived early in the evening, and the four men agreed to meet at a popular seafood restaurant in Palo Alto. Webb put the question to the researchers as coffee arrived: Would they be interested in teaming up with Damon Biotech on monoclonal antibody production, using the technology that Damon had already proven for NCI?

The Damon team had no way of knowing that Levy and Miller were actually a couple of steps ahead of them. In fact, they were now preparing to form their own company in Palo Alto, called BioTherapy Systems, for producing anti-idiotype antibodies for selected cancer patients. They had even discussed the concept with other companies in the hopes of acquiring financial and technical support. By year-end, they hoped to have forty or fifty of these patients as clients. The problem, they explained, was that they needed third-party financing.

No, they said to Jarvis' question, they didn't know very much about Damon's encapsulation process, although they'd certainly heard about it.

"How are you going to be preparing the antibody?" Webb asked.

The men replied they were going to be using mice.

"How long will it take to make antibody for a single patient?"

"About a year, we figure."

"And how many patients have you treated during the past three years?" asked Jarvis.

"Ten," replied Miller. Webb shook his head.

"Ten patients in three years. That's not a very practical time frame, is it?"

Webb brought the men up to date on the NCI work, then came to the point of the meeting: Damon wanted to work with them. If they agreed, Biotech would make antibodies for three of their patients, at no charge. It was up to the California men to refine the treatment protocol; Damon would submit the clinical results to the government for an IND—Investigational New Drug—application. Finally, Damon would provide the $2.5 million needed for laboratories, salaries, and equipment, in return for which it would acquire 80 percent of BioTherapy Systems.

THE CELL BUILDERS

The men left the restaurant at about 9 P.M. For Webb and Jarvis, it was midnight, and they were tired. As they climbed into their cars, Ron Levy told his visitors that he and Miller would like to think about the offer for a couple of days.

CHAPTER ELEVEN

THE CELL BUILDERS

Jack Christie began to get better during the first week of 1985. It could have been the interferon, or perhaps the COP treatment, or a combination of the two. For Ken Foon, the initial clue was in the routine paraprotein analysis that he ordered when Christie arrived at Frederick.

For most of 1984, the protein concentration had been bouncing between 200 and 400 milligrams—much better than when he'd entered the program, but still too high for the anti-id. Now the paraprotein had leveled off at just below 200. The question was, would it remain at that level or were the parent cells simply mustering their chemical strength, waiting for the chance to rebound? Before he decided on the next step, Foon wanted a closer look at the enemy.

"I hate like hell to do this to you, ol' pal, but I need another aspirate."

"Aw shit, Ken . . ."

"Actually, I just want to see your pretty little tush again, darling," Foon whispered seductively.

The aspirate confirmed the message: There were still some cancerous cells lurking deep within the marrow, but far fewer than there had been on Christie's previous visit. Abrams and Foon decided to order a complete series of tests, as though Jack had just walked in for the first time.

"I don't want you to get all excited now," Foon said the next day, "but there's a chance—just a chance, nothing sure yet—that you're going into remission. I think what I want to do is take you off the interferon for a while and just watch things for a month or two. Check in with someone back in Texas every couple of weeks, then one of you call me with the results."

But there were still those cancerous B-cells. "Think we should still go ahead with the anti-id?" asked Jack. He was almost hoping that Foon would answer in the affirmative; he'd waited almost a year for the antibodies and now felt strangely cheated that he might not receive them. Dammit, they were made from *his* cells. He wanted them—he *deserved* them.

Foon had also been thinking about the anti-id. After a conference with Abrams and another physician at Frederick, he had ruled it out, at least for the time being. "I'm not sure I see the point, Jack. It isn't entirely risk-free, you know, and the circulating id is still too high. So what would be the benefit? Let's just do nothing for now. Keep an eye on things . . ."

The next day a laboratory technician in Frederick sealed the nine grams of anti-idiotype from Damon into a small glass vial, labeled it, and placed it in a freezer.

The plane was only half full, so he was able to pull up the armrest and stretch across the seat. He tried to read, but his mind wandered continually. Sleep was out of the question. So he stared out the window, trying to guess the identities of the cities that were coming alive with their pinpricks of light. As if reading his mind, a passing flight attendant informed him that they had had to follow a slightly altered course this afternoon because of heavy storms moving into the Atlanta area; that was Nashville he was looking at. Christie stared at the city through the darkening skies. He thought about Bob Oldham, wondered if he were down there just now.

He had started to call Eileen from Frederick the night before, but then changed his mind. He wanted to see her face when he told her the news. And he wondered what else he would tell her. That even if he was really in remission—and it could be months before he could know for sure, before any physician could confidently state that it wasn't just his cells playing cruel tricks on him —he would still be a cancer patient for several more years? That the disease might launch a second, more vicious attack without warning? And what then?

And suppose that the anti-id, if he ever got to use it, proved to be a flop? He and Foon had talked about that several times, of course. Back to chemo, maybe. Or perhaps the relatively new procedure, called the autologous bone marrow transplant, in which the bone marrow is actually removed from the anesthetized patient, irradiated to destroy the cancerous cells, then replaced. He had discussed the technique with some people at the Dana-Farber Cancer Institute in Boston in June 1984, when he and Eileen were visiting his parents. The transplant was not entirely risk-free, of course—his disturbed marrow would make him highly vulnerable to infection, for one thing—but there had been some encouraging results. And unlike the procedure in which bone marrow is received from a donor, there would be no risk of rejection. He'd think about it. . . .

But not now. It was getting noticeably darker outside, even though they were heading southwest. He was too puzzled to think clearly now, unsure of whether he should be excited or depressed. And he was suddenly tired.

He closed his eyes and tried to drift off to someplace besides Houston, far away from Frederick.

He spotted Eileen as soon as he emerged from the jetway into the boarding area at Houston Intercontinental. When she didn't accompany him on the trips to Frederick, she always made it a point to greet him in something bright and colorful; this time was no exception. His eye was caught immediately by the cheerful yellow turtleneck and the matching knit fisherman's cap she had installed at a rakish angle. Walking hand in hand toward the main terminal, he leaned over and said something in her ear.

EPILOG

Outside my window, the unusually mild New England winter of 1984–85 struggled in vain to become what we jokingly call spring. The naked trees swayed and creaked under a northwest wind, the dull gray skies promised yet another icy baptism. Watching a car sliding helplessly around a corner, I thought again about the creased Boston lobsterman I'd met once. "Around here the only difference between the two seasons is that the snow's warmer in April," he'd said. I think he was right.

I tossed aside the last of the papers that had gradually become an eight-inch stack on my desk—technical journals and trade magazines, mostly, along with a few newspaper articles and press releases. During the past year and a half I had involuntarily fallen into the habit of skimming every publication I could find, looking for news of the hybridoma companies. By now, all the names were beginning to sound alike—Hybritech, Centocor, Bio-Response, Genetic Systems, Damon Biotech, Celltech—and it was becoming increasingly difficult to keep their identities separate.

A decade after Köhler and Milstein published their report, the hybridoma was still trying to become big business. It seemed that new companies were being formed almost weekly, most of them dedicated to immunoconjugates, the weapons consisting of drug molecules linked to antibodies. Multimillion-dollar contracts were being awarded, and with them new promises were being made to detect more diseases and perhaps cure many of them.

More and more, I found myself of two minds about it all. On

the one hand, it was exciting to know that I had witnessed a birthing of sorts, even though the observation had been a retrospective one; I had watched the hybridoma evolve from a laboratory curiosity to a familiar medical tool. And although only one man had been cured by the hybridoma (and even that happy news was still being tempered with caution in many circles), I had no doubt that that one man represented an important frontier. There would be other frontiers to be crossed, new miracles to be performed, and it would be interesting to watch and see which of the dozens of companies now scrambling for recognition would finally succeed.

Yet I couldn't help but wonder about the extent to which corporate profits would preempt the needs of the people who stood to benefit from the technology. There were more than a few observers who were wondering the same thing. Suppose, they asked, that there was a disease that afflicted only a few thousand patients, but that could be detected or treated with monoclonals; would those patients be ignored simply because they made up too small a market? Would those patients benefit from the kind of research dedication and enthusiasm that Jack Christie had enjoyed? Who would make such decisions? And who would there be to raise an objection?

By the end of 1985, Damon Biotech counted eighteen customers for its contract services (including the continuing interferon work for Roche); only two years before, the company could boast of only one. The new clients included such prestigious names as Eli Lilly, Serono Diagnostics, and the Scripps Institute; in this latter partnership, Damon Biotech will supply the first antibodies ever to be tested against human lung cancer.

Earlier in the year, Damon announced that it was about to begin selling antibodies to Japanese pharmaceutical companies. Close on the heels of the Japanese venture came word of Damon's plans to begin construction of its new European facility —Damon Biotech Ltd.—near Edinburgh, Scotland. There it would combine Encapcel with a newly acquired genetic engineering technology to produce something called tissue plasminogen activator (a chemical that appears to be useful in treating coronary blood clots) and other biological products. Nigel Webb was named as chief executive officer of the subsidiary in addition to his present duties as president.

In late 1984, Damon also entered a joint venture with Connaught Laboratories, the company that had supported Frank Lim's pancreatic islet work four years earlier. The new venture (named Vivotech) will concentrate on the use of encapsulated islet cells for treating diabetes. Fittingly, Ed Lurier is presently chairman of the Vivotech board.

At BioTherapy Systems, Rich Miller and Ron Levy were working with about twenty B-cell lymphoma patients by early 1986, creating hybridomas to be grown into anti-idiotype antibodies as Damon made the antibodies. Although the anti-id concept is still highly experimental, the California men are more convinced than ever that custom-made antibodies—either alone or hooked to a drug or radioisotope—will one day become the treatment of choice for many forms of cancer.

To almost no one's surprise, Ken Foon became the University of Michigan's new chief of hematology in June. It would be a double red-letter month for him, he said—his wife Rebecca was due to deliver their third child that month. With two girls at home, the couple had been excited to learn that child was a boy.

He was looking forward to leaving Frederick. He had always considered northern Maryland as something of a racist region, and "we weren't sure we wanted to raise our kids there. Besides, I'll be living closer to my family now; I'm excited about that. And I'll have the chance to do a lot of the things I wanted to do at Frederick but never got to do because of budgets or administrative work." Although the Frederick B-cell lymphoma anti-id program had eventually grown to include ten patients, it was now undergoing an extensive reassessment. Among his primary ambitions at Michigan is the reactivation of his anti-id work, and he's considering the possibility of having the university become a new-treatment testing site for work done by Levy and Miller.

Does he regret his four years with NCI? "Absolutely not," he said. "For all the politics and bureaucratic and financial constraints, I'm thrilled that I was able to put in that time. I don't think I would have been able to learn as much as I did about cancer anywhere else. . . ."

Paul Vasington resigned from Damon and successfully underwent bypass surgery at Boston's Beth Israel Hospital in early 1983. During recuperation, he was able, for the first time in his professional life, to really think about his future. What does a middle-aged biologist do with the rest of his career when his company has decided he's unneeded?

In Vasington's case, he finds a partner, rents a converted warehouse in Norwood—a few miles south of Damon on 128—and forms Karyon, a new company specializing in cell culture and monoclonals. At last report, Karyon had just received a contract from NCI to develop new techniques for cloning human lung cancer cells.

He chose the name of his company for two reasons. First, he said, it was something of a play on words: "I definitely wanted to carry on the work that I'd started at Damon. I was convinced, and still am convinced, that it's important work, and that I could do it better than Damon Biotech was doing it."

There was another reason for the name: "Karyon" is derived from the Greek word for "cell."

Franklin Lim, the inventor of the encapsulation process that launched a company, is now managing his own company—Lim Technology Laboratories—in Richmond, Virginia. He describes his work as developing "enabling technologies" for the biotechnology industry, such as cell culture, encapsulation, cell fusion methods, biosensors, and gene transfer. He still consults for Damon Biotech on their encapsulation technology.

In a seventh-floor office overlooking Boston's Park Square, Ed Lurier—the man who lost a wife to diabetes and consequently helped create an important new method for growing cells—now serves as vice president of Gryphon Ventures, a small firm that specializes in arranging funding for promising new technology companies. Although Gryphon itself has little or no formal connection with technology (nor with Vivotech), Lurier still cannot pass up any article or report on diabetes research, and he's more convinced than ever that when the disease is finally cured, it will be through a technology very similar to the one first designed by

Lim, Sun, and Vasington. Lurier left Damon Biotech in April 1984 and now lives with his second wife in Brookline.

Since early 1985, Paul Abrams has been vice president of NeoRx, a young Seattle company that was launched by a group of people from NCI and private industry. Among other programs, NeoRx is researching new technologies for producing immunoconjugates—the molecules for tumor-imaging and therapy that consist of an antibody linked to a drug or radioisotope.

While he's grateful for his years at Frederick, he had leaped at the opportunity to leave the Maryland heat and humidity. And while funding is always a problem in a young company, he thinks it's less so now than at NCI. "There was only so much money to go around at the institute," he explained as he watched the tankers chugging slowly along Puget Sound. "And if you were able to get all the money you needed for your program, that usually meant that it was taken from someone else, someone who needed it just as much as you did. In that sense, money is less of a problem in a company like ours."

In the small town of Franklin, Tennessee, just south of Nashville, Bob Oldham is now the scientific director and director of BioTherapeutics, Inc., and as much the maverick as ever. Less than a year after its founding, the company has already drawn fire from researchers—inside and outside the medical establishment he criticized so often—for designing customized cancer treatments in exchange for research fees reaching into the tens of thousands of dollars. To a large extent, the treatments are based on such still-unproven concepts as monoclonal antibodies and interferon; as such, they are not considered reimbursible by Medicare or most other insurance programs. His therapies, in other words, are limited to only the wealthiest cancer patients (although he is now working on an innovative insurance plan for cancer victims receiving biotherapy).

If he's bothered by such criticisms, he doesn't let on. Although he concedes that there will always be a role for conventional treatments such as drugs and surgery, he's still convinced that he and a few others will preside over an important new era of cancer therapy. When we last met, he was planning to write a novel about cancer research and his role as a chief architect of the Fourth Modality.

I last saw Jack Christie on an unusually warm and hazy afternoon in February 1985. It had been nearly four years since his diagnosis. We both happened to be visiting San Diego at the time —he to attend a seminar with Ken Foon, I to attend to some personal business or other—and had arranged to meet for an hour at one of the cafeterias at the UCSD Medical Center. Arriving at the tail end of the lunch hour, I had trouble spotting him amid the throngs of students. When we finally caught each other's eye, we found a cleared plastic-topped table in a corner. He checked his watch often during our meeting, explaining that Ken was going to take his girls to Balboa Park in the afternoon; Jack would meet them there later. Then Foon wanted to stop at a couple of produce stands to stock up on citrus fruits to bring back to Maryland.

Jack was ten or twelve years older than most of the others milling through the noisy hall, but he seemed to fit comfortably into the surroundings. He could be a grad student, perhaps, or maybe a postdoc. It was only up close that one could see the gray hairs beginning to sprout at the temples, the thin but deepening lines at the corners of the eyes. He was wearing his Texas uniform again—open-collar silk sport shirt, two chains around the neck, Italian-cut slacks, expensive Western boots.

He looked good, and I told him so. Certainly more relaxed than the first time we'd met—more accepting, perhaps, although that term misses his aura of determination, his conviction that the fight itself is every bit as important as the outcome. That fight was far from over, he knew; his adversary had called a temporary truce, nothing more. Sooner or later the battle was almost sure to resume—he would discover a swollen node, perhaps, or awaken in the middle of the night to find his sheets soaked with sweat. And this time the battle would be a more ferocious one. "But it's easier to accept that if you don't think there's something malevolent about it," he told me. "So many people think that their cancer is a punishment, or that God has it in for them or something. You have to think of it as just a screwy toss of the dice, that's all."

When he first realized he was in remission, he had the odd feeling that he'd been cheated. He and Foon had waited anxiously for the anti-id, and they had shared a growing sense of excitement that they were about to join a very small group of pioneers in cancer research. Yet he'd realized that there had been no promises, no assurances. In one of his conversations with Rich Miller in California, Miller had stressed: "This whole program is still very tentative, Jack. We're still trying to learn if the anti-id alone is sufficient for this type of disease, how and when to administer it, whether we have to link a toxin to it. We're still not even entirely sure what these things do in the bloodstream."

Like Levy, Miller was often angered at the public relations efforts that were increasingly surrounding monoclonals, the promises that the fabled "magic bullet" had finally been cast. "It's going to be one more weapon for the arsenal, Jack," Miller told him. "But I don't think anyone believes that it's going to be the only weapon."

Jack had received no treatment of any kind for two or three months now, and was still almost completely symptom-free.

"So now what?" I asked him.

"There are so many options for me now, so many things opening up. If and when the disease catches fire again, Ken and I will discuss going ahead with the anti-id therapy, but at Michigan. And there are other choices. I might go back on interferon, or consider the bone marrow transplant, or maybe resume the chemo. It depends on a lot of things. What I feel good about is that I've got so many bright and dedicated people to work with me. Sometimes I think about patients like me who were diagnosed just ten or fifteen years ago; they had so much less to look forward to than I have. . . ."

He had been reading a great deal, he said, and spending much of his spare time attending conferences on anything that might bear on his future: hybridomas, monoclonals, interferon, cancer research—anything that would help him get a better grip on his disease and play a bigger role in managing it.

There had been a letter a few months before, in the Correspondence section of the *New England Journal of Medicine,* and Jack had made a copy of it. Titled "Lessons in Living with Cancer," it had been written by a Seattle physician who had been diagnosed with lung cancer a few years before. The cancer had responded well to treatment at first, the physician wrote, and seemed to disappear. Then it had returned, with a vengeance. It was in his bones now, and in his brain and in another portion of his lung. There was no reason to think that he would be around two years hence.

But the fight had not gone out of him. The wretched drug therapy, the constant fragrance of death, the statistics that gave him such a pitiful chance—none of it had yet conquered him, just worn him down from time to time. "I get tired of being frightened by each new symptom," he had written, "of feeling sorry for myself, and of fearing that the system for handling my disease is not proving effective. I sometimes feel like giving up and saying, 'I have done enough. Why should I have to keep working so hard? Why does it have to be me? Why can't I be completely well again?' " More than most people, Christie understood the emotions that lay behind those words. And he had something else, something that the man in Seattle may not have had: He had witnessed firsthand the exciting early days of a new era in medicine, and had even had a hand in its shaping. He felt privileged to have been a pioneer of sorts—even a reluctant one.

There had been some important lessons during the past years, he said. Money was no longer at the center of his life, for one. As Eileen often said, having it merely frees the mind for other things. He recognized that his remission had nothing to do with his prosperity; he had received that for free, assisted by men and women who had demanded nothing in return.

He had once sought solitude, had barricaded himself from human involvements. Now he sought them out—from among his troubled and hurting patients, mostly, but also from even casual acquaintances, cherishing even the briefest touching of souls. Every involvement, even the most fleeting and superficial, had added something to his life. He wanted more.

And he had learned to look ahead, not back. The physician in Seattle had learned too; Jack had underlined a passage, and slid the paper across the table to me:

In each of the last three autumns, I have wondered whether to plant the tulip and daffodil bulbs for the spring bloom or not bother. Now, again this past spring, a glory of living color rewarded me, and once again I have planted for next spring's blooming.

It was nearly two o'clock, and he had to leave. Ken and the girls were waiting. We walked outside together, shook hands, and then he was gone, half-walking, half-jogging across the broad patio outside the cafeteria. I watched him for a while, until he was finally swallowed up in the crowds of laughing, shouting students.

I think that he was going to go plant some daffodils. . . .